"An extremely well-done instructional package."
—William Zachmann, ComputerWorld

"As high quality a book as you can get... It integrates the computer and text better than anything I have ever seen."
—Robert Alonso, Computer Currents

Now you can learn the C programming language quickly and easily. The C Workshop integrates a book with tutorial software that gives you private lessons at your personal computer.

Besides quizzes and online help for the terms and symbols of C, the C Workshop offers you over 100 program exercises. Complete an exercise using the built-in full-screen editor, press a key, and the compiler and Soft Tutor™ report back to you. If your program produces incorrect output, the C Workshop shows you an example. Because the system is in RAM memory, you can instantly change your program and get immediate feedback.

The C Workshop teaches you C even if you have never programmed before. Its complete coverage and flexibility make it ideal for people of all programming backgrounds.

Everything you need to learn and start using C is contained in the C Workshop. Unlike books which add a diskette of sample programs, the C Workshop is a complete learning environment with unique feedback and guidance.

"The heart of this process is a powerful editor and compiler so easy to use that I recommend them for any instructional environment."
—Sorel Reisman, IEEE Software

"What I learned in five days with your book and software has taken me over a month before... This product is a winner."
—Al Patrizio, Richmond, California

The C Workshop

by Charles Pine

Cover design: BMR, David Crossman
Cover art: Rosiland Solomon
Interior art: Benjamin Dann
Phototype services: Desktop Publishing, Inc.

Wordcraft
3827 Penniman Avenue
Oakland, CA 94619

ISBN 0-917419-12-X
Library of Congress Catalog Card Number: 87-50662

Printed in the United States of America.

10 9 8 7 6 5 4

Contents

Registration form

License

Preface

A computer is an infinity of machines, each created by a program. The *C Workshop*, consisting of interactive software and this book, has everything you need to learn C and write programs.

You answer quizzes and complete program exercises using the built-in editor. The compiler translates your program to computer instructions. Once it runs, the Soft Tutor™ reports when an exercise is wrong, giving you an example of the problem. Otherwise, it confirms that you've completed the program correctly.

You may also write and save your own programs using the programming environment (editor, compiler-linker, and runtime library). Because the system remains in RAM memory and gives virtually immediate feedback, you can develop programs at an extremely fast pace. Your compiled programs may be run on their own without the *C Workshop*.

At all times a context-sensitive help key supplies operating information and details of the C language itself, such as the precedence chart of operators, examples for each C word and symbol, and descriptions of the library functions.

Some exercises ask you to learn C by doing. Others pose significant intellectual challenges which develop your ability to think about algorithms, the recipes of programs.

Organization of Material

The book assumes no previous programming knowledge. It covers the essential concepts of structured programming; the mechanics, special features, and tricky points of C; and the manipulation of important data structures.

Chapters 1 and 2 get you started using the software and book. They also introduce the fundamental concepts of structured programming. If you already know a programming language, you may work quickly through these chapters.

Chapter 3, "Reading and Writing C," is an informal preview. It guides you through several program exercises in order to help you become comfortable with C.

Chapters 4 through 10 methodically cover C names, functions, expressions and statements. The essential unit of C programs, the function, is stressed as the organizing concept.

Chapters 11 through 16 explore the architecture of data: arrays, pointers, and structures. These features of C give it power to arrange and access data in systematic ways. Some of these topics, like pointers, have a reputation for mystery, but you will find that the method of completing program exercises and receiving immediate feedback makes these subjects easy and even fun.

These chapters also explain the preprocessor and the library, including standard disk functions.

Chapters 17 and 18 show you how C easily handles common data structures, like linked lists, and operations on them like sorting. These topics in computer science are introduced without requiring prior experience with them.

Chapter 19 discusses assembly language interfacing and the organization of large projects.

Chapters 20 and 21 are manuals on advanced use of the *C Workshop* library, editor, and compiler.

Development System

Although menus and help screens eliminate hard to remember command sequences, the editor was designed to require a minimum of keys to enter, locate and modify text. If you already have a favorite word processor, the facility for customizing editor keys eliminates annoying conflicts in the meaning of a key combination. Screen output may be routed through the BIOS where required, or written directly to video memory for almost instant display.

You can write prototype versions of programs, save the source text, and combine and recompile modules with virtually any other C development system on the market. The *C Workshop* has a full feature compiler conforming to the Kernighan and Ritchie standard, including floats, longs, and bit fields. Some ANSI extensions such as unsigned longs and re-usable member names have been added.

Because both the compiler and your source code reside in RAM memory, the compiler processes over 5,500 lines per minute. Utilizing the *C Workshop*, you can concentrate on the goal of your program.

School Edition

A school edition of the *C Workshop* is available; it requires less memory. Maximum program size is reduced; split screen editing and customizable parameters are not supported. All other features are identical.

An Evolving Tradition

Wordcraft, founded in 1981, has created and published C language tools since 1985. This package is our latest product. Although based on the experience of its predecessors, the *C Workshop* has a more responsive and capable split-screen editor, a complete compiler, and an on-line help system. The textbook is completely reorganized and significantly expanded.

Humanity continually discovers new industries as it assumes wider stewardship of the world. Like many young fields, the computer industry attracts both the best and worst types of people. It is a pleasure to thank the fine persons who encouraged, reviewed and made suggestions for this project, including Wilson T. Price, Hector O. Conde, James Eakin, Timothy Holland-Davis, Roy Cunningham and Paul Ross. Ilona Graham, Fred Cisin and many users of earlier Wordcraft products offered helpful reports and opinions.

CHAPTER 1
Getting Started

Read this before you use the C Workshop the first time!

This chapter tells you how to start using the C Workshop. It also introduces the basic concept of programming.

The following instructions apply to the C Workshop for the MS-DOS or PC-DOS operating system, version 2 or greater, running on a computer with an industry standard BIOS.

Your computer must be turned on and the operating system loaded ("booted").

1. Make a Working Copy

The first thing to do with your purchased copy of the C Workshop is to make a working copy.

Format blank disks. Copy the files on the original C Workshop disks to them; consult your operating system manual if necessary. Your working copy may be on 360Kb, 1.2Mb or 3.5" disks.

Keep the original disks in a safe place and use the working copy.

2. Register Your License

Complete and mail the registration page at the back of this book. Licensed users are entitled to notice of corrections and updates and to support in case of malfunctions by the C Workshop.

3. Install the Program

Before you use the C Workshop the first time, you must install it. Put the working copy of Disk 1 in a drive. Since the installation process will both read and write to the disk, make sure the drive is correct for your disk. *Normally, you should not write to a 360KB disk in a 1.2MB drive.*
Run the program CWINST. From the operating system prompt, enter

```
>cwinst
```

CWINST will ask you for a name. Enter a name as you want it displayed on the screen, ending with the Return or Enter key.
When the installation is complete, a message will remind you how much RAM memory the C Workshop needs. The MS-DOS program CHKDSK tells you how much memory is available. If necessary, you can free memory by removing virtual disks (sometimes called ramdisks), memory-resident utility programs, and unnecessary device drivers (installed by DEVICE commands in the MS-DOS file CONFIG.SYS).

Start the C Workshop

Starting from a floppy diskette.
Put the disk with the file CW.EXE in the current drive.
You start the C Workshop by executing the program CW. For example:

```
>cw
```

The program may ask you to insert a disk with files it needs, normally Disk 2. You may put the disk in another drive or swap disks in the current drive, enabling you to use the C Workshop on a computer with only one floppy drive. Enter the drive letter; you may enter a directory path, too. ("Enter" means type the information, then press the Enter or Return key.) For example,

```
b:
```

or

```
c:\cw
```

Starting from a hard drive.
After installation, you may copy all files on the working diskettes to a subdirectory of a hard drive.
Log into that directory, then start the program

```
>cw
```

Startup options.
A later chapter discusses more elaborate ways of organizing files and starting the program from different drives. You can also control several other features of the C Workshop, go directly to a specific screen, or begin editing a file. Consult the chapter on advanced use of the C Workshop for details.

Getting into the Workshop.
The C Workshop will show its copyright message and a few other lines of information. Press a key when asked; if you have changed your mind and do not want to start the program, pressing Ctrl-C here will return you to the operating system.
The opening display will start, relating the features of the C Workshop. You can press a key at any time to interrupt it and begin the tutorial. Until you know what the various functions keys do, press the *PgDn* key, located on the lower right side of most keyboards.
Every time you press the *PgDn* key, the next screen will appear. Try this key once or twice, then try the *PgUp* key, which takes you back a screen.

This Book and the C Workshop Software

This book and the software are coordinated so that you can study C at your computer and away from it.

All instructional material on the screen is in the book, but the book contains extensive discussion of topics as well as examples and exercises. If you have never programmed before, the easiest way to learn is to read the book, turning to the computer when you come to Self Test questions and program exercises. If you have programming experience, you may want to use the screen tutorial most of the time; when you need to know more about a subject, turn to the book.

A page reference in the upper right corner of each screen shows where the screen occurs in the book. This reference gives the page number, followed by a letter if more than one screen starts on a page in the book. For example, screen 101B would be the third screen on page 101.

You can always move between the book and the software using the page numbers.

What Is a Program?

This section and the next one explain the basic concepts of programming.

Before you write a program, you need an idea and then a plan. The idea is your concept of what you want the computer running your program to do. The plan of how the task will be done may exist in several different forms: notes and specifications, diagrams, and recipe-like explanations (sometimes called "pseudocode").

The size and documentary form of your plan are not the crucial points. Whether you write a small program from informal notes, or you participate on a team writing a large group of programs according to detailed specifications, the important thing is that you have an idea and a plan before you start writing C statements.

A program exists in at least two forms. One is a sequence of statements written in a programming language. A fragment of a C program might look like this:

```
score = part1 + part2;
if (score > 93)
    report ('A');
```

The statements would be stored in a file that you can read on the screen or from a printout. This is the source text, or source code. It is nothing more than letters and special punctuation, like a novel. Although these statements must follow certain rules, the source program is still text for the human brain rather than instructions ready to be executed by computer circuits.

The other form, often called the object program, is a coded file of operations that the computer can perform. We cannot read this list of operations (except very tediously, character by character, once we know some codes).

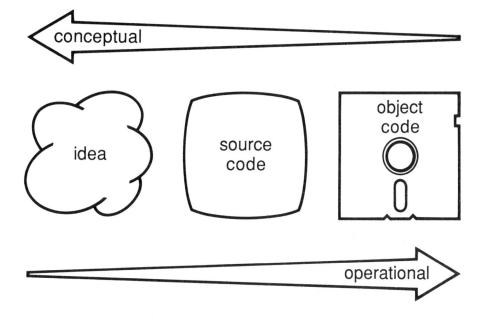

Programming: from idea to instructions

One of the amazing things about programming is that special programs called compilers can process the source text into an object form. The compiler expects the source text characters to follow each other according to certain rules, such as the rules of the C language.

Programs make the computer act like a word processor or a calculator. They turn the computer into a machine that accepts, stores, and manipulates lists. If the computer is connected to other machinery, like a printer or a robot, a program can make the computer control the machine. Programs accept input disk files and create new output files.

CW.EXE is an object program that performs the functions of the C Workshop. The source text was written in the C programming language. A group of programs that operate on source files and intermediate files were used to translate the source code into the object program.

The Programming Cycle

You write a program using the editor. The compiler in the C Workshop converts your source code into computer instructions. If the program can be translated completely into object form, we say the program compiled.

Results produced by your program must be tested for validity. A program that compiles obeys the rules of C syntax, but this does not guarantee that it performs the intended function.

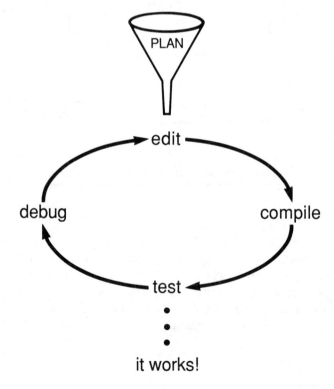

When you complete a program exercise, the C Workshop makes the computer execute your object program and tells you whether the results are correct. If they are wrong, the Workshop points out an example of the problem with your program, and you edit it and try again.

Editing, compiling, testing and debugging make up the steps of the programming cycle. You repeat the cycle until the program is correct.

As you learn to program in C, you can write, compile, and run your own programs. Then it is up to you to determine whether the results of a program are correct. If not, you have to find the error in your program (a process called "debugging") and rewrite it. This cycle is the general pattern of developing programs.

CHAPTER 2
Operating the C Workshop

8

This chapter shows you enough about the operation of the C Workshop to get you started using it.

It also discusses the idea of structured programming.

Most of the keys used to move around the tutorial are function keys. These are the keys with *F* and a number, not the numeric keys.

8A

The *PgDn* key advances to the next screen. To go back a screen, press the *PgUp* key.

The *F1* key is the help key. When you are using the tutorial, it explains how to use the function keys to move around the C Workshop.

The *F10* key is your gateway to the editing and programming environment, as will be explained shortly.

When you want to quit the C Workshop, press *F2*.

8B

Some of the screens have questions for you.

Press the *PgDn* key to see a question on the next screen.

SELF TEST   **8C**

Self Test questions take up the lower part of the screen. You can answer the question or use screen keys like *PgDn* to skip it.

Questions in the C Workshop

A) must be answered
B) may be skipped

Which is correct, A or B?

9

Some screens display the beginning of a program exercise. When you press *F10* for Program on these screens, you enter the programming environment. There you complete the exercise and see whether your work is correct.

However, when the current screen is *not* a program exercise but simply information like this screen or a question, pressing *F10* enters a blank programming environment ready for you to experiment on your own. While you are first learning C, you will want to start programming only when the current screen displays a program exercise.

9A

The next screen has a completely written program. It is *not* a beginner's program, and you should not expect to understand it. However, running it will show you how much a single screen of C source code can do.

For the next screen, you should do the following:

Press *PgDn* to go to the program screen.

Press *F10* to start the programming environment. The menu at the bottom of the screen will change.

Press *F3* from the editing menu. It will ask you to press a key to compile and run. The program plays a little game with you.

9B

```c
/*  Example program in C */
/*  After pressing F10, PRESS F3 to run. */

main()      /*  guess numbers using binary search */
{
int low, high, mid, c;

    low = 1;
    high = 1000;
    printf ("Think of a number between 1 and %d\n", high);
    puts ("Press key when ready.");
```

```
    getchar();

    do  {
        mid = low + 1 + (high - low) / 2;
        printf ("\nIs it greater than %d? y/n:", mid - 1);
        c = getchar();              /*  input a key */
        if (toupper (c) == 'Y') /*  'y' to 'Y' */
            low = mid;              /*  must be in upper range */
        else
            high = mid - 1;         /*  must be in lower range */
        } while (high - low);   /*  while there is a range */

    printf ("\nYour number is %d.\n", high);
}
```

10

When you selected *F3* on the editing menu, the C Workshop compiled the program and ran it. The program played a guessing game with you (later we will see how it works).

To leave an exercise, use the *F2* Quit option. You will leave the editing and programming environment and return to the tutorial.

The *F1* key is the Help key. It gives you different information in different situations, so try it any time you need help.

10A

The next screen contains a simple program. First, just go to the screen and run the program.

10B

```
/*  Display a message */

/*  After pressing F10, PRESS F3 to run.
    The program will be compiled and run.   It writes
    a message to the screen.
*/

main()
{
    puts ("The well-read cardinal picked through the leaves.");
}
```

11

The program is really yours. To see this and practice with the editor, you can change the message contained within the quotation marks.

On the next screen the program is repeated. Before you run it this time, use the arrow keys to move to the message. You can alter the message by typing over it and using the Insert and Delete keys.

11A

```
/*  Use the editor to rewrite a message */

/*  PRESS F10 to start exercise. You are now ready to edit it.
    Using the arrow keys, MOVE the cursor to the message in
    quotation marks.
    REWRITE the message by typing over it and using the Insert
    and Delete keys.
    The F1 Help key tells you more about the edit controls.
    When you have changed the message, PRESS F3 to run.
    The program displays your message on the screen.
*/

main()
{
    puts ("The well-read cardinal picked through the leaves.");
}
```

11B

The next section in the book explains the basics of using the editor, including the idea of cursor position, control keys, and blocks of lines.

Your Full-Screen Editor

When you press *F10*, you go to the editing and programming environment. The menu at the bottom of the screen assigns new commands to the function keys.

Pressing *F1* for Help displays a menu offering different kinds of help. One of the letter selections shows you the editing functions and their keys. You use these keys for moving around the text and altering it.

You can change the keys that perform different editing functions. The following discussion assumes that the default key assignments have not been changed.

If this is your first full-screen editor, the basic concept is simple. The text (the source code of a program unless you decide to write a letter to a friend) is a continuous flow of lines. The screen shows one screenful of text at a time.

Your position on the screen is marked by the cursor. It is the highlighted cell that moves when you use the arrow keys, for example. If you enter text by pressing an ordinary character key, it goes where the cursor is. New text at the end of the program is simply added. If text already exists at the cursor, your new material normally overwrites it.

However, you can press the *Ins* key, and you will see INSERT in the lower right part of the screen. This causes new characters to be inserted, pushing the rest of the line forward as each new character is typed. Text that overflows a line goes onto a newly created line below.

Inserting changes back to overwriting when you press the insert key again.

Pressing the Return or Enter key while editing ends a line. If the cursor is in the middle of a line, the carriage return will divide the line in two. If the cursor is at the beginning of the line, pressing Return creates a new line to work on.

Other keys cause larger movements through the text. For example, the *Home* key moves the cursor to the beginning of the line. Immediately pressing it again moves the cursor to the top of the screen.

Control key combinations perform some actions. You activate them by holding down the *Ctrl* key and tapping the specified letter key at the same time. For example, *Ctrl Y* deletes the entire line at the cursor. Do not hold the *Y* key down, because the key automatically repeats when you do that.

To carry out some operations, you mark blocks of text. Move the cursor to the start of the text you want to mark and press the control key combination for a block mark. (You can look up this combination using the Help command.) This action inserts a block marker. Do the same thing at the end of the block. Then you can move the cursor somewhere else. Pressing the Block function key presents a menu of block actions, such as copying, deleting or moving a block.

The block menu is a typical menu in a window. It accepts your command, performs it, then disappears. If you want to perform another block operation, simply press the block function key again. When the menu is waiting for your letter command, you can press a function key instead; the block menu goes away and the new menu appears. The Edit function key, *F10*, simply returns to text editing. In general, to abandon any menu in a window, press the Edit function key.

The entire text exists in memory chips in the computer while you edit. This memory space is called the edit buffer. At some point you probably want to save text onto disk, either the entire edit buffer or a marked block. Press the Out command key. The output menu will appear.

In the C Workshop, text files on disk have names from one to eight characters. They also have a file extension, up to three more characters following a dot after the filename proper. By convention, files of C program source text get an extension .C.

You may also print the block of text on paper if a printer is connected to the computer. Make sure the printer is turned on and ready. Select the Out menu, then its printer option.

The editor has more features, such as the ability to work in two edit buffers at once on a split screen. A later chapter discusses advanced use of the editor.

SELF TEST   13

The cursor marks the spot where

A) the next character will go
B) a line should be deleted
C) the text ends

Which is correct, A, B or C?

13A

C — A Structured Programming Language

C is one of a number of languages that encourage structured programming. A structured program is organized into strictly separated blocks, and each block is structured as either a short sequence of statements, a choice between alternatives, or a loop.

An *un*structured program is written as long sequences of statements whose flow of execution is altered by GOTO operations that may transfer control to any other statement.

Here is an example of unstructured statements.

1   Do something
2   If A < B goto 6
3   Do something
4   If C < D goto 7
5   Do something
6   Do something
7   If N < MAX goto 1

The result is often called "spaghetti code" because the control flow can get so tangled. Programs become difficult to grasp as a whole and a nightmare to test, correct and modify.

To remedy these problems, computer scientist Edsger Dijkstra and others introduced the idea of structured programming.

A structured program consists of short blocks of statements (from a couple to one or two dozen). Blocks may call other blocks to be executed. Within a block, only three types of flow are allowed:

1) a short sequence of statements

        statement 1;
        statement 2;
        statement 3;
        *

2) an alternative: a choice of executing one of two or more sub-blocks depending on a test of a condition

        if condition is true
            {
            statement 1 for true;
            statement 2 for true;
            } *

```
else
    {
    statement 1 for false;
    statement 2 for false;
    } *
```

Note: The example above is not written in C. When we want to illustrate a programming idea without regard for details of a particular language, we use statements that read like English but are organized like a programming language. This is called pseudocode.

The final type of structured program flow is

3) a loop: a sequence of statements executed repeatedly while a test condition is fulfilled

```
while (condition is true)
    {
    statement 1;
    statement 2;
    }
*
```

A block of statements can only begin at the top. That is, in a strictly structured program, no statement ever throws control into the middle of another block. The exit points for leaving a block are well defined, too; in the above pseudocode, asterisks (*) show these places.

An operation in a statement may trigger another block of statements. After they are executed, control resumes following the operation that invoked the block.

```
score = part1 + part2;
if (score > 93)
    report ('A');
a_tally++;
```

As you will learn later, the line `report ('A');` causes a group of statements in a function called `report` to execute. When they are done, control resumes with the line `a_tally++;` and proceeds.

The important fact is that when an operation invokes a block of statements, control will return at the end of the block to the point just after the invoking operation. This system of blocks invoking blocks, each of which is built from the three elementary types, is both powerful and organized.

Another advantage of structured programming is that the programmer can organize the code on the page, using indentation to reflect the logical structure of the program. Notice how the test and loop blocks are indented in the pseudocode above.

Dijkstra proved that a structured program can do anything that a GOTO tangle could do. The discipline of structured programming does not sacrifice any capabilities of the computer. Experience has shown that structured programs are easier to write, test and correct than unstructured ones, as well as easier to modify.

Structured programming is a style of thinking and working. Some languages have the facilities for structured programming, C among them, but even so, it is possible to use C in an unstructured way. Responsibility for good style belongs with the programmer.

Here is a comparison of a program written in unstructured Basic and structured C. Although some versions of Basic have facilities for structured programming, it is still true that many programs written in Basic are unstructured and hard to read.

```
10   N = 0
100  INPUT "Age?", A
110  INPUT "Weight?", B
120  N = N + 1
200  IF WTFN (A, B) > 0 GOTO 600
300  PRINT "Weight is not excessive for age"
310  IF N < 20 GOTO 100
320  END
600  PRINT "Weight is excessive for age"
900  END
```

This program has non-symmetric logic: it examines up to 20 people but stops as soon as an excessive weight is processed. However, the source code does not make this fact apparent quickly. By contrast, the corresponding structured code in C visibly displays the situation.

```
/*  Structured C code translated from unstructured Basic */

#define TRUE    1
#define FALSE   0
#define MAX     19

main()
{
int trials, age, weight, excess;

    excess = FALSE;     /*  starting assumption */

    for (trials = 0; trials <= MAX && excess == FALSE; trials =
trials + 1)
        {
        age = get_age();
        weight = get_weight();
        if (comp_age_wt (age, weight) > 0)
            puts ("Weight is not excessive for age");
        else
            {
            puts ("Weight is excessive for age");
            excess = TRUE;
            }
        }

    exit (excess);
}
```

Even though the C syntax may be new to you, it is apparent that the principal logical structure is some kind of loop dependent upon the variable trials. Within this loop, an alternative is selected based on the age and weight.

Other contrasts between the unstructured program that happens to be written in Basic and the structured program in C are as follows:

—Manipulation of the loop variable occurs throughout the code in the Basic program and is concentrated on one line in C.

—The long names in the C example are more easily understood than the single letters and abbreviated names in Basic.

—The Basic program has two scattered END statements; the structured example reads from top to bottom.

—Certain tasks in the C program, such as inputting the age and weight, have been isolated in their own blocks of statements (which are named but not shown here).

SELF TEST   **18**

The flow of control in a structured programming language is

A) strictly sequential except for jumps
B) organized as sequences, alternatives, and loops
C) like parallel strands of spaghetti

SELF TEST   **18A**

After you have an idea and a plan, the programming cycle typically goes in which sequence:

A) compile, edit, test
B) edit, compile and link, test, debug
C) link, edit, compile, test
D) edit, test, debug, compile

Exercise. An algorithm is stated in pseudocode:
Set a variable *i* to 1001
A: If *i* is a prime number
    Display *i*
    Stop
Add 2 to *i*
If *i* is greater than 1050
    Display "No primes between 1001 and 1050"
    Stop
Else
    Goto A

Rewrite the pseudocode so that it uses only the three block forms allowed in structured programming (no goto's!). You may use braces to put an entire block in place of a single statement in another block.

Exercise. Rewrite this algorithm following the rules in the preceding exercise:

Set a variable *i* to 101
A: Set a variable *j* to 10
B: If *j* goes evenly into *i*,
        Display *i* and *j*
        Stop
Add 1 to *j*
If *j* is greater than or equal to *i*
        Goto C
Else
        Goto B
C: Add 1 to *i*
If *i* is greater than 200
        Stop
Else
        Goto A

Hint: Define another variable *flag* and set it to 0 at the start. At appropriate places, set the flag to 1, and at other places decide what to do based on whether the flag is 1 or 0.

CHAPTER 3
Reading and Writing C

This chapter introduces enough features of C so that you can write programs. After this chapter we will take up each aspect of C and study it in depth; subsequent exercises rely on informal knowledge of C that you will gain here.

The main() Point

We will look at each part of the simple program we have already run.

```
/*  Display a message */

main()
{
    puts ("The well-read cardinal picked through the leaves.");
}
```

Anything enclosed between /* and */ is a comment. It is for human enlightenment. The compiler that translates your program ignores comments.

In a C program, instructions are grouped in functions. This program has only one function called main; most programs have several functions. Each one is a group of statements organized to perform a specific task. When you write a function, it always has a pair of parentheses after it, which may contain input for the function to work on.

```
main()
{
    puts ("The well-read cardinal picked through the leaves.");
}
```

Statements belonging to the function are enclosed within braces { }. In this example, main has one statement in it.

21

A C program always begins running at a function called main. Statements in a function may invoke other functions, and all the functions in your program are ultimately descendants of the ancestor, main().

The program starts execution at main. The statement between the braces { } belongs to main. It concludes with a semicolon, C punctuation for ending a statement. A C statement ends at a semicolon, not at the end of a line.

21A

The only statement in this main invokes another function, puts. The code for this function is in another file. A C program may extend over a number of source files. Each source file is compiled separately into an object file.

Another tool, the linker, combines object modules into a single program ready to run. For example, the linker searches a file that has the object code for puts and a number of other commonly used functions.

When you run a program in the C Workshop, it automatically starts the compiler then the linker.

21B

In our example, the statement invokes puts and gives it a parameter, also called an argument, which is input for the invoked function. Here, a short piece of text about a cardinal, called a string, is the input. String text is put in double quotation marks. Like all function parameters, the string is enclosed in the parentheses following the name of the function.

22

Depending on what input a function expects, the parameter may be a number or variable instead of a text string.

```
main()
{
    get_lucky (7);
}

main()
{
    mark_spot (x);
}
```

SELF TEST   **22A**

A function's statements are enclosed within

    A) ()   parentheses
    B) { }   braces
    C) /*   */

SELF TEST   **22B**

A C statement ends with a

    A) period   .
    B) semicolon   ;
    C) end of a line
    D) right parenthesis   )

SELF TEST   **22C**

`main` invokes another function, `puts`. It is found and combined into the program by the:

    A) editor
    B) compiler
    C) linker
    D) program itself

Using and Displaying Some Numbers

Let's create a function that does something to a variable.

A variable is a named memory location that holds a value. In the next program the variables are named `answer` and n.

When we invoke such a function, we need to pass it a value for the variable and obtain a result from the function.

The next screen has a program that uses numbers. It is ready to run.

23A

```
/*  First program using integers */

/*  After pressing F10, PRESS F3 to run the program. */

main()
{
int answer; /*  working integer variable */

    answer = double_it (5);
    printf ("The result is %d", answer);
}

double_it (n)
int n;        /*  declaration of function parameter */
{
    return (n + n);
}
```

23B

One new object in this program is the definition of the variable `answer`.

Right after an open brace {, you may declare objects that exist within the block enclosed by the pair of braces.

The first word of this declaration is one of the keywords in C, `int`. An `int` is a whole number within a range set by the computer and compiler. In this Workshop, `ints` range from -32768 to +32767. (The computer uses base two numbers; these are the limits for signed numbers with sixteen binary bits.)

This particular integer is named `answer`. Upper and lower case are different; it would be wrong to refer to this same object later as `ANSWER` or `Answer`.

Why does an `int` have such strange boundaries? The computer you are using stores numbers in binary format instead of our familiar powers of ten. An `int` has 16 binary digits, or bits, one of which keeps track of the sign. Two to the fifteenth power is 32,768. (An appendix discusses hexadecimal and binary numbers.)

24

Now let's skip for a moment to the invoked function, `double_it`. (We use this clumsy name because `double` is another C keyword.) It, too, works with an integer variable, but n is declared in a different place.

```
double_it (n)
int n;   /*  declaration of function parameter */
{
```

A variable listed in the parentheses after the name of the function is a parameter, sometimes called an argument. Earlier, `puts` had an entire string of text as its parameter. The function `double_it` has an integer parameter n.

Each parameter should also be declared after the argument list and before the opening brace. Here we read that n is an integer.

24A

Besides receiving passed values, a function may return a value. The function `double_it` returns the value of an expression.

```
return (n + n);
```

Back at `main`, the variable `answer` is assigned the value returned by the function `double_it`.

```
answer = double_it (5);
```

In other words, a function that returns a value may take the place of a variable within an expression. The returned value is used in the computation just like the value of a variable. (Consequently, a function may return only one value.)

The function `main` invokes another one, `printf`.

```
printf ("The result is %d", answer);
```

Like `puts`, `printf` is found in a library, and it displays information on the screen.

The `printf` function has a varying number of parameters, in this case two. The first is always a string in quotes, and it may have special formatting codes that begin with the percent sign `%`. Here `%d` tells `printf` to display a decimal integer value. The remaining `printf` parameters are the values to use for the `%` codes. Here, the value of `answer` is used for `%d`.

Later we will learn about other `printf` codes like `%c`, `%x` and `%u`.

The first argument for the `printf` function is called the control string. Every time it has a `%` code, the value of a parameter is substituted for the percent code. If the control string has two percent codes, that invocation of `printf` had better have two more parameters.

```
printf ("He won %d then lost %d", round1, round2);
```

The parameters need not be distinct, but the count must match.

```
printf ("He lost %d, yes, %d", betA, betA);
```

This might seem trivial, but remember that the same value may be displayed using different percent codes. The variable supplies the quantity; the percent code governs how it is displayed, for example, in hexadecimal rather than decimal notation.

SELF TEST   **25A**

```
split (hair1, hair2)
int hair1, hair2;
{
int fee;
    /* (code omitted) */
}
```

In this function a parameter is

A) `split`

B) `fee`

C) `hair1`

SELF TEST   **26**

Suppose another function `triple` returns three times its parameter. When these statements execute

```
answer = triple (7) + double_it (2);
printf ("%d is the result", answer);
```

the screen shows

___ is the result

What number appears at ___?

On the next screen, the program exercise uses the Soft Tutor built into the C Workshop. After the exercise runs, the Soft Tutor reports that you completed the exercise correctly, or it reports that the exercise produces incorrect results, giving an example of what is wrong.

                                                                              26A

```
/*  Program with function to triple a number */

/*  COMPLETE this program so that triple() calculates
    and returns three times its input parameter.
    Follow the example of the double_it() program.
*/

main()
{
int answer; /*  working integer variable */

    answer = triple (5);
    printf ("The result is %d", answer);
}

/*  Here you WRITE the function  triple  similar to
    double_it  in the previous program.
*/
```

Syntax Errors and the Soft Tutor

If the compiler cannot make sense of a statement, or if it is contradictory to some other statement, the compiler generates an error message. The mistake is called a syntax error.

In the C Workshop, you see these messages one at a time in a window on the screen. You use menu selections to look at the next or previous messages.

The compiler often discovers a problem after the real error. Always look back in a program if the reported error line seems acceptable.

The function key that normally starts the compiler is relabeled *ERR* when there are errors. You can edit your program and review the messages by pressing this key. When you are ready to try compiling the program again, use the menu selection that discards the error report. The function key goes back to *Run* and you can try again.

A completely different kind of error check is the Soft Tutor. It examines a program that runs to see what kind of results it produces. You might go back to the computer and deliberately write `triple` incorrectly in order to see the Soft Tutor at work. For example, you could make the function return n + n.

Although your program passes 5 to `triple`, the Soft Tutor examines how your function would process other values. If the Soft Tutor finds a mistake, it tells you, in most exercises, about a value that is not handled properly. After all, the point is to write `triple` so that it returns a correct result for any integer.

When you want to see how your function handles different values, you may edit the program to alter the input data (except in certain cases where a comment warns you not to change them). However, you should not change the rest of the program outside the function you are writing, because the Soft Tutor may not work properly. Similarly, if you save an entire program exercise in a disk file and read it back later, the Soft Tutor will not work.

The Soft Tutor tests results, not methods. You are free to write a function the way you think is best and to employ any techniques you know.

You will see the Soft Tutor report only after completing certain program exercises; the results of other exercises are obvious from the screen display.

28

Character Codes

Suppose people agree on a standard numeric value for each letter of the alphabet. Then an `int` can represent a letter. Letters, digits, punctuation and some other characters are represented this way in C using single quotation marks.

```
response = 'A';
```

The single quotes tell the C compiler: look up the standard number for the character A and use it as the value. Most computers use the ASCII standard to assign numbers to characters. In this code, a capital A is 65, B is 66, and so on. (An appendix discusses the ASCII standard.)

28A

Some ASCII codes represent actions that do not print ink on the page. In C, these are represented with an escape sequence. C takes one character, the backslash (\), and designates it as a symbol that escapes into a new realm of information. The character following the backslash is not an ordinary character; it signals an action to be performed.

For example, \t represents a tab. The newline \n starts a new line.

```
next_char = '\n';
```

Even though it takes the backslash character and a letter to represent the code, the object is still a single integer value. For example, newline has the value 10.

28B

The special non-printing codes may be used within strings of text, too.

```
printf ("The culprits are\nDon\nJon\nRon");
```

This would display as

```
The culprits are
Don
Jon
Ron
```

29

You could write a block of statements

```
score = 94;
grade = 'A';
printf ("\tScore = %d\n\tGrade = %c", score, grade);
```

A tab would occur at the start of this statement.

Note also the new code, `%c`. It causes `printf` to interpret the integer value, here 65, as a character code and display the resulting character, **A**.

SELF TEST   29A

When the above statements execute, `printf` displays

```
A)  Score = 94      Grade = A
B)  Score = 94
    Grade = A
C)      Score = 94
        Grade = A
D)      Score = 94
        Grade = 'A'
```

29B

```
/*  Discover some ASCII codes */

main()
{
int code;

    code = 'A';     /*  assign a value to variable */

/*  WRITE a printf statement here to display  code  as a
    character and also as an integer value.
    Hint: Use %d and %c in the printf control string,
    then use  code  twice for value parameters.

    When your program does what you want, experiment by
    changing the value assigned to  code  above and
    rerunning the program.
*/
}
```

30

Another kind of number is the `float` like 136.25. It may have a fractional part, and its range is far greater than the -32768 .. 32767 range of `ints`.

Note: we use *a..b* to represent the range from *a* through *b* inclusive. This notation borrowed from mathematics is not part of C.

30A

```
/*  Display a floating point number */

/*  Just go to the programming environment and
    run this program.
*/

main()
{
int m, i_answer;
float f_answer;

    m = 25;
    f_answer = m / 2.0;
    i_answer = m / 2;
    printf ("Half of %d is %f\n", m, f_answer);
    printf ("The integer half of %d is %d", m, i_answer);
}
```

30B

A `float` has a fractional part. It is usually contained in the computer as a binary fraction and exponent, although you write it in C as a decimal number.

A `float` constant may be represented with a decimal point (for example, 2.0) in order to distinguish it from an integer constant (like 2).

The `printf` code for displaying a `float` is `%f`.

The internal representation of a `float` is completely different than that used for integers. Consequently, the computer operations performed when +, for example, is used to add them are different from the instructions for integer addition.

Incidentally, the previous program showed a flexibility of C. Several variables of a given type may be declared at once.

```
int m, i_answer;
```

31

```
/*  Experiment with floating point */

/*  Try some experiments on this program.  Go to the
    programming environment and run it.
    Then, change 2.0 to 2, run the program again, and
    observe the result.
    Next, change %f to %d and notice the garbage that
    results.
    What does this tell you about coordinating arguments to
    printf?
*/

main()
{
int m, i_answer;
float f_answer;

    m = 25;
    f_answer = m / 2.0;
    i_answer = m / 2;
    printf ("Half of %d is %f\n", m, f_answer);
    printf ("The integer half of %d is %d", m, i_answer);
}
```

SELF TEST   **31A**

When you changed 2.0 to 2 in the preceding program, the result was different. This indicates that m / 2, eventually assigned to **f_answer**, was computed using

A) floating point arithmetic
B) integer arithmetic

32

First Look at if-Statements

Statements in a function execute in sequence until a control structure alters the flow of execution. One control mechanism is the if-statement.

```
if (a > b)
    scale (a);
```

The test condition in parentheses is evaluated. If it is true (if a is greater than b), the statement scale (a); is executed. Otherwise, it is skipped.

```
a = 2;
b = 1;
if (a > b)
    scale (a);
```

This sequence of statements will invoke scale.

SELF TEST   **32A**

```
a = 10;
b = 15;
c = 7;
if (a > b)
    c = 14;
```

What is the value of c after these statements?

SELF TEST   **32B**

A)   if a < b
            c = 14;

B)   if (a < b)
            c = 14;

Which form is correct, A or B?

32C

```
/*  Return result based on if-statement */

main()
{
int history;    /*  score on History exam */
```

```
        history = 75;
        printf ("A score of %d ", history);
        history = adjust (history);
        printf ("is an adjusted score of %d", history);
}

adjust (score)
/*  If score is over 70, increase it by 10.
    Otherwise, its value is unchanged.
    Return: score.
    WRITE this function with statements to return
    the proper value.
*/
int score;
```

33

The simple if-statement takes action if and only if the test condition is true. To take action when the test condition is false, use the `if-else` construction.

```
    if (a > b)
        scale (a);
    else
        scale (b);
```

The else-clause specifies what to do when the statement is false (in this example, when a is less than or equal to b).

Notice that both execution statements end with semicolons.

33A

Technically, the parentheses in an if-statement enclose an expression whose value is true (non-zero) or false (0). The expression is evaluated and tested. If the result is non-zero, the execution statement after the test expression is executed. If the result is 0, this statement is skipped, and the else-clause, if present, is executed.

33B

A single execution statement ends with the usual semicolon. To do several things in an if-else statement, enclose them in braces.

```
    if (a == b)      /*  == tests for equality */
        {
```

```
c = 1;        /*  = assigns value to  c */
notify();
d = scale (c);
}
```

The enclosed statements make a compound statement. Notice that no semicolon follows the closing brace }.

Notice, too, that = assigns the value of the expression on the right-hand side to the variable on the left side. An entirely different symbol, ==, tests whether two expressions evaluate to the same value, in which case the result is true, otherwise false.

34

```
/*  Classify score as passing or failing */
/*  (F1 has help on moving the cursor to end of text) */

main()
{
int score;

    score = 75;
    printf ("A score of %d ", score);
    if (grade (score) == 0)
       puts ("is failing.");
    else
       puts ("is passing.");
}

grade (score)
/*  Return: 1 if score is 70 or over,
            otherwise return 0.
    WRITE this function with if-else to test the score and
    return 0 or 1 (not the value of the score).
*/
int score;
```

34A

TRUE and FALSE

When a C expression is tested for truth or falsehood, its value is compared with 0. If the expression evaluates to 0, it is false; otherwise, it is true.

By convention, most functions that programmers write assign the value 1 when assigning the true-value to a statement. However, when a test is made, any non-zero value is taken as true.

Instead of writing 1 and 0 in our programs, we may write TRUE and FALSE, if we put these statements at the beginning of our C program:

```
#define TRUE    1
#define FALSE   0
```

The `#define` lines are examples of *preprocessor* statements. Unlike all others, these statements stop at the end of the line; they do *not* use a semi-colon.

SELF TEST   35

```
#define TRUE    1

    flag = TRUE;
```

What is the value of `flag`?

SELF TEST   35A

```
#define MAX_ROW    24
#define MID_ROW    12

    row = MAX_ROW - MID_ROW;
```

What is the value of `row`?

Every time the preprocessor sees TRUE in your program, it substitutes 1, and similarly it replaces FALSE by 0. This is merely a replacement of source text. Then the preprocessor gives the statement to the compiler proper, which sees text containing 0 rather than FALSE.

Programs are much easier to read if they have descriptive terms instead of arbitrary, "magic" numbers in them. You can understand a program faster when it refers to MIN_PAY, WIDTH, and TAB than to 862, 80 and 9.

By convention, we capitalize defined names like TRUE, FALSE and other symbolic constants.

We have introduced several features of C informally so that you can read and write program exercises. The following chapters take up the parts of C one by one.

CHAPTER 4
Names and Functions

CHAPTER 4
Names and Functions

CHAPTER 4
Names and Functions

This chapter begins with some formalities you must observe when you create names for variables, functions, and other objects. Then it examines in detail how C is built up of functions. They invoke other functions; pass and return values; and make use of two kinds of data, local and global.

Functions, `ints` and other objects have names, such as `main`, `answer`, and n. A name, or identifier, may be made up of letters, digits, and the underscore character (_). For example,

```
sum_of_digits
```

The first character of the name must be a letter or the underscore character, not a digit. It is not a good idea to start names with an underscore character, because the compiler and library system traditionally begin names that way. For example, a library might have a function `_flush`, and if you give a function the same name, the linker (which combines library code with the object code for your program) might complain that two functions have the same name.

One of the most important rules about C syntax is this one:

UPPER and lower case are different!

Unlike many other languages, in C `main`, `MAIN` and `Main` are all different identifiers. There is a convention so strong it is almost a rule: use lowercase for all variables and functions. Uppercase is used for names of constants, like `FALSE`.

Once an identifier starts, it continues for the longest possible unbroken sequence of letters, digits, and underscores. In practice, identifiers are separated by white space, various operators, and the punctation marks of the language. White space consists of blanks, newlines, and tabs (and the more obscure vertical tab and form feed). Operators include symbols like +, *, =, !, and ==. The last one in this list reminds us that the symbol for an operator may take up more than one character. Punctuations consists of parentheses, semicolons, braces, and the like.

How long can an identifier be? It depends on the particular compiler. Furthermore, an identifier has not one but two length limits. A name can only be some number of characters long. In addition, only the first so many characters are significant. In some systems, for example, identifiers may be up to 16 characters long but only the first eight are significant. The compiler cannot tell the difference between `process_first` and `process_last` because they are identical through the first eight characters. The remaining characters only add to readability. The names could be changed to

```
first_data_read
```

and

```
second_data_read
```

In this Workshop the maximum length and significant characters of an identifier are both 18 characters.

Because compilers differ in the maximum and significant name lengths they recognize, you must exercise care choosing names if you want your program to be highly *portable*. The portability of a source program refers to the quantity of changes it needs to be compiled and executed in another programming and computing environment. The fewer changes that source code needs, the more portable it is.

37

Names for identifiers must obey the following rules:

1. Identifiers begin with a letter and may consist of letters, digits, and the underscore character (_).

2. UPPER and lower case are different.

3. By convention, variables and functions have lowercase names, while uppercase is used for names of constants.

4. Identifiers have a maximum length and a maximum number of significant characters. These vary in different C systems.

SELF TEST   38

Which is a legal declaration of a variable?

A) `int 1st_love;`
B) `int true_love2;`
C) `int buffer.1;`

SELF TEST   38A

Is
```
int sum_of_digits;
```
the same as
```
int Sum_of_digits;
```

A) yes
B) no

SELF TEST   38B

According to conventional style, the preferable declaration is

A) `int sum_of_digits;`
B) `int SumOfDigits;`
C) `int SUM_OF_DIGITS;`

                                                                          38C

Functions

Operations performed by a C program are organized into groups called functions. As we saw, a C program begins with `main`, a function that invokes other functions. The compiler and linker always arrange to start execution of the program at `main`. From there, a program may descend through levels of functions indefinitely.

Organizing Programs from the Top Down

C is one of several languages designed for top-down programming. The idea is to divide the task into several phases, each handled by a function. Then you consider each phase as a task and break it down into further sub-phases, handled by their functions. The most general task is thought of as being at the top, and the sub-tasks are regarded as being further down.

Top-down programming is an orderly way to organize a programming project. Your analysis of a problem should lead to a top-down conception of major tasks divided into sub-tasks.

After making this analysis, you can write the functions in any convenient sequence. Many programmers start at the top, then write some some low-level functions (usually handling input and output). They go back and forth, working toward the "middle" levels of the program.

Functions are not organized in strict, mutually exclusive ranks from top to bottom. A work function that displays a certain item of data on the screen, for example, might be invoked by several functions at different levels above it. In fact, we shall see functions that invoke each other.

Top-down programming is a style of work, not something inherent in a language. However, C has features, like functions, that encourage top-down programming.

Syntax of a Function

A function has six major parts.

```
float                                  <1>
lab_test (sample_number, time, date)   <2> <3>
int sample_number, time, date;         <4>
{
double max, min;                       <5>
float purity;
    /*  (code here) */                 <6>
    return (purity);
}
```

These parts are the 1) type of the function, 2) name, 3) parameter list, 4) parameter declarations, 5) local declarations, and 6) statements. The first four parts are sometimes called the header, and the latter two parts are called the body of the function.

The first part of a function, indicated by the first `float` in the example, declares what kind of object the function returns to the expression in which it was invoked. Because the code within the function ends with the statement

```
return (purity);
```

it is necessary to declare that the function "is" a `float`.

Until now we have not seen this part of a function, because the C compiler assumes that anything the function returns is an `int` unless declared otherwise.

Newlines and blanks are both white space, so it means exactly the same thing to write

```
float lab_test (sample_number, time, date)
```

As a matter of style, we prefer to put the type of the function on its own line.

After the name of a function comes its parameter list. Parameters are also called arguments. They are values copied and made available to this function. The parameters of a function are listed within parentheses and separated by commas. Even if there are no parameters, parentheses are required to indicate that the identifier is the name of a function.

As a matter of style, this book prefers to put a space between a function name and its parameter list when there are parameters

```
triple (n)
```

but to omit the space when there are no arguments

```
reset_keyboard()
```

Either way, the function name is an identifier that ends at a space or left parenthesis.

After the list of parameters come their declarations. For each parameter there should be a declaration. Compilers assume a listed argument is an `int` if you omit its declaration, but it is good practice to declare all parameters explicitly.

The parameter name is known only to the function, not to its invoker. When one function invokes another, they should agree on the number and types of the parameters, but the names may be the same or different. If a statement in `main` is

```
result = scale (x, y, z);
```

the function may be declared

```
scale (x, y, z)
int x, y, z;
```

or

```
scale (r, s, t)
int r, s, t;
```

with absolutely no difference in program operation.

The fifth part of a function is the declarations of the local data objects. These follow the opening brace rather than preceding it. They are known only to the function. In other words, if you write two functions

```
double_it (m)
int m;
{
int n;
    ...
```

and

```
triple (p)
int p;
{
int n;
    ...
```

there are two distinct objects both named n. The program is not confused, because any reference within `double_it` refers to its n, while any reference within `triple` refers to its n.

The last part of a function is the statements that follow the declarations within braces. This is the action part that does the work.

A function concludes its work when it encounters `return` in the execution of its statements or when it simply arrives at the closing brace. Execution resumes within the function that invoked this one, immediately following the point at which the invocation occurred.

Although a function executes once each time that it is invoked, there may be several `return` statements in it.

```
decide (score)
int score;
{
    if (score > avg)
        return (TRUE);
    else
        return (FALSE);
}
```

Some programmers prefer to rewrite such functions so that they have only one `return` at the end.

```
decide (score)
int score;
{
int result;
    if (score > avg)
        result = TRUE;
    else
        result = FALSE;
    return (result);
}
```

A function may simply finish execution without returning a value. This occurs when it arrives at its closing brace, or when it comes to a `return` statement that has no expression.

```
open_door ()
{
    if (have_key ())
        {
        unlock_door ();
        return;     /*  function has done its job */
        }
    else
        cry ();     /*  display "Waa-a-a-a" on screen */
}
```

One of the more common typing errors when writing functions is putting a semicolon after the parameter list.

```
calculate()      /*  CORRECT */
{
/* ... */
}

calculate();     /*  WRONG */
{
/* ... */
}
```

The compiler will often detect and report that there is a mistake a few lines later, so look back at earlier lines to find the problem.

43

Top-down programming is implemented in C by breaking tasks into subtasks, then writing all of them as functions. When one function invokes another, they communicate data by passing arguments to the invoked function and returning a value to the invoking function.

Within a function's braces, local variables known only to the function may be declared.

SELF TEST   **43A**

```
float
calc_avg (a, b, c)
int a, b, c;
{...
```

This function returns a value of type

A) `float`
B) `int`

SELF TEST   **43B**

```
triple (n)
int n;
{
int result;
    ...
```

The local variable for this function is
A) above the opening brace ({)
B) within the function braces

C) in the parentheses

Invoking Functions and Passing Arguments

In an expression that combines objects using operators, for example,

```
b + c
```

the objects may be variables, but they may also be function invocations.

```
triple (5) + c
```

Because a function may return one value of a certain type, such as int, the expression makes sense using it instead of the value of a simple variable.

Even if a function returns nothing, a statement may consist of a function invocation.

```
open_door (3);
```

This function might cause the computer to output a signal to the relay controlling door #3, without returning a value. Since the statement does not depend on a value for further computation in an expression, that is acceptable.

Naturally, a function can do both things: perform actions and return a value. Suppose a function start_scale turns on an electronic scale and returns the measured weight. A program might have the statement

```
weight = start_scale (2);
```

The function invocation process consists of the following steps:

1. A copy of the value of each parameter is passed to the invoked function; in this example, the program passes the value 2 to start_scale.

2. The invoked function executes, using the passed parameters. We assume that this function outputs a signal to a relay that starts a scale and receives a weight reading. The action performed by a function may be divided into a) actions performed by the function itself, and b) actions caused by still more invoked functions.

3. The function may return a value of its declared type to the invoker.

4. The invoking statement resumes from where it was suspended, perhaps using the returned value in an expression.

When a C function passes a parameter, a copy of the value is passed. Suppose we have the statements

```
int door_number;

    door_number = 3;
    open_door (door_number);
```

A copy of the current *value* of `door_number`, 3, is passed. Within the function `open_door`, that value is stored in a separate location named by the parameter declared in its arguments. Anything the function does affects only its copy there, not the variable in the invoking function. This arrangement is named "call by value."

Every time a function is invoked, it begins anew with the argument values passed during that invocation.

Occasionally, it will be necessary for a function to alter the value stored in a variable, rather than to work with a copy of the value. We will see that this is possible by using a pointer to deliver the address of a variable to a function. However, even in this case the pointer parameter consists of a copy of an address.

We have seen that a function invocation may construct the value to be passed by enclosing a constant in the argument list

```
    open_door (3);
```

or by enclosing a variable whose value is passed

```
    open_door (door_number);
```

Since a value is passed, the argument may be an expression that evaluates to some value of the specified type:

```
    open_door (his_door + 1);
```

In fact, the expression for an argument may contain its own function invocation:

```
    open_door (calc_max (his_choice, her_choice));
```

This statement invokes the function `calc_max`, giving it the values of the two choice variables. We assume that `calc_max` returns a value, which is immediately passed to `open_door` as that function is invoked.

The invocation of a function and its declaration should agree on the number and type of parameters. It is generally up to you the programmer to insure this agreement. If you have written

```
open_door (door_number, hall_number)
int door_number, hall_number;
{
/* ... */
}
```

then you will have a problem if some other function has a statement like

```
    open_door (dn);
```

which passes only one argument. You will also have a problem with a program fragment like

```
double fdn;
int hn;

    open_door (fdn, hn);
```

which passes a `double` value (which is a variety of floating point number) to a function that expects an `int` parameter.

For this reason, it is difficult in C to create a function that accepts a variable number of parameters. It must be possible, because the `printf` function has an additional argument for each `%` code in its control string argument.

```
    printf ("Hello.  No control codes here!\n");
    printf ("Please open door %d\n", door_number);
```

Most functions are written with a constant number of parameters.

(How does an exception like `printf` work? It knows that it gets at least one parameter, the control string. By counting the occurrences of valid `%` codes in the string, it knows how many more arguments there are.)

It is your responsiblity as programmer to maintain consistency in number and type of function arguments. One reason for this is the ability of C to compile a program whose source code may be in two or more files. A statement in one file may invoke a function in another file. The compiler processes each file separately; while it processes the invocation statement, it has no idea about the invoked function.

The next screen is a program screen. One function invokes another that invokes another function, and so on. The "bottom" function is the same `triple` that you wrote previously.

```
/*  Program with several levels of functions */

/*  COMPLETE this program so that triple() calculates
    and returns three times its input parameter.
    PREDICT before running what statements you will see on
    the screen and in what order.
*/

main()
{
int answer; /*  local variable */

    answer = sub_function1 (5);
    printf ("The result is %d", answer);
}

/*  (This program is longer than a single screen.  The
    F1 Help key tells you the editing commands; one of
    them takes you to the bottom of the program text.)
*/
sub_function1 (n)
int n;
{
    puts ("This is the execution of sub_function1().");
    n = sub_function2 (n);
    return (n);
}

sub_function2 (m)
int m;
{
    puts ("This is the execution of sub_function2().");
    return (triple (m));
}
```

```
/*  WRITE the function triple() as you did before.
    (If you saved it on disk, the Get choice on the
    programming menu will bring it into this program.)
*/
```

48

The preceding program showed several layers of functions. Although `sub_function1` and `sub_function2` did not do very interesting things, each did accept an argument, invoke a "lower down" function to get some work done, accept the value returned, and return it.

48A

```
/*  Program with invocations across two levels of functions */

/*  COMPLETE the work function below. */

main()
{
int n, ans;

    n = 5;
    ans = sub_function1 (n);
    printf ("Twice %d is %d\n", n, ans);
    n = 6;
    ans = dbl_w_pride (n);
    printf ("Twice %d is %d\n", n, ans);
}

sub_function1 (n)
int n;
{
    puts ("  This is an execution of sub_function1.");
    n = dbl_w_pride (n);
    return (n);
}

dbl_w_pride (m)
/*  Return: r set to twice the value of m.
*/
int m;
{
```

```
int r;

/*  WRITE a statement here to calculate  r  from m */
    puts ("I don't care who invoked me.");
    return (r);
}
```

49

The preceding program has a function invoked by functions at different levels above it. Each time dbl_w_pride executes, it receives a value, stores it in a local variable m, and performs its statements.

In fact, each time the function executes, it is allocated an entirely new memory location for m.

49A

```
main()
{
int m, n;

    m = 5;
    n = double_it (m);
    printf ("m = %d and n = %d", m, n);
}

double_it (m)
int m;
{
int n;

    n = m + m;
    m = 17;
    return (n);
}
```

This program has a silly statement (m = 17;), but the question is, is it a damaging statement to m in main?

SELF TEST   **49B**

The above program displays

```
    A) m = 17 and n = 34
    B) m = 17 and n = 10
    C) m = 5 and n = 10
```

50

The silly statement occurs after the passed value has been used in the computation, so the assignment of 17 to m has no effect on the answer n.

50A

```
/*  Program with error in use of local variable */

/*  Try to run this program.
    Notice the error message from the compiler.
*/
int answer1, answer2;

main()
{
int m;

    m = 5;
    answer1 = scale (m);
    answer2 = n + answer1;   /*  is NOT 5 + 5 + 5 + 4 */
    printf ("%d", answer2);
}

scale (n)
int n;
{
    return (n + n + 4);
}
```

50B

If you compiled and ran the preceding program, you received an error message. By the time main tries to compute answer2, n has lived and died in scale. The compiler warns that n is not defined in main.

50C

You may write an expression to create the value passed to a function.

```
    test_tiny (flt2 - flt1);
```

50D

```
/*  Use expression to pass an argument */
```

```
/*  COMPLETE the indicated statement in  main
    without invoking another function.
    Simply calculate the second parameter
    by writing an expression.
*/

main()
{
int n;

    n = 5;
    display (n,          /*  COMPLETE THIS LINE */
}

display (m, n)
/*  Display a number and its triple
*/
int m;  /*  the number */
int n;  /*  three times the number */
{
    printf ("Three times %d is %d", m, n);
}
```

51

Global Data

A variable may be declared outside all the functions of a program. It is called a global variable, and it exists during the entire execution of the program.

51A

```
/*  Program with global data */

/*  DECLARE an integer  salary  here */

main()
{
int weeks;

    weeks = 4;
    calc_salary (4);
```

```
    disp_salary();
}

calc_salary (weeks)
int weeks;       /*  number of weeks this check period */
{
    salary = weeks * 473;   /*  multiply by weekly rate */
}

disp_salary()
{
    printf ("Salary is %d\n", salary);
}
```

The global data object `salary` is not passed from `main` to the other functions of the program, nor is it declared as an argument or local variable of functions.

If you define a local variable with the same name in a function, the compiler assumes that all references within the function to `salary` refer to the *local* variable.

The rule that descriptive variable names are better than short, mysterious ones applies especially to global data. Typically, an object is made global because many functions throughout the program refer to it. Because of the distances from the object declaration to the function code, the variable name should remind you what it contains. Although functions may sometimes use indexes named `i` and numbers named `n` without confusion, global variables should always be more descriptive.

Space is reserved for a global variable before the program begins execution at `main`, and this same storage holds the variable throughout the program. Any function that assigns a new value affects what the next function to access the variable will find there. This is different from passing parameters between functions.

Global data should be used sparingly. It is exposed to changes by any function, and what one function does may confuse other functions and lead to unintended results. A few key variables defining the environment of a system may need to be global data; functions should usually communicate information by way of passed parameters and returned values.

53

```
/*  Local variables outrank global variables */

int rank;

main()
{
int score1, score2;

    score1 = 94;
    score2 = 89;
    calc_rank (score1, score2);
    printf ("Rank is %d\n", rank);
}

/*  EDIT this function so that  main  displays the
    correct value for rank.  Do not change  main.
*/
calc_rank (score1, score2)
int score1, score2;
{
int rank;

    if (score1 >= score2)
        rank = 1;
    else
        rank = 2;
}
```

SELF TEST   **53A**

Although legal to a compiler, which of the following should never be a global variable?

```
A) int i;
B) int read_index;
```

Exercise. How many different C identifiers are there that are exactly three characters long? Remember that max is different than MAX. However, aaa is indistinguishable from aaa (exchanging the first and second a's).

Exercise. The function shoddy has the curious property of returning the sum of its two arguments the first two times it is invoked, after which it returns -1 every time. Write shoddy and write main invoking it five times.

Note: When you press *F10* to Program on a screen without a program exercise, you can write your own program. However, the Soft Tutor will not be here to tell you whether your program produces correct results.

Exercise. Will one, none, or both of these programs compile and run?

```
main()
{
int main;

    main = 1;
    printf ("%d", main);
}
int main;
main()
{
    main = 2;
    printf ("%d", main);
}
```

CHAPTER 5
Fundamental Data Types

Variables and constants always have a type. We have used two data types informally, `int` and `float`. Now we will learn more about the fundamental data types of C. The `int` is only one of several kinds of integers. The character type is a subspecies of integer. Floating point numbers come in two types.

Varieties of Integers

The most frequently used type is the `int`. The `int`s are a finite subset of the infinite collection of mathematical whole numbers

...-3, -2, -1, 0, 1, 2, 3, ...

The greatest and least values for an `int` depend upon the computer and the implementation of C. On so-called 16-bit microcomputers, C typically permits an `int` to range between -32768 and 32767 inclusive. C on a 32-bit DEC VAX computer has `int`s in the range -2147483648 to 2147483647. As we have seen, these peculiar numbers are the decimal values of powers of two.

We have omitted commas in order to get used to the fact that they are not allowed when writing C constant numbers.

```
i = 10000;  /*  legal */
i = 10,000; /*  invalid; compiler will complain */
```

Nor are decimal points allowed in integer constants, because they indicate that the constant is a floating point number.

```
i = 1.0;    /*  floating constant */
```

The compiler will not complain, because it is possible to convert and assign a floating point number to an integer number. But the results of an expression may not be what you expect.

It is legal to write

```
i = -1;
```

but as a matter of syntax -1 is regarded as an expression in which an operator, the unary minus, is applied to an integer constant.

Integers may be combined according to the usual arithmetic operations, like addition and multiplication.

```
int n, r, s, t;

  n = r + s;
  t = r * s;
```

However, while mathematical integers may become as great as necessary, C integers cannot exceed their range. If the arithmetical value of an expression exceeds the limits of the data type, the result is unpredictable. The compiler cannot give you an error message. When the program runs, the computer does not check for illegal values. Your program may run, but the results will probably be wrong. For example,

```
int a, b, c;
  a = 30000;
  b = 30000;
  c = a + b;      /*  unpredictable result in  c */
```

57

In addition to the plain `int`, C has other integer data types, including unsigned `int`, `long int`, and `short int`. All of these may be declared, and in declarations the word `int` is optional.

```
unsigned u;      /* same as  unsigned int u; */
long debt;
short rank;
```

An `unsigned int` is always non-negative, but it represents more positive values. In this Workshop, the range is 0..65535.

A `long` takes values in the same or a greater range than a plain `int`, depending on the computer and compiler. In this Workshop, the range of `long`s is

```
-2147483648 .. 2147483647
```

inclusive. Arithmetic using `long`s takes more time.

A long constant is written with a trailing L.

```
long molecule_count;
    molecule_count = 120000000L;
```

When you pass a constant to a function, the compiler does not know what type of argument the invoked function expects. Suppose you write

```
process (40000);
```

Is this an `unsigned int` or a `long`? The C Workshop compiler passes the former. However, if you write

```
process (100000);   /* better: 100000L */
```

it will pass a `long`, the only type this constant can be.

Other compilers behave differently. Be explicit about `long` constants.

57A

```
/*  Pass appropriate type of constant */

/*  CORRECT the constant so the program display is correct */

main()
{
```

```
    process (40000);
}

process (x)
long x;
{
    printf ("You passed me %ld", x);
}
```

Currently, only a few systems implement another variety of integer, the unsigned long. The C Workshop has unsigned longs in the range 0..4294967295.

The ranges and even the existence of integer data types depend on the machine and compiler. Some types may be effectively identical. For example, on a VAX the long has the same range as an unmodified int. The C language does guarantee that a short has a range no greater than an int, and that a long has a range as least as great as an int.

The two most common implementations are for 16-bit microcomputers using the 8088 or 80286 microprocessor and for 32-bit VAX-style minicomputers.

	Microcomputer	Minicomputer
int	16 bits	32 bits
short	8 or 16 bits	16 bits
long	32 bits	32 bits

In this Workshop a short is the same as an int.

58

Summary of integers:

An int is a whole number within a certain range, -32768 to 32767 in this Workshop. Probably 95% of all numbers used in C are plain ints, and most of the rest are unsigned ints.

Integer arithmetic must stay within the bounds of the range, or unpredictable results occur.

Integer constants have no commas or decimal points.

The unsigned int, or simply unsigned, is non-negative and usually represents twice as many positive integers.

The `long` and `short` integers have ranges that may be greater and narrower, respectively, than plain `int`s.

To learn the exact range of a data type, consult your compiler, because ranges vary by type of computer.

SELF TEST   59

The proper C statement using an `int` constant is

    A) n = 1.0;
    B) n = 32,767;
    C) n = 12000;
    D) n = 40000;

SELF TEST   59A

A C Workshop program has the following:

```
unsigned int m;
   m = 40000 + 3;
```

What is the value of m?

SELF TEST   59B

A C Workshop program has the following:

```
int m;
   m = 40000 + 3;
```

What is the value of m?

    A) 40003
    B) depends on the compiler
    C) 7235

                                                          59C

```
/*  Binary guessing game using unsigned integers */

/*  This is the guessing game you saw earlier.
    The maximum number allowed is higher.
    EDIT the  int  declarations to  unsigned int.
    Then run the program. */

main()
```

```
{
int low, high, mid;

    low = 1; high = 50000;    /*  (high could be 64K-1) */
    printf ("Think of a number between 1 and %u.\n", high);
    puts ("Press key when ready.");
    getchar ();

do  {
    mid = low + 1 + (high - low) / 2;
    printf ("\nIs it greater than %u? y/n:", mid - 1);
    if (toupper (getchar()) == 'Y')      /*  'y' to 'Y' */
        low = mid;             /*  must be in upper range */
    else
        high = mid - 1;        /*  must be in lower range */
    } while (high - low);      /*  while there is a range */

    printf ("\nYour number is %u.", high);
}
```

60

As the preceding program showed, there is a control code allowing `printf` to display unsigned integers: `%u`.

To display a `long`, put the letter `l` between the percent sign and the `d`.

```
printf ("Our species emerged %ld years ago", 1000000L);
```

60A

Hexadecimal and Octal Notation

In many situations, hexadecimal notation is more convenient than decimal for representing unsigned constants. These are indicated in C with the prefix `0x`.

0x10 is 16 decimal.

0x100 is 256 decimal.

0x10A is 266 decimal.

If hexadecimal arithmetic is new to you, see the appendix on it. In fact, this would be a good time to experiment with the index. By pressing the *F4* key and entering the word you want, you will go to the index. The first part of the word, like "hexadec," is sufficient.

61

The `printf` control code for displaying an unsigned integer in hexadecimal notation is `%x`. A long integer may be displayed in hexadecimal by using the "middle-fix" `l`.

```
printf ("Occupied memory is %x (hex) bytes\n", 0x4000);
```

displays

```
Occupied memory is 4000 (hex) bytes
```

and

```
printf ("Free memory is %lx (hex) bytes\n", 0x10000L);
```

displays

```
Free memory is 10000 (hex) bytes
```

Octal notation uses base eight. Although it is helpful when using computers with memory cells of 24 or 48 bits, these sizes are rare today. Octal constants are signaled with a 0 at the beginning, and `printf` displays values in octal using the `%o` control code.

```
printf ("The ASCII value of A in octal is %o", 0101);
```

displays

```
The ASCII value of A in octal is 101
```

The same display results from

```
printf ("The ASCII value of A in octal is %o", 65);
```

That is, the format of function input need not be the same as the format of its output. After all, the most common code is more like the following:

```
n = 65;
printf ("The ASCII value of %c in octal is %o", n, n);
```

61A

The char Data Type

Characters, such as letters, digits, punctuation, special characters and the newline, blank (space), and tab are represented in computers by whole numbers. The ASCII code uses the numbers 0..127. Capital A is coded as 65, the digit 3 is coded as 51, etc. Some mainframe computers use the EBCDIC code. Both are merely conventional assignments of an integer to represent a character.

In C the data type `char` (pronounced "kar" or "char") is another variety of integer. It occupies one byte, or eight bits, of storage, which provides enough values to represent the coded character value.

```
char response_key;

    response_key = 65;
    response_key = 'A';
```

Character constants are represented within single quote marks. An 'A' is different than the string of text "A" that might occur as the parameter of the `puts` function.

The *escape* character \ with a letter represents the otherwise unrepresentable characters:

Table of non-printing character constants

Name	Escape sequence
Newline	'\n'
Tab	'\t'
Null (binary 0)	'\0'
Double quote	'\"'
Single quote	'\''
Backslash	'\\'
Carriage return	'\r'
Formfeed	'\f'
Octal bit pattern	'\ooo'
where the ooo are three octal digits	

Like all `char`s, these occupy one byte.

Besides being used as character constants within single quotes, these escape sequences may appear in strings of text. We have frequently written statements like the following:

```
printf ("End a line with a newline character.\n");
```

The newline character is ambiguous. Its action is to move to the start of the next line. In MS-DOS systems, the program must transmit a carriage return and a line feed to MS-DOS to get this result. In the UNIX operating system, where C was born, a line feed gets this action. Typically, MS-DOS C compilers represent a \n as a line feed (ASCII code is decimal 10), but the library functions like `printf` and `puts` output the two characters MS-DOS needs.

Is it possible to have a negative character? Given a C system that represents a `char` in a byte, the values 0x80 through 0xFF may represent positive values in the range 128..255 or negative values -128..-1. In the C Workshop, a `char` is unsigned, but you may declare a `signed char`. Some compilers by default regard a `char` as signed. The importance of this situation occurs when type conversions are performed between a `char` and an `int`, which we will study in a later section.

63

```
/*  Use escape sequences in printf */

/*  COMPLETE the program so that it displays the following:

    I say, "'Escape sequences' begin with a backslash (\)."

*/

main()
{
    printf

/*  COMPLETE this statement.
    You may put the argument on a separate line.
*/
}
```

63A

Floating Types

To represent some of the numbers that lie between integers, C provides two floating data types, `float` and `double`.

```
float voltage;
double current;
```

Floating types represent numbers with a fractional part. Until now, we have used the word "range" to describe the distance from the greatest integer to the least (in the sense of approaching negative infinity). Floating types have a range in a different sense: it is the limits of the largest and smallest (in the sense of closest to zero) of the positive numbers that can be represented. Floating types represent negative numbers, too, but the range is defined this way. Another, independent quality of floating types is their precision: the number of significant decimal (or binary) places of a value.

Just as an implementation of C may not provide any larger range for `longs` than for plain `ints`, a `double` may or may not have greater range and precision than a `float`.

Some new C systems have a type `long double`. It may offer greater range and precision.

There are no `float` constants; they are all `double`. One way to write them is with a decimal point.

```
float voltage;

    voltage = 5.0;   /*  a power supply this precise? */
    voltage = 3.178;
```

As with integer constants, commas and spaces are not allowed. Note that the variable `voltage` is declared as a `float`, but the constant is of type `double`. When the value is assigned to the variable, a conversion occurs automatically.

Another way to represent floating constants is with the use of scientific notation. Some examples are the following:

```
float current, power;

    current = 2.841e-5;
    current = 0.2841e-4;
    current = 0.02841e-3;

    power = 98.28E4;
    power = 9828E2;
    power = 982800e0;
```

A decimal point or an exponential part is required. The exponential part begins with e or E. The exponent (power of ten) is an integer value, possibly negative to represent numbers with absolute value less than one.

It is legal to write the floating constant 1. but for readability, 1.0 is preferable.

The quantity in scientific notation is the mantissa, which precedes the e, times ten raised to the exponent. Ten raised to zero is one, and ten raised to negative powers are tenths, hundredths, thousandths, etc. The constants assigned to current above represent the same quantity, as do those assigned to power.

One way to display a floating value in a printf expression is with the control code %f.

```
printf ("Voltage = %f", voltage);
```

This code may be used whether voltage is a float or a double, because the value is always converted to a double before being passed as a parameter.

Another control code %e displays the value in exponential form.

In addition, you may control the number of character places occupied by the displayed value and the number of digits shown past the decimal point (the default is six decimal places). The options are numerous and detailed; consult the index for detailed specification of printf controls if you are interested.

Many real numbers may only be approximated in value by floating types. In a binary machine, 1/3 is such a number. All machines represent pi only approximately. Furthermore, when floating types are combined in arithmetic expressions, some precision is usually lost; results are not exact. It is rarely much good to write a statement like

```
if (voltage == 1.0)
    shut_down();
```

for this reason. Better is

```
if (voltage < 1.0 + eps)
    shut_down();
```

where eps is a small number guaranteeing a safety factor.

Numerical analysis is the study of losses of precision due to rounding, truncation, scaling, overflow and underflow.

Although we will present the essential information about floating types, we will not study them in depth. There are three reasons. First, numerical analysis is an entire subject in itself, and anyone who uses floating types more than casually should know something about losses of precision. Second, computers are used for many problems that are more symbolic than numeric. Third, a programmer can often solve tasks that seem to require floating types by using integer scaling techniques (discussed later in this book).

SELF TEST   66

Which is the valid floating constant?

```
A) 1230
B) .123-9
C) 1,230e0
D) 0.123e-1
E) 0.123 0e1
```

SELF TEST   66A

A very poor C system has `float` and `double` with precision of one decimal place.

```
v1 = 1.03;
v2 = 1.07;
if (v1 == v2)
    shut_down();
```

Does `shut_down` execute?

```
A) yes
B) no
```

Exercise. Write a short program that displays the following sentence, filled in.

```
The numerical ASCII value of a \ is __
```

Exercise. Code the following program in the C Workshop and change only one character so it displays a common sentence.

```
main()
{
unsigned int n;

    n = 64206;
    printf ("You must %u the facts", n);
}
```

CHAPTER 6
Expressions and Operators: I

In this chapter and the next, we build elementary C statements by forming expressions with operators. There are arithmetical, logical and other kinds of operators. The C language derives part of its power (and also some tricky aspects) from the special action of various operators.

Operators make things happen. They take one, two or three operands, each of which is a value of a variable, constant, or invoked function. Most operators produce a new value of a certain data type.

Because an operator consumes one or more values and yields a value, operators with their operands may be combined in expressions. The expression may then be said to evaluate to a value. Some expressions are

```
response_key + 1
x
5 - sum (first, second)
'A' + max (m, n)
```

You can imagine that as a program executes it maintains an "expression accumulator," which holds the current value that has been evaluated, and its type. The simple expression

```
x
```

places the value in the variable **x** into this expression accumulator, for example.

Assignment

A fundamental operator is assignment (=). It has two operands. The assignment operator places the value of the expression on its right-hand side into the place named on the left-hand side.

```
m = n + 1
```

If we make the expression into a statement by ending it with a semicolon,

```
m = n + 1;
```

this in effect clears our imaginary expression accumulator. That is, we can no longer rely on it to have a meaningful value.

Informally, we have been writing code like

```
if (x)
    do_it();
```

The expression accumulator has the value of **x** when the keyword `if` examines it to determine whether or not to `do_it`. Thus, it makes sense that the parentheses enclose an expression, while the action part of `if` is a statement.

Unlike arithmetic, it makes no sense in C to write

```
n + 5 = 20; /* NONSENSE */
```

This symbolism specifies no place for the assignment operator to store the value 20.

On the other hand, the mathematical contradiction

$x = x + 1$ (implies $0 = 1$)

may become the C statement

```
x = x + 1;      /* fine C */
```

which says, add the value of **x** and 1 and store the result in the location for **x**.

In formal discussions of C and sometimes in compiler error messages, you will see the term *lvalue*. It refers to an object with a definite place in memory. The term suggests a legitimate left side of an assignment. If you write

```
n + 7 = 13;
```

a compiler might explain the error by saying "need an lvalue."

We have seen that the assignment operator in C is different than the mathematical equality relation, even though they use the same symbol =. In this respect, virtually all computer programming languages are like C and unlike mathematics. However, C goes on to treat assignment as an operator in the full sense, alongside traditional operators like + and *. For example, the statement

```
n = 3 + (a = b) + 4;
```

is perfectly legal C, although not very useful. After this statement executes, the value of b will be stored in a as well as the value of 3 + b + 4 being stored in n.

70

```
/*  Example of assignment within assignment */

/*  PREDICT what this program will display.
    Then RUN it.
*/

main()
{
int a, b, n;

    b = 2;
    n = 3 + (a = b) + 4;

    printf ("n = %d and a = %d", n, a);
}
```

A more useful instance of treating assignment like any operator is the statement

```
if ((c = read_keyboard()) > 32)
    do_it();
```

This statement says, invoke the function and assign the value it returns to c, then compare this value (which is now in our imaginary expression accumulator) to 32. If the value is greater than 32, invoke do_it. Whether or not the function is invoked, the keyboard has been read and the key value has been stored in c. This is compact, and the object code generated by the compiler may be a little shorter, too.

SELF TEST   71

Which is a C expression?

```
A) x - 3 + y;
B) alpha_count + gamma_count
C) m n - 4;
```

SELF TEST   71A

Which is a valid C statement?

```
A) 5 - 3 = 2;
B) i = j = k = 0;
C) 2 = 5 - 3;
D) key = 'A' + 1
```

                                                                                            71B

```
/*  Another example of assignment within statement */

/*  Don't change this program.  Just STATE in English
    what it will do when the user presses different
    upper and lower case letters.  RUN the program
    to see if you are correct.
*/

/*  getchar() returns the next key pressed */
/*  putchar() displays a character */

main()
{
int c;

    puts ("Press a key");          /* prompt user */
    if ((c = getchar()) == 'z')    /* == tests for equality */
        c = toupper (c);           /* convert to uppercase */
    putchar (c);                   /* display the character */
}
```

Arithmetic, Precedence, and Associativity

C has operators similar to traditional arithmetic operators. They are combined according to rules of precedence and associativity.

Integer arithmetic has five basic operators. Assume a = 14 and b = 5.

Addition	+	c = a + b;	19
Subtraction	-	c = a - b;	9
Multiplication	*	c = a * b;	70
Quotient	/	c = a / b;	2
Modulus	%	c = a % b;	4

Division has two results, a quotient and a remainder, so the language gives you operators for obtaining the one you want.

```
/*  Compute value of pocket change */

main()
{
int n, d, q, h, sum;
int dol, cent;                      " DIME.C

    n = 5;
    d = 2;
    q = 3;
    h = 1;

    sum = calc_change (n, d, q, h);
    dol = sum / 100;
    cent = sum % 100;
    printf ("This pocket has %d dollar(s) and %d cents",
        dol, cent);
}

calc_change (nickels, dimes, quarters, halves)
/*  Return: total cents in these coins.
    WRITE this function.
*/
```

```
int nickels, dimes, quarters, halves;    /*  count of each */
```

Division has some peculiarities. The divisor should not be zero. If it is, the program may halt, or the computer may crash. The handling of negative quantities depends on the particular compiler and computer. For example, after the statements

```
a = -14;
b = 5;
c = a / b;
```

the value of c may be -3 (the largest integer less than the mathematically defined quotient) or -2 (the smallest integer greater than the mathematical quotient).

If we replace the last statement by a modulus computation,

```
c = a % b;
```

the value of c may be -4 or 4. The sign depends on the implementation. See the section on compiler specifications for details about the C Workshop compiler (or put the statements above in a small program and see what comes out). Most modulus computations are performed on pairs of positive integers.

73

Many expressions combine several operators. For example,

```
d = a + b * c;
```

The question is, does C add a and b then multiply by c, or does it multiply b and c then add the result to a? The answer is decided by C's rules of precedence. Multiplication, quotient and modulus have higher precedence than addition and subtraction. This means that the multiplication in an expression without parentheses is performed before the addition.

According to precedence, the value of

```
4 + 3 * 2
```

is 10, not 14.

If you want to add a and b before multiplying by c, you may override the rules of precedence by using parentheses.

```
d = (a + b) * c;
```

The multiplication operator and the two division operators all have the same precedence. If we write

```
d = a * b % c;
```

we need to know whether C multiplies a and b then computes the modulus after division by c, or whether d is the result of multiplying a times the result of b % c. It is obvious that the order of operations can seriously affect integer calculations. (The precision of floating type computations may be affected, too.)

Rules of associativity resolve the ambiguity. Within a group of operators having the same precedence, associativity specifies that C applies the operators either from right to left or in the reverse direction. Some precedence levels go one way, and some go the other way. However, all binary operators (the ones that have two operands) associate left to right, with the important exception of assignment.

Therefore, the result of

```
7 * 8 % 5
```

is 1 (remainder of 56 divided by 5), not 21.

74

To determine the order of action in evaluating an expression, analyze each parenthetical grouping first. Apply the rules of precedence, higher before lower. Finally, within a precedence level, follow the direction of associativity left to right or right to left.

An appendix of this book has the standard C chart of operator precedence and associativity. The chart is also one of the screens shown when you press the Help key.

One tiny problem about combining operators remains. When a commutative operator is repeated

```
d = (a + b) + c;
```

the order of evaluation is unknown to you. A commutative operator is one which does not care if the two operands are reversed. In the above statement, the C compiler is allowed to evaluate the sum of a, b, and c in any order, even though parentheses are present. This liberty permits the compiler to produce more efficient code at times. For example,

```
d = (7 + a) + 1;
```

may be coded as machine instructions adding 8 to a.

If the order of operations matters to you (for example, in tracking floating type precision), break the action into two statements.

```
temp = 7 + a;
d = temp + 1;
```

This technique takes advantage of the fact that a statement begins with no assumptions about the imaginary expression accumulator.

Let us return briefly to the assignment operator. When we write

```
c = a + b;
```

the expression has two operators. Because assignment is an operator, it could conceivably be that the value of a is assigned to c and then the value of b is added. The expected result occurs because addition, like all operators except one obscure one, has higher precedence than assignment.

Assignment differs from other binary operators in that it associates from right to left. This rule is what makes the statement

```
i = j = 0;
```

work. First the value 0 is assigned to j, working from the right. Then the value in the expression accumulator, 0, is assigned to i.

SELF TEST   75

```
b = 18; c = 4;
a = b % c;
```

What is the value of a?

SELF TEST   75A

```
b = -18; c = 4;
a = b / c;
```

After these statements, the value of a is

A) -4

B) 4

C) -5
D) depends on compiler
E) 5

SELF TEST   **76**

```
p = 5; q = 2;
r = (p + q) * (p - q);
```

What is the value of r?

SELF TEST   **76A**

```
m = 5; n = 2;
a = (m - n) * (m / n);
```

What is the value of a?

SELF TEST   **76B**

```
j = 7; k = 2;
i = (j / k) + (j % k);
```

What is the value of i?

SELF TEST   **76C**

```
a = 14;
b = 5;
c = 2;
```

What is the value of a + b * c ?

                                                                 76D

```
/*  Use the arithmetic operators */

main()
{
int p, q, r;

    p = 9; q = 3;
    r = transform (p, q);
    printf ("%d and %d are transformed to %d", p, q, r);
}
transform (p, q)
/*  Return: the sum of p and q, plus
```

```
    twice the difference of q from p, plus
    the product of p and twice q, plus
    three times the quotient of p divided by q, plus
    the remainder of p divided by q.
    WRITE this function.
*/
```

77

Conversion of Data Types

Generally, we have kept each type of data to itself, adding `int` to `int` but not to `float`. Fortunately, these barriers are leaped easily with a few rules about conversion of data from one type to another.

The three most common situations are assignment, arithmetic conversions, and passing arguments to functions.

Consider the statements

```
float f_pressure;
int i_pressure;

    f_pressure = 2.7;
    i_pressure = f_pressure;
```

Assignment converts the type of the value on the right side to the type of the lvalue into which it is stored. In this case, a `float` is truncated to an `int`. That is, the value of `i_pressure` is 2.

On the other hand, the statements

```
    i_pressure = 2;
    f_pressure = i_pressure;
```

have no quantitative effect, although the data type is converted. (Because a `float` is stored in a different format and often in more bytes than an `int`, the type conversion is more than conceptual.)

An important case of conversion during assignment has to do with `char` and `int`.

```
char menu_key;
int option;
```

The effect of the statement

```
option = menu_key;
```

depends, for certain values of the `char`, upon the C implementation. A `char` may be treated as a signed or unsigned quantity. In some instances, it does not matter. The byte that represents the ASCII value of *A* as a `char` keeps the value 65 decimal or 0x41 in an integer word regardless of whether sign extension occurs or not.

The fun begins with negative `char` values, especially the value -1. As a byte this is 0xFF; as a word, it is 0xFFFF. Suppose some special key combination on the keyboard could generate 0xFF. Then the above statement will store either 0xFF in `option` (no sign extension) or 0xFFFF (sign extended).

In C terminology, the `char` data type may be `signed` or `unsigned` depending on the computer. You must know what your compiler does. The C Workshop compiler defaults to unsigned characters.

Many functions return -1 to indicate that no input is available or that an error occurred. The standard library function `getc()` returns the next character in a file or -1 if none is available (typically, the end of file has been reached). Suppose we have

```
char c;
```

and that our C system does not extend the sign in assigning a `char` to an `int`. We write

```
c = getc (file);
if (c == -1)
    windup();
else
    process_letter();
```

While the file has characters, they are processed. When `getc` returns -1, the assignment to `c` truncates the quantity to 0xFF (always when chopping an `int` value to a `char`). The comparison then compares 0xFF to -1 (an integer constant, 0xFFFF in hexadecimal). This comparison is never true, and the computer locks up trying to process 0xFF again and again.

Ordinary ASCII codes are never negative; in fact, C requires that the standard character set must be represented by positive values. But -1 is frequently used as described, and some extended ASCII patterns may use the negative characters 0x80 through 0xFF.

The easy way to avoid potential problems using some compilers is to change the type declaration. By declaring `int c;` we store the integer returned by the function into an integer.

If our program reads a file into a large array, it will be important to declare the array as a collection of `char` rather than `int` in order to save a vast amount of space. The idea is to get the `int` and store it by truncation into the array after it has been tested and processed. When a character is extracted from the array, it may be converted back to an `int`.

Moral: maintain values as integers until it is necessary for space reasons to store them as characters.

Some compilers recognize and obey declarations like

```
unsigned char c;
signed char c1;
```

and careful use of these types will pin down the action to your intention.

SELF TEST   79

```
int u, i;
char c;
signed char s;

    c = 0x8D;     s = 0x8D;
    u = c;
    i = s;
```

After these statements, does u equal i?

A) yes

B) no

Assignment makes some other conversions. Assigning a `long int` to a plain `int` or `char` truncates the high-order bits. When a `double` is assigned to a `float`, the quantity is rounded or truncated to fit, depending on the compiler.

79A

Assignment promotes one type to a "larger" type without loss of information, such as `int` to `double`. Assignment in the opposite direction loses information in some way.

Because the treatment of `char` may be as a signed or unsigned quantity, the assignment to `int` must be watched wherever the sign may be negative. The case of -1 is common. We recommend that you carry the value along as an `int` as far as possible. In any event, you must know your compiler's rule.

80

Arithmetic Conversions

If a program declares

```
int i;
float f;
```

we must ask how

```
    i + f
```

is computed. The answer is that the values of `i` and `f` are converted to `double` and then added!

This conversion applies only to evaluating the expression; the locations `i` and `f` continue to hold type and value as they were declared and assigned.

80A

There is a set of "usual arithmetic conversions" for combining the operands of binary operators that accept arithmetical data types.

First, if either operand is `char` or `short`, its value is promoted to `int`.

If an operand is `float`, its value is promoted to `double`.

Roughly, these first two rules say that integer arithmetic is performed versus character arithmetic, and that floating type arithmetic is performed at the `double` level.

Then if the operands are mixed types, a series of rules promotes the "lower" type to the higher:

If either operand is `double`, the other value is promoted to `double` and the result is `double`.

Otherwise, the same kind of rule is applied for `long`.

Otherwise, the same kind of rule is applied for `unsigned`.

80B

Note: as some compilers support new data types, like `long double` and `unsigned long int`, the rules acquire more detail to handle them. The basic idea is to promote the lesser type. If in doubt, investigate your compiler's documentation, or write a short test progarm.

81

Conversion of Function Arguments

The arguments of a function are expressions, even if they have only one operand. That is, we may invoke

```
process (x);
```

or

```
process (2 * x + y);
```

81A

Consequently, conversions are performed in evaluating the expression that is the argument. Even if we write

```
char c;
    process_option (c);
```

the rules state that a `char` value in an expression is promoted to an `int` value. This happens regardless of whether the definition of the function reads

```
process_option (option)
int option;
    ...
```

or

```
process_option (option)
char option;
    ...
```

81B

In the latter case the passed integer value will then be stored in a character location, possibly truncated.

Most often a problem occurs not because a type is promoted but because of over-reliance on automatic promotion. Normally, you can pass `char` or `int` without worry, and you can pass `float` or `double`. However, a function that requires a `double`, like the typical library routine `fabs`, yields nonsense and possibly a program crash if you write

```
int n;
    f = fabs (n);         /*  WRONG */
```

The simple argument expression n undergoes no conversion to any kind of floating type, so an `int` is passed where a `double` is expected.

82

Arguments may be whipped into shape. One way would be to create another variable.

```
int n;
float f_n;

    f_n = n;
    f = fabs (f_n); /*  float promoted to double */
```

However, this technique creates unncessary objects, complicating the source text and wasting computer time. A better way is to use a *cast*. The cast is an operator (you'll find it on the precedence chart). It is written by putting the desired type specifier in parentheses before the expression.

```
    f = fabs ( (double) n );
```

A cast is a unary operator that changes the type of a value. Note that the value is converted to the specified type only for this expression; in memory n remains an `int`.

SELF TEST   **82A**

```
int i;
float f;

    f = 3.812;
    i = f;
```

What is the integer value of `i`?

SELF TEST   **82B**

```
char c;
int i;
    i = -1;
    c = i;
```

The value of c is
   A) -1
   B) 0xFFFF
   C) depends on compiler
   D) 0xFF

SELF TEST   **83**

```
char c;
int i;
    c = -1;
    i = c;
```

The value of i is
   A) -1
   B) 0xFFFF
   C) depends on compiler
   D) 0xFF

                                                                           83A

```
/*  Write a cast */

extern double fabs();    /*  tells compiler of non-int return */

main()
{
int a, b, c, d, n, abs_n;

    n = -13;

    abs_n = fabs (n);
/*  REWRITE this statement with a cast so that the
    resulting display is correct.
*/

    printf ("The absolute value of %d is %d", n, abs_n);
}
```

Incidentally, the extra declarations in the preceding program are solely for your protection. Without a cast, fabs may throw your computer into an endless loop. The declarations help neutralize the effect of a misguided `fabs`; the trick is specific to this situation.

84

On the next screen is a program exercise asking you to add two unsigned integers. The function that does the work is asked to ensure that the sum will not exceed the range of unsigned integers.

This program uses the maximum value of unsigned integers, which varies with the computer and the compiler. To complete the program, you need to use the maximum unsigned integer value to determine whether you can add the second number to the first. That is, does the magnitude of the second number exceed the remaining interval left by the first number?

84A

```
/*  Add unsigned integers, avoiding overflow */

#define MAX_UNS  0xFFFF      /*  C Workshop limit */
extern unsigned u_add();     /*  Declare what fn returns.
                                 Compiler needs to know
                                 for non-int return type. */

main()
{
unsigned int u1, u2, s;

    u1 = 0xC284;
    u2 = 0x2001;

    s = u_add (u1, u2);
    if (s == 0)
        printf ("Sum exceeds range");
    else
        printf ("%u + %u = %u", u1, u2, s);
}

unsigned
u_add (u1, u2)
/*  Return: sum if within range of unsigned integers
            0 otherwise
    Invoker must not submit 0 + 0.
    WRITE this function.
```

```
*/
```

Exercise. Put parentheses in the indicated statement so the program compiles and displays its message.

```
main ()
{
int a, b, c;

    b = 4;
    c = 1;
    a = b + c = c;        /*  needs ( ) */
    if (a == 5)
        printf ("Correct");
}
```

Exercise. Write a function `fraction` that accepts two integers and displays the quotient as a mixed fraction. For example, `frac (17, 3)` should display 5 2/3. The fraction need not be reduced to lowest terms.

Exercise. Declare n so that this program displays exactly 102 numbers in the C Workshop. (If your program keeps going much further after 102 numbers are displayed, press Ctrl-Brk to stop it.)

```
main ()
{
    more (100);
}

more (n)
/*  NEED DECLARATION */
{
    printf ("%d\t", n);
    if (n == 255)
        return;
    else
        more (n - 1);
}
```

Exercise. The longs and unsigned integers in a C compiler are defective, but a programmer desperately needs a function `show_thrice` that displays three times its positive integer input. Write this function for your colleague. Hint: you may find it useful to have a statement

```
printf ("%d%d%d%d%d\n", ten_thouses, th, hun, t, u);
```

CHAPTER 7
Expressions and Operators: II

This chapter looks at more operators, including relational, logical, and bit-wise operators. Two sophisticated arithmetic operators, increment and decrement, are also introduced. Finally, compound assignment operators and the three-term conditional expression are studied.

Relational and Equality Operators

Relational and equality operators compare values and produce 0 if the comparison is false or a non-zero value (1) if the comparison is true.

Tests use these operators. For example, when we write

```
if (a < b)
    report (b);
```

the less-than operator < produces a 0 or a 1. If the result is non-zero, `report` is performed; otherwise it is skipped.

These operators are:

Greater than   >
Less than   <

Greater than or equal	>=
Less than or equal	<=
Equal	==
Not equal	!=

Notice that the comparison for equality is different than assignment. We write

```
if (a == b)
    c = a + 3;
else
    c = a + 4;
```

88

The operator is a single unit of C (called a token by compiler writers) made up of one or two characters. In order to fuse the two characters into one symbol, no blanks are allowed between them, no more than blanks are allowed in variable names.

```
if (i < = j)        /*  WRONG */
    do it (i);      /*  WRONG */

if (i <= j)         /*  CORRECT */
    do_it (i);      /*  CORRECT */
```

If i == j then j == i, too, but as we saw, this is not true for assignment.

Assignment (=) is not commutative; it stores the value of an expression on the right side into an lvalue, a legitimate place in memory for storing values. The equality operator is commutative; it compares the values of two expressions and generates a value 1 or 0. This value is not stored; it merely occupies our imaginary expression accumulator.

88A

The precedence of the relational and equality operators is below that of the arithmetic operators, so we may evaluate expressions before making comparisons.

```
a = 5;  b = 3;
if (a < 2 * b)
    do_it ();
```

Since 5 is less than 2 times 3, we do it.

For the same reason, the test

```
(i < j)
```

has the same result as that of

```
(i - j < 0)
```

The precedence of the relational operators is one level higher than that of the two equality operators (== and !=).

89

The usual arithmetic conversions are performed when applying the relational and equality operators. For example, if a program has the statements

```
char c;
int i;

   if (c < i)
       do_it();
```

the value of the char c is converted to an int. Recall that if the value of c is 0xFF, it depends on the compiler whether this value is promoted to 0x00FF or 0xFFFF for the comparison with i.

SELF TEST   **89A**

What is the value of 0 <= 0 ?

SELF TEST   **89B**

```
   a = 1; b = 2; c = 3; d = 4;
   if (a == b - 1)
       d = c;
```

What is the value of d after these statements?

SELF TEST   **89C**

```
   a = 1; b = 2; c = 3; d = 4;
   if (a != b - 1)
       d = c;
```

What is the value of d after these statements?

SELF TEST   90

```
p = 1; q = 2; r = 3;
if (r > p)
    q = p;
```

What is the value of q after these statements?

SELF TEST   90A

```
p = 1; q = 3; r = 4;
if (p < r)
    r = q;
```

What is the value of r after these statements?

SELF TEST   90B

```
a = 1; b = 2; c = 3; d = 4;
if (a <= b)
    d = c;
```

What is the value of d after these statements?

SELF TEST   90C

```
a = 1; b = 2; d = 4;
if (a >= b - 1)
    d = b;
```

What is the value of d after these statements?

SELF TEST   90D

```
int a, b, m, n;
    m = a; n = b;
    if (a < b == m < n)
        printf ("Propositional logic creates no new truth");
```

(You should know the precedence of the operators to answer this.)
These statements execute the `printf` statement

    A) sometimes, depending on all of a, b, m and n
    B) always
    C) never
    D) sometimes, depending only on the values of a and b

91

Relational and equality operators produce a value of 0 or 1. Remember, though, that the action of an if-statement executes whenever the test expression has *any* nonzero value.

```
if (test_size())
    de_allocate();
```

Do not assume that `test_size` returns 0 or 1. It might well return 0 or the actual size. The above code is reliable, while the following code is not.

```
#define TRUE 1
#define FALSE 0

    if (test_size() == TRUE)   /*  BAD.  Might return size > 1 */
        de_allocate();
```

On the other hand, comparison with 0 is fine.

```
    if (test_size() != FALSE)
        de_allocate();
```

91A

The first program in the C Workshop demonstrated a number guessing game. You might remember that it asks

```
Is it greater than %d?
```

even when `mid` and `high` are equal. In this case the program could ask directly about one number. You can dress up the program by testing for equality and asking

```
printf ("Is your number %u? y/n:", m);
```

when the midpoint and high bound are equal.

91B

```
/*  Binary guessing game with dressed up question */

main()
{
unsigned low, high, mid;

    low = 1; high = 50000;   /*  (high could be 64K-1) */
    printf ("Think of a number between 1 and %u.\n", high);
```

```
    puts ("Press key when ready.");
    getchar();

do  {
    mid = low + 1 + (high - low) / 2;

/*  TEST mid and high for equality.  If they are equal,
    ask the user if this is his number; else, ask the
    old question. */

        printf ("\nIs it greater than %u? y/n:", mid - 1);


    if (toupper (getchar()) == 'Y')      /*  'y' to 'Y' */
        low = mid;                /*  must be in upper range */
    else
        high = mid - 1;           /*  must be in lower range */
    } while (high - low);         /*  while there is a range */

    printf ("\nYour number is %u.", high);
}
```

92

An Irritating Mistake

One of the most irritating mistakes is writing

```
    if (i = 7)
```

when you intend

```
    if (i == 7)
```

The first, erroneous form will assign 7 to i and then evaluate whether i is non-zero (true) or zero (false). In other words, the assignment places the value in our imaginary expression accumulator. Since 7 is non-zero, the execution statement for the if is performed. In addition, the value of i is corrupted.

92A

Although relational operators occur most frequently in the test expression of if-statements and other control structures, you can use them profitably in

many situations. For example, an interactive program asks the user to press
'Q' to quit or another key to continue. Here is a function to do the job.

```
ask_continue()
/*  Return: TRUE/FALSE quit/continue  */
{
int c;
    printf ("Press Q to quit, any other key to continue:");
    c = toupper (getchar());   /*  accept q or Q */
    return (c == 'Q');
}
```

The expression c == 'Q' evaluates to 1 or 0, and this value is returned.
Even shorter, you may combine the last two lines and omit the variable c by
writing

```
    return (toupper (getchar()) == 'Q');
```

93

```
/*  Use relational operator without if-statement */

#define TRUE    1
#define FALSE   0

main()
{
int jackpot;    /*  must be lower case */
int key;

    jackpot = 'i';
    puts ("Tap letter keys until you discover the secret one.");
    puts ("(Or press Ctrl-Brk to quit.)");

/*  (This loop is studied later.) */
    do  {
        key = getchar();
        printf (" ");
        } while (play (jackpot, key));
    puts ("\nYou got it.");
}

play (secret, key)
```

```
/*   Return: TRUE if user pressed key OTHER THAN jackpot key.
          FALSE if presses jackpot key.
     User is allowed to press upper or lower case key.
     WRITE this function.  Can you do it without using an
        if-statement?
     There is a library function tolower().
*/
int secret;      /*  jackpot key in lower case */
int key;
```

94

Logical Operators

Logical operators typically combine the results of relational or other tests. For example, whether someone must be registered to fight in a war depends on both their sex and age; a program used by the Selective Service would test both.

The token && stands for *and*.

The token | | stands for *or*.

```
a = 1;   b = 2;   c = 3;   d = 4;
if (a < b && d >= c)
    do_it();
```

Since 1 is less than 2 and 3 is less than 4, we do it.

94A

The *and* operator && yields a 1 if both expressions have true (non-zero) values. If either expression or both evaluate to 0, the and-ed value is 0.

The *or* operator | | evaluates to 1 if either or both expressions are non-zero; the value is 0 if and only if both expressions evaluate to 0.

Although logical operators often combine relational test expressions, they may be used to combine other expressions. The statement

```
int a, b, c;
    c = a && b;
```

makes sense: c has a value of 1 or 0 (true or false) depending on the values of a and b. Here the two expressions are simply single variables.

Remember to write the double characters && and | |, because later we will see that the single characters have completely different meanings. The compiler will accept what you write, although it would *not* be what you intend.

```
/*  Determine draftability of person */

#define TRUE    1
#define FALSE   0

main ()
{
int s;

    s = screen (19, 'M');
    if (s == TRUE)
        puts ("You are expected to be registered.");
    else
        puts ("You are not required to be registered.");
}

screen (age, sex)
/*  Return: TRUE if male and 18 or over,
            FALSE otherwise.
*/
int age,
    sex;    /*  'M' or 'F' is passed */
/*  WRITE this function using  && */
```

The && operator has precedence over the || operator; in an expression a || b && c, the higher precedence && will be applied first, then the result joined by || to a to produce the result.

```
    if ((have_nickels() || have_dime()) && ok_by_mom())
        buy_candy();
```

Parentheses are required to alter the precedence and test for change first, then see whether Mom gives permission. Without parentheses around the first two terms, a child who had nickels could buy candy, even if Mom said no (provided this family executes C programs).

In mathematical logic, not C, "and" is sometimes represented by the multiplication sign and "or" by the plus sign. Just as multiplication has precedence over addition, and-ing has higher precedence than or-ing.

96

All the relational and equality operators have higher precedence than the logical operators.

```
a = 1;   b = 2;   c = 4;   d = 4;
if (a < b && c >= d)
    do_it();
```

In these statements a is compared to b and c to d before the && is applied.

96A

An important point about C logical operators is this:
Evaluation proceeds from left to right and *stops* as soon as the truth value is known.
Suppose a program ends when the user presses Q. We want to ask the user if he really means to quit. We might write

```
if (key == 'Q' && ask_confirm())
    windup();
```

So long as the menu key is not 'Q,' the logical operator && knows immediately that it must evaluate to 0. It ignores the second operand, the function `ask_confirm`. This is what we want: do not ask the user whether he really wants to quit until the quit key is pressed.

96B

You cannot write

```
i = 1;
if (17 < i < 29)
    do_it (i);
```

and get the result you might expect from mathematical notation. Relational operators are evaluated left to right and produce 1 or 0, which represent true and false only by convention. First,

```
17 < i
```

is evaluated as false, producing 0. Then the evaluation of

```
0 < 29
```

is true, even though i is not in the specified range. Instead, you must use a logical operator to combine the value of the two separate tests.

```
if (17 < i && i < 29)
    do_it (i);
```

SELF TEST   97

What is the value of 0 && 0 ?

SELF TEST   97A

Assume that triple returns three times its argument.

```
i = 10; j = 14; m = 2;
n = 3;
if (i < j && (n = triple (m)) < 4)
    advance ();
```

When these statements execute, is advance invoked?
   A) yes
   B) no

SELF TEST   97B

After the statements

```
i = 14; j = 10;
m = 2;
n = i;
if (i < j && (n = triple (m)) < 4)
    advance ();
```

what is the value of n?

                                                                               97C

```
/*  Determine whether character is alphabetic */

#define TRUE    1
#define FALSE   0

main ()
```

```
{
int c;

    c = ';';
    if (is_alpha (c))
        printf ("%c is alphabetic.", c);
    else
        printf ("%c is not alphabetic.", c);
}

is_alpha (c)
/*  Return: TRUE if c is in ranges 'A'..'Z' or 'a'..'z'.
            FALSE otherwise.
    WRITE this function.
*/
```

98

A Unary Logical Operator

The arithmetic operator – is actually two operators, a binary operator in statements like

```
    d = j - i;
```

and a unary operator in contexts like

```
    if (a < 0)
        a = -a;
```

A unary operator has one operand. The logical not operator ! changes 0 to 1 and any non-zero to 0.

```
    if (!(a <= b))
        do_it();
```

means do it if, in effect, a is greater than b.

98A

The most common use of ! is to express a test for 0.

```
    if (!key)
        key = CR;
```

is the same as

```
if (key == 0)
    key = CR;
```

Similarly,

```
if (key)
    process();
```

is the same as

```
if (key != 0)
    process();
```

SELF TEST   99

```
a = 0;
if (!a)
    b = 3;
else
    b = 4;
```

What is the value of b after these statements?

SELF TEST   99A

```
n = 268;
m = !!n;
```

What is the value of m after these statements?

99B

Increment and Decrement Operators

So far the most peculiar aspect of C compared to other programming languages has been the nature of assignment as an operator.

Now we introduce the increment and decrement operators, which even more than assignment give C its special flavor.

99C

Increment and decrement, symbolised ++ and --, are unary operators: they apply to a single operand.

```
c = a - i++;
```

This statement does two things. It subtracts i from a, storing the result in c. It also increments i for the next time the program uses it (as a loop index, for example). If

```
a = 3;
i = 7;
c = a * i++;
```

then after these statements execute, the value of c is 21 *and* the value stored in i is 8. The action on i is called a *side effect*. It is important to be aware of side effects.

SELF TEST   **100**

```
m = 6;
i = 1;
n = m + i++;
```

What is the value of i after these statements?

                                                                                100A

```
/*  Simple example of increment operator */

/*  PREDICT what this program will display.
    Then RUN it.
*/

main()
{
int a, n;

    a = 2;
    n = 3 + (a++) + 4;

    printf ("n = %d and a = %d", n, a);
}
```

                                                                                100B

You may apply the ++ and −− operators to a variable before its value is taken in an expression, too. In that case, write the operator before the variable.

```
a = 3;
```

```
i = 7;
c = a * ++i;
```

This time, i becomes 8 before the expression is evaluated; consequently, c has a value of 24.

This action is called pre-increment or pre-decrement, as opposed to post-increment or post-decrement.

SELF TEST   **101**

```
m = 6;
i = 1;
n = m + --i;
```

What is the value of i after these statements?

101A

Because of side effects, some statements using increment or decrement are ambiguous and bad programming.

```
n = 4;
m = ++n + n;
```

When n is pre-incremented, what is used the second time n appears in the statement? The answer is, we do not know. The compiler is free to evaluate addition in any order, since

$$x + y = y + x$$

mathematically speaking. Addition is "commutative."

Therefore, the statement could assign 5 + 5 to m or 5 + 4. It is better to write two statements

```
n++;
m = n + n;
```

or

```
m = 2 * ++n;
```

101B

Increment and decrement are different from adding or subtracting 1. They alter the contents of a variable, while + 1 or - 1 in an expression affects only the value of the expression.

```
a = ++b;          /* value of b  changed */
```

is different than

```
a = b + 1;        /*  value of  b  unchanged */
```

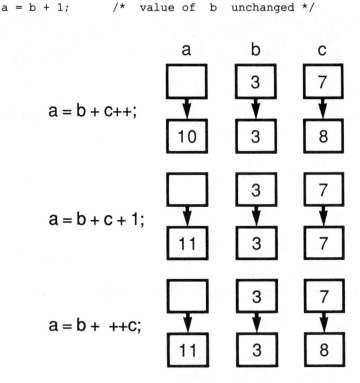

The increment operator

102

    Increment and decrement operators apply only to a variable, not an expression or constant.

```
x = (y + z)++;     /*  WILL NOT COMPILE */
c = a + 1++;       /*  WILL NOT COMPILE */
```

This makes sense, because the expression has no stable storage place that could be incremented or decremented for later use. The imaginary expression accumulator has no named place of storage. We use assignment to put a value in a variable. And a constant must stay constant.

In technical language, the increment and decrement operators apply to lvalues. An lvalue is a place where an object of data is stored during and after a statement. Values that exist only while an expression is evaluated are not lvalues.

103

To peek ahead, these operators are very useful in moving through arrays. We will often see statements like

```
c = message[i++];
```

which fetch a character from an array and simultaneously advance the index i.

```
b = 2;
a++ = b + 1;          /*  BAD */
```

It might seem perfectly clear what these statements should do, but the compiler will not allow the increment of a.

103A

Because the increment and decrement operators cause side effects, you must be careful when using them in combination with logical operators.

```
if (m < MAX_M && i++ < MAX_I)
    proceed();
```

If m is less than its limit, the logical && is determined to be false without evaluating its second operand, the expression i++ < MAX_I. Consequently, i is not incremented. Note that this is true for pre-increment, too.

SELF TEST   **103B**

```
a = 3; i = 7; c = 2;
d = (a + i++) * c;
```

What is the value of d?

SELF TEST   **103C**

```
a = 3; i = 7; c = 2;
d = (a + ++i) * c;
```

What is the value of d?

SELF TEST   **104**

```
a = 1; b = 2; c = 3; d = 4;
if (a >= b--)
    d = b;
```

What is the value of d after these statements?

SELF TEST   **104A**

```
a = 1; b = 2; c = 3; d = 4;
if (a >= --b)
    d = b;
```

What is the value of d after these statements?

SELF TEST   **104B**

```
a = 1; b = 2; c = 4; d = 8;
if (++a <= b && --c < d - 6)
    d = b;
```

What is the value of c after these statements?

SELF TEST   **104C**

```
a = 1; b = 2; c = 3; d = 4;
if (++a <= b && c < --d)
    d = b;
```

What is the value d after these statements?

104D

On the next screen is a program that simply counts down to zero. It uses the decrement operator. All you have to do is run the program. It uses a do-while control statement, which we will study later.

If you feel brave, run the program again after changing the decrement expression to a simple subtraction of one. Remember that the decrement operator alters a variable, while subtracting one merely affects the expression being evaluated.

Making this change will cause the program to go into an endless loop. In this and many instances, but not all, you can break an MS-DOS computer out

of a loop by pressing Ctrl-Break (or Ctrl-Scroll Lock). Otherwise, you will
need to restart the computer.

105

```
/*  Count down using decrement operator */

/*  First, RUN this program and observe its display.
    Then change
        i--;
    to
        i - 1
    When you RERUN, be prepared to stop the endless loop.
    Use Ctrl-Break (Ctrl-Scroll Lock) to stop the program.
*/

main()
{
    count_down (30);
}

count_down (n)
int n;
{
int i;

    i = n;
    do {
    printf ("\t%d", i);      /*  tab and number */
    } while (i-- > 0);       /*  test whether done */

    putchar ('\n');
}
```

A Brief Overview of Computer Architecture

The concept of *lvalues*, required for the assignment operation and the increment and decrement operators, is related to computer architecture. The C
language reflects the typical organization of a serial procedural computer.

This structure is also called von Neumann architecture, named for the mathematician who formalized the idea in the 1940s.

A computer has memory storage, registers, and a program counter. Both the program itself (a sequence of machine instructions) and the data are stored in memory. The only thing that tells the computer whether a memory location should be interpreted as an instruction or data is the program counter, a special register. Suppose the program counter begins with the value 100. The computer reads the value stored at memory location 100 and interprets it as a coded machine instruction. The program counter is automatically incremented.

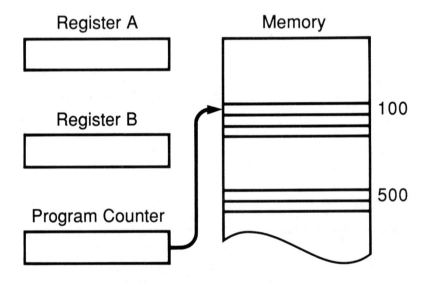

Typical computer architecture

Instructions cause various things to happen in memory and in a few special storage places called registers. An instruction might read a value from memory into a register, store a register value into a specified memory location, or add the value in one register to the value in another register.

Variables in C like `count` or `grade` are typically stored in memory. (A register may be dedicated to storing a variable.) Expressions are evaluated using the registers.

For example, when we write

```
c = a + b++ + 2;
```

the compiled machine instructions might do the following:

100 Load register A with value at 500 (where `a` is kept)
103 Load register B with value at 501 (where `b` is kept)
106 Add 1 to value at 501 (post-increment `b`)
10A Add register B to register A
10C Add 2 to register A
10F Store register A value at 502 (where `c` is kept)

There must be a designated location, here cell 502, to store the *lvalue* `c`. On the other hand, the value in register A is not attached to a specific variable. Instead, the register holds intermediate results while the expression is evaluated. This is the physical counterpart of the imaginary thing we have called the expression accumulator.

This fragment of a program is executed when the program counter steps through the values 0x100 to 0x10F. (The length of instructions varies; the program counter adds the proper length each time.) Some machine instructions alter the value in the program counter. For example, an instruction might say, "If the value in register A is 0, put 200 in the program counter." On the next machine cycle, the instruction at location 200 is read, and execution will proceed through 201, 202, etc. until another branching instruction alters the sequential flow.

You do not need to know machine instructions to program in C. However, having a general idea of computer architecture may help you understand *lvalues* and side effects.

Bitwise Operators

You may access and change the bits in an integer (not a floating type) using bitwise operators. Warning: the effects of these operators depend on the architecture of the particular processor.

&	bitwise and
|	bitwise or
^	bitwise exclusive or
<<	left shift
>>	right shift
~	one's complement

The bitwise *and* operates bit by bit.

```
n = 0x3 & 0x6;
```

This is the bitwise and-ing of 0011 and 0110, hence n is 0010 binary (higher order 0's not shown) or 2 decimal. This is different from logical and-ing (&&).

The bitwise &, | and ^ are useful for manipulating masks.

```
#define ASCII_MASK 0x7F     /*  binary 01111111 */

    m = 0xC2;
    n = m & ASCII_MASK;
```

A mask is a bit pattern used to isolate certain bits of an integer. The ASCII code uses the lower seven bits of an integer or character. By and-ing a value with the mask, we ensure that no higher order bits are set, isolating the ASCII character presumably embedded in n.

```
m           0xC2    0000 0000 1100 0010
the mask:           0000 0000 0111 1111
n           0x42    0000 0000 0100 0010 which is ASCII 'B'
```

A mask to be used with the bitwise *and* operator & should have a 1 in each bit position intended to stay as is and a 0 in each position that must be turned off.

Conversely, a mask for or-ing with | has a 1 in those positions that you want to insure on.

The exclusive-or ^ produces a 1 where its operand bits are different, that is, one is 1 and the other is 0. The mask operand should have a 1 in each position where you want to flip the bit in the other operand.

The one's complement ~ is a unary operator. It flips each bit; 1 bits become 0's and vice versa.

Suppose a computer controls a water project; a single line runs to each piece of machinery, and up to 16 items are wired into a memory word of the computer. Assume the least significant bit (bit 0) of m controls a pump; when the bit is 1, the pump is turned on and when the bit is 0, the pump is turned off.

```
#define PUMP_MASK   1

    m = m | PUMP_MASK;   /*  turns pump on */
    m = m & ~PUMP_MASK;  /*  turns pump off */
    m = m ^ PUMP_MASK;   /*  reverses state of the pump */
```

The above statements manipulate the pump control bit without disturbing the sluice gates, lamps, or whatever dam machinery.

The statements would probably use the corresponding compound assignment operators, to be studied later. They look like this:

```
    m ^= PUMP_MASK;
```

```
    m = 1;
    n = m << 2;
```

The left shift shifts the bits to the left, in this case by two places, filling the two low-order bits with 0. After the above statements, the value of n is 4. The operand on the right, which specifies how many places to shift, must be a non-negative integer and should not exceed the number of bits in the object whose value is to be shifted.

A *right* shift of an `unsigned` integer fills the high-order bits with 0. However, a right shift of a signed integer is machine dependent. On some systems it fills the high order bits with 0; on others, it propagates the sign bit into the high order bits opened up by the shift. Consequently, C code using >> may not be portable.

For non-negative numbers, shifts are equivalent to multiplying (left shift) and dividing (right shift) by powers of two. On most computers the shifts are much faster than equivalent arithmetic instructions.

SELF TEST   **110**

```
#define ASCII_MASK 0x7F

    m = 0xC3;        /*  'C' with high bit set */
    n = m & ASCII_MASK;
```

What is the value, in *decimal*, of n?

110A

More Assignment Operators

We often need to write statements to the effect

```
c = c + '0';
b = b * 2;
```

C has a set of shorthand operators that also help compilers produce tighter code. The above statements may be written

```
c += '0';
b *= 2;
```

110B

For each arithmetic operator, there is a corresponding compound assignment operator.

```
+=    -=    *=    /=    %=
```

The binary bitwise operators have compound assignment equivalents, too.

```
&=    |=    ^=    <<=    >>=
```

110C

```
    a = 7;
```

```
a += 1;
```

After these statements the value of **a** is 8. Now we see that the increment operator ++ is simply the special case += **1**.

The precedence of the compound assignment operators is low, the same as that of simple assignment. (If you have not looked at the precedence chart recently, take a look using the Help key.)

111

The whole expression after an assignment operator is computed first because of the low precedence of the shorthand assignment operators. In fact, assignments have lower precedence than all operators except one.

```
a *= b + c
```

is computed as

```
a = a * (b + c)
```

not as

```
a = a * b + c.
```

For readability, it sometimes helps to write parentheses around the right side of a compound assignment expression.

```
a *= (b + c);    /*  () perhaps helpful; not required */
```

SELF TEST   **111A**

The four statements

```
n *= 2;   n = n * 2;   n * = 2;   n += n;
```

A) are all the same
B) are not the same

SELF TEST   **111B**

```
m = 3; n = 4;
m *= n;
```

What is the value of **m** after these statements?

SELF TEST   **111C**

```
p = 40; q = 4; r = 5;
p /= q + r;
```

What is the value of p after these statements?

112

The ASCII digits '0'..'9' have the values 48..57 (which are conveniently 30..39 hexadecimal). By subtracting ' 0 ' from an ASCII digit, you get the actual value that it represents.

The program on the next screen asks you to convert an ASCII digit into the value it represents. You should be able to do the arithmetic using a compound assignment operator.

112A

```
/*  Convert ASCII digit to numeric value */

#define EXCEPTION    (-1)

main()
{
int c, binary_value;

    c = '7';
    binary_value = ascdigit_to_i (c);
    if (binary_value == EXCEPTION)
        puts ("Invalid ASCII digit");
    else
        printf ("ASCII code %d represents %d", c, binary_value);
}


ascdigit_to_i (c)
/*  Return: integer value that ASCII decimal digit represents
            EXCEPTION for invalid digit
    WRITE this function.  You should USE a compound assignment.
*/
```

112B

The Conditional Expression

We conclude this chapter with the conditional expression operator. It is the only ternary operator in C: it has three operands.

Suppose we want to set max to the maximum of a and b. One way to do it is to write the necessary tests.

```
if (a >= b)
    max = a;
else
    max = b;
```

113

A conditional expression can do the job, too.

```
max = (a >= b) ? a : b;
```

Between the assignment (=) and the statement punctuation (;) we have a conditional expression. It reads: evaluate the first operand

```
(a >= b)
```

If this value is true (non-zero), the expression evaluates to the value of the second expression, here a. If the value of the first operand is false (zero), the whole expression takes the value of the second operand.

113A

```
max = (a >= b) ? a : b;
```

Parentheses are not required, because the precedence of the ? : operator is below all the arithmetic and relational operators but above assignment. Therefore, the test expression up to the question mark is evaluated, then the conditional expression operator is applied, and finally the selected value is assigned to max.

However, many programmers use parentheses for easier reading.

113B

Formally, the conditional expression is of the form
e1 ? e2 : e3
where *e1*, *e2* and *e3* are expressions. The expression *e1* is evaluated; if it is true (non-zero), *e2* is evaluated and that is the value of the conditional expression. Otherwise, *e3* is evaluated.

Note that if *e1* is true, *e3* is not evaluated, so any side effects in *e3*, such as function invocations and increment operators, will not occur.

SELF TEST **113C**

```
c = (a % 2) ? 1 : 0;
```

What value does this statement assign to c?

A) a 1 if **a** is even
B) a 1 if **a** is odd
C) neither

SELF TEST   **114**

```
d = 7;
c = 10;
c = (c > 9) ? c + d : c + d++;
```

What is the value of **d** after these statements?

                                                                114A

```
/*  Convert ASCII digit using conditional expression */

#define EXCEPTION    (-1)

main()
{
int c, binary_value;

    c = '7';
    binary_value = ascdigit_to_i (c);
    if (binary_value == EXCEPTION)
        puts ("Invalid ASCII digit");
    else
        printf ("ASCII code %d represents %d", c, binary_value);
}


ascdigit_to_i (c)
/*  Return: integer value that ASCII decimal digit represents
            EXCEPTION for invalid digit
    WRITE this function.  This time USE a conditional expression.
*/
```

CHAPTER 8
Control Statements: I

We begin a detailed investigation of control statements. They combine simple statements using keywords like `if` and `for`, covered in this chapter. The next chapter covers additional control statements.

Operators and operands make up expressions. The simplest form of statement simply puts a semicolon after an expression.

```
i = 0;
```

There is actually a simpler statement:

```
;
```

It does nothing, but it is valid. Later we will see when it is useful.

Expression statements are executed one after another. Now we will look at more complicated statements that alter the flow of control from this simple sequential pattern.

The if-Statement

We have already used the if-statement, both in its plain form
```
if (a > b)
    scale (a);
```

and with an else-clause

```
if (a > b)
    scale (a);
else
    scale (b);
```

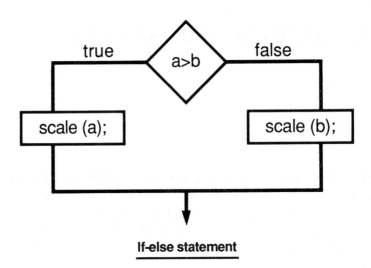

If-else statement

The test condition in parentheses is evaluated. If it is true (if a is greater than b), the statement `scale (a);` is executed; otherwise it is skipped and the else-statement, if any, is executed.

116

```
/*  Test adjacent letters */

main()
{
int result;

    result = precede ('j', 'k');
    printf ("Result is %c\n", result);
    result = precede ('a', 'c');
    printf ("Result is %c\n", result);
```

```
}

precede (first, second)
/*  Return: the first value if it is one less than second
            otherwise, return '*'.
    WRITE this function.
*/
int first, second;        /*  assumed to be letters */
```

117

In order to do several things after the test expression is evaluated, a compound statement is used.

```
if (a > b)
   {
   scale (a);
   display_scaled (a);
   }
```

The braces and their enclosed statements are together called a compound statement. Notice that there is no semicolon after the closing brace } .

117A

Technically, the parentheses enclose an expression whose value is non-zero or 0. The expression is evaluated and tested for non-equality to 0. Depending on the result, the if-clause is executed or, if present, the else-clause.

117B

```
/*  Compound statement in if-statement */

int tally;  /*  count persons subject to windfall tax */

main()
{
int income;

    tally = 0;
    income = 70;
    printf ("Pretax income: %d\n", income);
    income = windfall (income);
    printf ("Aftertax income: %d\n", income);
```

```
    printf ("Number of windfall incomes: %d", tally);
}

windfall (income)
/*  Return: if income is 50 or over,
               increment tally of windfall-taxed incomes
               and return income reduced by 10
            else return income
    WRITE this function.
*/
int income;
```

118

If-else statements may be nested. That is, the action statement to be performed when the test expression is TRUE (or when it is FALSE) may be another if- or if-else statement.

```
    if (age >= 18)
        if (weight > 180)
            consider_for_pros();
```

This says that if age is greater than or equal to 18 and weight is over 180, do the function that considers this person for the pros.

The inner if-statement is a single statement. The number of lines on which it is written is purely a matter of organizing the code for easy reading. No braces are used because there is no compound statement.

118A

The preceding example is rather simple. It could be replaced by

```
    if (age >= 18 && weight > 180)
        consider_for_pros();
```

However, nested statements become useful when there is an else-clause.

118B

```
/*  Classify characters as upper, lower or not letter */

int upper, lower;
int non_letter;

main()
```

```
{
    upper = lower = non_letter = 0;
    classify ('H');
    classify ('o');
    classify ('w');
    classify ('d');
    classify ('y');
    classify ('!');

    printf ("Upper : lower counts are %d : %d", upper, lower);
    printf ("\nOther characters: %d", non_letter);
}

classify (c)
/*  If the character is a letter, increment  upper  or  lower
        depending on whether it is upper or lower case.
    Otherwise, increment the count of  non_letter.
    WRITE this function.
    (You may use the library functions isalpha and tolower)
*/
int c;
```

119

The pairing of else-clauses is important to watch.

```
if (age >= 18)
    if (weight > 180)
        consider_for_pros();
    else
        advise_gain_weight();
```

The player will be advised to gain weight only if he is 18 or older and he weighs less than 180. Telling 17-year olds to gain weight is talking too soon.

119A

```
if (age >= 18)
    {
    if (weight > 180)
        consider_for_pros();
    }
else
    too_young();
```

When you nest if-else statements, the compiler pairs each else with the nearest previous if that has no else. If you want a different flow of control, use braces to indicate what you mean.

Here, we want to tell the person he is too young if he is less than 18. Even though there are no compound statements here, the braces are necessary to match else with the outer if.

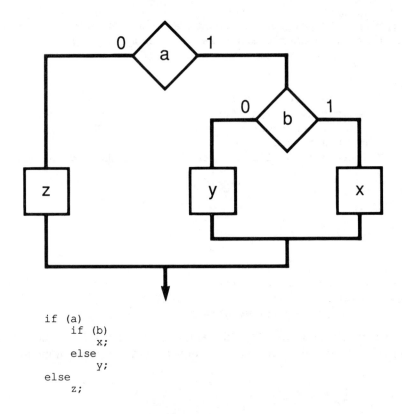

```
if (a)
     if (b)
          x;
     else
          y;
else
     z;
```

Nested if statement

SELF TEST   **120**

WITHOUT the braces, too_young() would be executed when

A) he is less than 18

B) he is 18 or over and weighs less than 181

C) he is less than 18 and weighs less than 181

121

It is good programming style to indent if-statements. Indentation helps your eye check that each level in a series of nested if-statements is in the correct place. The eye can also make a quick vertical check for matched braces.

The following two statements are equivalent to the compiler, but the second one will annoy most readers.

```
if (age >= 18)
    {
    if (weight > 180)
        consider_for_pros();
    }
else
    too_young();

if (age >= 18) {
if (weight > 180)
    consider_for_pros(); }
else too_young();
```

121A

In this Workshop, we indent to the next fourth column as a matter of convention. Often you see programs indented to the eighth column, but in our judgment nested statements run over the line too quickly.

We also line up the opening and closing brace of a block in the same column. Some programmers like to write

```
if (a < b) {
    scale (a);      /*  save a line */
    report();
    }
```

instead. The important point is that you and your colleagues adopt a style and stick to it.

A common use of nested if-else statements makes a three-way or greater decision. Here the usual style of indenting may be altered.

```
if (age > 0 && age < 18)
    minor();
else if (age >= 18 && age < 30)
    young_adult();
else if (age >= 30 && age < 65)
    middle_age();
else if (age >= 65)
    senior();
else
    error();
```

The final `else error();` is not strictly necessary, but it is an example of defensive programming. What if another part of the program assigned a negative age, for example?

```
/*  Grade test scores using if-else */

main()
{
int a;

    a = grade (95);
    printf ("The grade is %d", a);
}


grade (score)
/*  Return a grade according to the following table.
    WRITE this function.
    Grade    Score
    4        93 - 100
    3        85 -  92
    2        70 -  84
    1        55 -  69
    0         0 -  54
    Return  -1  if score input is out of range.
*/
```

123

```
/*  Rewrite conditional expression with if-else */

main()
{
int a, b, c, d;

    a = 1; b = 2; c = 3;
    d = test (a, b, c);
    printf ("Result is %d\n", d);

    a = 1; b = 3; c = 2;
    d = test (a, b, c);
    printf ("Result is %d\n", d);
}

test (x, y, z)
/*  Return: value equivalent to conditional expression.
    REWRITE this function so it uses if-else statements
    instead of the conditional expressions.
*/
int x, y, z;
{
    return ( (x > y) ? (x > z ? x : z) : (y > z ? y : z));
}
```

123A

Remember that there is no semicolon immediately following the test expression.

```
    if (n == 1)          /*  CORRECT */
        do_it();

    if (n == 1);         /*  WRONG */
        do_it();
```

As we will see later, there are occasions when you want to do nothing after testing the expression. You should put the semicolon on the next line to make your intent clear.

```
    if (key == 'X')
        ;
    else if (key == 'A')
```

```
        menu_a();
    else
        next_menu();
```

124

When the compiler gives you an error message saying that an `else` is not matched with an `if`, an unwanted semicolon may be the bug.

```
    if (n == 1);      /*  INCORRECT SEMICOLON */
        do_it();
    else
        sleep();
```

Often you know your program must read a character from a file or perform a similar action, but the program then must test for an exception or end condition before proceeding.

```
#define EOF (-1)

    c = getchar();
    if (c == EOF)
        windup();
    else
        process (c);
```

There is a more compact way to write the code.

```
    if ((c = getchar()) == EOF)
        windup();
    else
        process (c);
```

We must always read the next character, but whether we proceed as usual or begin winding things up depends on a test. Because a C expression may contain a function invocation, the compact arrangement shown above is common.

124A

The next screen asks you to complete a program. To discourage overuse of scarce programming talent, the government enacts a tax on company expenditures for programmers. Every month a company generates a tax liability based on its programmer payroll. The monthly tax need not be paid in full, only certain minimums. The balance is carried forward to the next month, at which time the tax liability for that month is added and the new amount due is calculated.

Insiders know, however, that this tax is likely to be repealed in a few months and all the accrued tax liability forgiven. Therefore, they write in some provisions enabling military contractors and investment bankers to postpone more tax liability than other companies.

The tax formula and program are on the next screen.

125

```
/*  Calculate programmer tax payable */

/*
    (Translating this rule can be difficult.)
    For each month, if the total tax accrued is 1000 or more,
the company must pay 750 or half the tax (half dollars
rounded down), whichever is greater, except that if the
company is a military contractor or investment banking firm
and the accrued tax is between 1000 and 1199, the payable
amount shall be half the tax or 550, whichever is greater.
    The remaining tax accrued is carried over and added to
the tax liability generated during the next month, at which
time the payment rule is applied again.
*/

main()
{
int jan_tax, feb_tax, mar_tax, bus_code;
int mar_due;

    jan_tax = 1060; feb_tax = 800; mar_tax = 540;
    bus_code = 'M';
    mar_due = calc_mar_due (jan_tax, feb_tax, mar_tax, bus_code);
    printf ("For tax liabilities %d, %d, %d, March due is %d\n",
        jan_tax, feb_tax, mar_tax, mar_due);
}

calc_mar_due (jan_tax, feb_tax, mar_tax, bus_code)
/*  Return: tax payable for March
    WRITE this function and any helpful work functions you need
*/
```

```
int jan_tax, feb_tax, mar_tax;   /*  tax liability for month */
int bus_code;                    /*  'M' for military contractor
                                        or investment banker
                                     0 for all others
                                 */

calc_due (accrued, bus_code)
/*  Return: amount due for the month.
    Suggestion: write this function and use it above.
    Otherwise, delete these lines.
*/
int accrued;          /*  previous plus this month */
int bus_code;
```

126

The for-Statement

The three types of program flow in a structured program are the short sequence (a list of statements), alternation (conditional statements like the if-statement), and the loop. One of several C statements that create repetitive loops is the for-statement.

126A

```
#define MAX_INPUT      30

int i, sum;
    for (i = sum = 0; i < MAX_INPUT; i++)
        sum += i;
```

There are three statements in parentheses after `for`. The first is executed once only when the `for` starts; it is the initialization statement.

At the "top" of the loop is the middle statement, the test. If the expression evaluates to true (non-zero), then the execution statement below the `for` line is performed (in this example, the addition to `sum`). If the test statement evaluates to false (0), the `for` terminates immediately.

After the execution statement, the third or loop statement in parentheses is performed, here incrementing `i`. Control then goes back to the test statement.

SELF TEST   **127**

```
n = 0;
for (i = 0; i < 5; i++)
    n += i;
```

What is the value of n after these statements execute?

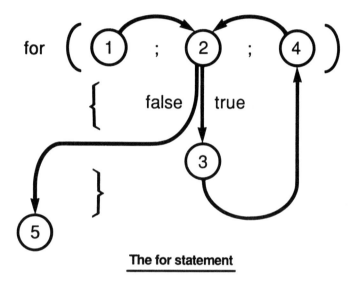

The for statement

                                                                        127A

Aside: Debugging Hints

Although it is quite possible to make errors in any programming statement, a mistake in a loop can easily cause your computer to lock up or crash. A loop that never stops because the test condition is always satisfied simply repeats. If nothing is displayed while the program is in the loop, you see nothing happening and may have to restart the computer. A loop that starts writing values at some location and keeps writing without end will sooner or later overwrite some vital part of memory, perhaps causing the computer to do strange things.

For these reasons, we take a little time to discuss debugging.

Play mental computer.

If a program does not produce correct results, you need to find the errors (called "bugs"). First, read the program slowly, or what appears to be the crucial part of a large program. Imagine in your mind what variables each statement affects, the values it assigns to them, and where it directs program flow. Just as a proofreader looks at the actual words that the letters on a page spell, you can find many errors by reading step by step through the program.

C statements often have side effects. When an expression invokes a function, everything that happens in the function is a suspect for the cause of the bug. As you imagine what happens in an expression, you also need to remember that increment and decrement operators change variables, and the new values may be throwing the program off later.

Use the printf microscope.

Another technique is to insert `printf` statements to examine the value of variables at different points in your program. For example,

```
i = getchar();
if (i = 'A')
    count++;
printf ("i = %d, count = %d", i, count);
```

will quickly show you that the value of i is always 65 (the ASCII code for *A*) because the test inside the `if` has an assignment (=) instead of the equality test (==).

Divide and conquer.

If you have no idea where a problem is, use a divide and conquer tactic. Insert a `printf` statement that tells you whether the bug occurs before or after a point that in some sense is roughly halfway through the execution of the program. Based on what you discover, remove the `printf` statement and insert one to divide the suspect code in half. This is a programmer's equivalent to the binary search algorithm that underlies the number guessing program at the front of the book.

Look back to find syntax errors.

When the compiler reports an error in a statement, the cause of the error often lies before that statement.

Tighten the spiral.

This is not a debugging method but a way to avoid bugs. Do not write 50 lines and then test them. Instead, code only a little bit, then test it. That is, tighten the development spiral that goes through editing, compiling, testing and debugging. When you discover mistakes, you know that the new code is wrong, or it specifically is involved in some interaction with the rest of the program. This knowledge narrows the problem considerably.

Practice "forcing."

Related to debugging, forcing compels your program to do its job on selected test data, especially data at the boundaries. For example, the statement

```
if (count++ <= MAX)
    do_it();
```

may appear to work fine while `count` is well below the permitted maximum. By forcing this statement to be executed on values of `count` at `MAX` - 1 and `MAX`, you may discover an error, such as having written `<=` when you need `<`.

Keep a notebook; talk to others; walk away from it.

Write down the causes of errors as you find them. You may find yourself making the same kind of mistake repeatedly for awhile. Review the list when a new error shows up. Describing a problem to someone requires you to be precise, and probable errors may occur to you as you talk. If a bug is especially hard to locate, do some other things for awhile, then come back to the problem with a mind that has escaped from its rut.

Now we resume our study of `for`.

129

```
/*  Compute a triangle number */

#define EXCEPTION (-1)

main()
{
int i, t;
```

```
    printf ("The sum of the first %d positive integers is %d",
            4, triangle (4));
}

triangle (n)
/*  Return: sum of the first n positive integers,
            EXCEPTION if n is invalid (0 or negative).
    WRITE this function.
*/
int n;  /*  you may assume  n <= 180 (no long answer) */
```

130

The program on the next screen gives you an opportunity to set more interesting limits on a loop variable.

130A

```
/*  Display ASCII codes for A..Z */

main()
{
    display_az();
    putchar ('\n');
}

display_az()
/*  Display the ASCII values for the letters A..Z
    in hexadecimal.
    WRITE this function.
    %x is the printf control code for hexadecimal.
*/
```

130B

The next exercise uses an array, which we have not studied yet. A `for` loop is frequently used to process a large amount of similar data objects, and as it happens, arrays are convenient devices for holding such data.

However, the array has been isolated from the rest of the program. Your program invokes a function that we have written; do not change this `get_ts` function. In general, functions may be used to isolate parts of a program from each other.

```
/*  Count 1's in a string of 1's and 0's */

char test_string[80] = {"010110101101110101011011"};

main()
{
int count;

    count = tally_ones();
    printf ("%d 1's", count);
}

tally_ones()
/*  Return: count of '1' characters in test_string.
    WRITE this function.
    INVOKE get_ts() to access each character.
*/
{

}

get_ts()
/*  Return: next character in test_string.
            binary 0 when no more available.
    Written for you.  Do not change it.
*/
{
static int index = 0;
int c;

    if (!(c = test_string[index++]))
        index = 0;
    return (c);
}
```

The for control mechanism is extremely flexible. Its initialization, test, and loop statements are not limited to changing and testing a loop variable i. They may be any statements, including invocations of functions.

```
#define CR  0x0D;        /*  ASCII carriage return code */
```

```
for (i = 0; (c = getchar()) != CR && i <= MAX_INPUT; i++)
    process (c);
```

The test condition of this loop is fairly complicated. Every time it is executed, the function `getchar` is invoked, returning a character in `c`. Notice the use of parentheses.

We want to stop when the user presses the Return key. We must also stop when we fill the memory for the characters.

132

Nor are all the statements inside the parentheses of `for` required. However, two semicolons are always required, and their position indicates absent statements.

```
for (i = 0; i < 3; )                 /* no loop statement */
    i = double_it (i);

for (key_count = 0; ; key_count++)   /* no test statement */
    if (c = inkey())
        return (c);

for ( ; ; )     /* no init, test, or loop statement */
    if (c = inkey())
        return (c);
```

The execution statement may be a compound group of statements, grouped in braces just like the statements in a function.

SELF TEST   **132A**

```
n = 0;
for (i = 0; triple (i) <= 12; i += 2)
    n++;
```

```
/*  Assume that triple() returns triple its argument.  */
```

What is the value of n after these statements?

SELF TEST   **132B**

```
n = 0;
for (i = 0; i <= 3; )
    {
    n += i;
    i++;
```

```
    i = double_it (i);
    }
```

What is the value of n after these statements?

133

Remember that a compound set of statements has no semicolon after the closing brace.

In the previous question, i is 0, then 2 (0 incremented to 1 and doubled), and then 6, at which point the test fails.

133A

A fan of the CP/M operating system (popular in the late 1970's) claims that a toupper function which converts a character to uppercase may be accomplished by bitwise and-ing the character with 0x5F. The next screen asks you to write a program testing this idea.

133B

```
/*  Test an idea for a toupper function */

main ()
{
    examine ('a', 'z');
    printf ("\nPress a key to continue:");
    getchar (); puts ("\n");
    examine ('Z' + 1, 'a' - 1);
    printf ("\nPress a key to continue:");
    getchar ();  puts ("\n");
    examine ('0', '9');
    printf ("\nHow do the results look to you?");
}


examine (lo, hi)
/*  In the range lo..hi inclusive, display the
    ASCII characters and the results returned by mask ().
    WRITE this function with a for-statement.
*/



mask (c)
/*  Return: c bitwise and-ed with 0x5F.
    Written for you.
```

```
*/
int c;
{
    return (c & 0x5F);
}
```

134

Even the execution statement in a for-loop can be empty, simply a semicolon. This might be the case if you wish to advance an index until a test condition is met.

```
for (i = 0; get_ts(); i++)
    ;
```

Assuming that `get_ts` gets successive characters of a string, the loop continues until `i` has counted the characters. In C, strings by convention end with a binary zero.

134A

The test expression may be absent.

```
count_keys()
{
int count, c;

    for (count = 0; ; count++)   /*  no test expression */
        {
        c = getchar();
        if (process (c) == FALSE)
            return (count);
        }
}
```

With no test expression, the convention is that it is true. The loop will be performed until something within the execution statements, like a `return`, stops the loop.

SELF TEST **134B**

In the above function `count_keys`, is the last keypress (the one that makes `process` report FALSE) counted?

A) yes
B) no

135

You can perform multiple initialization and loop statements by joining expressions with a comma. The expressions are evaluated from left to right. Instead of writing

```
n = 100;
for (i = 0; ...
```

you may write

```
for (n = 100, i = 0; ...
```

The comma is the lowest priority operator on the precedence chart. The comma join is an operator, not punctuation like the commas that separate parameters in a function.

Rarely is the C comma operator used outside a `for` loop. However, it may be used elsewhere with parentheses as needed.

135A

```
/*  Silly use of comma operator */

/*  Study and predict what this program displays.
    Then just RUN it.
    By using inner parentheses, the invocation of
    of pass_values from main enables us to write a
    comma operator.  Notice its effects.
*/

main()
{
int n;
    pass_values (1, (n = 10, n+3));
}


pass_values (a, b)
int a, b;
{
    printf ("My first argument is %d\n", a);
    printf ("My second argument is %d", b);
}
```

136

The next program determines whether a number u is prime. By examining the remainders of u % i for an appropriate range of i, you can tell if u is prime.

A prime is evenly divisible by only itself and 1. We usually say that 1 is not prime, but 2 is.

136A

```
/*  Determine whether a number is prime */

#define TRUE     1
#define FALSE    0

main()
{
int prime_flag;
unsigned u;

    u = 81;
    prime_flag = test_prime (u);
    if (prime_flag)
        printf ("%d is prime", u);
    else
        printf ("%d is not prime", u);
}

test_prime (u)
/*  Return: TRUE if u is prime, FALSE if not.
    WRITE this function.
    Hint: Write a for-loop to check remainders.
*/
unsigned u;      /*  handle u >= 0 */
```

136B

Like the if-statement, for loops may be nested.

```
for (r = 0; r <= MAX_ROW; r++)
    for (c = 0; c <= MAX_COL; c++)
        {
        setcur (r, c);
        output_star();
```

```
            }
```

These statements range over all combinations of r and c representing all positions on a console screen. At each position, the cursor is moved there and an asterisk displayed. (For most computers this routine is inefficient, but that is beside the point here.)

First r is 0 and the inner loop is performed for all values of c from 0 through MAX_COL; then r is 1 and the inner loop is repeated in full, and so on.

SELF TEST   137

In the previous nested loop, the stars are displayed by

A) rows
B) columns
C) diagonally from the upper left

                                                                          137A

Note that a single for with a pair of comma-joined loop statements does *not* do the same thing as a nested for loop.

```
    for (r = c = 0; r <= 10 && c <= 10; r++, c++)
        {
        setcur (r, c);
        output_star();
        }
```

SELF TEST   137B

The above loop displays asterisks

A) in a solid box
B) in a horizontal line
C) diagonally from top left toward bottom right
D) in a column

                                                                          137C

```
   for (r = 0; r <= MAX_ROW; r++)
       {
       /* A -- do something at beginning of row */
       for (c = 0; c <= MAX_COL; c++)
           {
```

```
        setcur (r, c);
        output_star ();
        }
    }
```

If we want to do something at the beginning of each row, we put the statement(s) at *A*. Notice that additional braces are needed around the compound statement to be performed for each row.

138

If we want to generate all the permutations of heads and tails when a coin is tossed four times, we can use nested `for` loops.

The outer loop represents the first toss; we can let a variable `t1` range from 0 to 1 (tails to heads). Each inner loop will represent a further toss, utilizing variables `t2`, `t3`, and `t4`.

Within all the nested for-statements, we have each of the four variables set to tails or heads, and we can perform any analysis required by our problem. For example, we can test the sum

```
t1 + t2 + t3 + t4
```

for a certain number of heads.

138A

```
/*  Count cases of m heads in 4 coin tosses */

main()
{
int count, heads;

    heads = 3;
    count = toss (heads);
    printf ("%d heads occur %d out of 16 cases.", heads, count);
}


toss (exact)
/*  Return: count of cases with exact number
    of heads among all permutations of tossing
    a coin 4 times.
*/
int exact;
{
```

```
int t1, t2, t3, t4, count;

    count = 0;
    for (t1 = 0; t1 <= 1; t1++)
/*  COMPLETE this function with nested for's */
```

139

We will write a program that displays the ASCII characters and their values in a neatly arranged table.

If you save the completed object program on disk as a .COM file, you can run it whenever you want to see the ASCII codes.

In order to avoid control codes whose display action might disrupt the table, we will display the printing values only, ranging from blank (0x20) through 0x7F.

The major requirement will be to display the characters in columns. However, we do not know yet how to display columns, and in any case, it is slower than displaying rows. Therefore, we will display the top row of each column, then the second row, etc.

We must display 96 codes, showing the ASCII character and its hexadecimal value. Let us display eight codes per row; therefore the number of rows will be

```
#define ROWS 12 /*   (hand calculated: 96 values/8 per row) */
```

Once we know how many rows there are, we know that each column will show the code 12 greater than its neighbor to the left. Let a variable `row_start` be the starting ASCII value of the row. The first row begins with the code for blank, 0x20, and the rows increment until `row_start` exceeds 0x20 plus the number of rows. Our outer loop counts off the rows:

```
    for (row_start = 0x20; row_start < 0x20 + ROWS; row_start++)
```

We should start each row with a newline in order to get from the end of the previous row to the next row down at the left margin. Then we are ready to display eight values, which may be counted off using an inner for-statement:

```
        for (col = 0; col < 8; col++)
```

Within the loops we know the ASCII value at the start of the row, namely, `row_start`, and each column displays the value that is ROW greater.

Finally, in order to allow for a partial last row, we may check the value against the limit 0x7F before displaying it.

```
/*  Display the printing ASCII character values */

main()
{
    disp_ascii_table();
}


#define ROWS 12     /*  (hand calculated: 96 values/8 per row)
*/


disp_ascii_table()
/*  Display the printing ASCII codes 0x20..0x7F.
    Print eight values and characters per row.
    Arrange so values go down in column.
    WRITE the indicated statement below and
    judge your display when the program runs.
*/
{
int row_start, col, ascii;

    printf ("ASCII printing codes in hexadecimal\n");

    for (row_start = 0x20; row_start < 0x20 + ROWS; row_start++)
        {
        /*  print a row */
        putchar ('\n');
        for (col = 0; col < 8; col++)
            {
            /*  WRITE the statement to calculate  ascii
                for this row and column */

            if (ascii <= 0x7F)   /*  allow partial last row */
                printf ("%c  %x\t", ascii, ascii);
            }
        }
}
```

Exercise. A town has avenues First through Tenth and cross streets First through Tenth. Despite the neat grid of streets, the terrain is uneven. It is given by the function

```
calc_height (x, y)
/*  Return: height at x, y.
*/
int x, y;   /*  avenue and street */
{
    return (2*x*x + 2*y*y - 20*x - 22*y + 141);
}
```

A nearsighted person at an intersection can see as far the next intersection in each of the four directions. He walks to the lowest intersection, or stays where he is if all of them are higher. He never leaves the town.

Write a program that, given the starting intersection, reports the final intersection to which the nearsighted man walks. Does the man always end up at the same intersection?

Suggestion: write at least two functions, one that reports whether and how the man moves from a given intersection, and a higher-level function that searches for as long as the man keeps walking.

CHAPTER 9
Control Statements: II

142

If you know Basic or Pascal, you have seen how the C keyword `for` is defined more generally than their counterparts. Now we will see how other repetitive control statements are consistent with the general for-statement.

142A

The while-Statement

The while-statement is logically equivalent to a for-statement without initialization or a loop expression.

```
#define MAX_INPUT       30

int i, sum;

    i = sum = 0;
    while (i < MAX_INPUT)
        {
        sum += get_addend();
        i++;
        }
```

The expression in parentheses is evaluated, and the execution statement performed if the result is non-zero; when the expression becomes false, the program proceeds directly to the following statements.

In a `for` loop, the test statement is performed, then the execution statement only if the test result was true. Otherwise, the execution body is not performed.

Because `while` is a special case of `for`, the same concept governs the action. The test is a pre-test, and the execution statement(s) may never be performed.

```
i = 4;
while (i < 3)
    do_it();
```

This sequence would never execute `do_it`.

Conceptually, `while` is a special case of `for`. Some compilers take the reverse view: they extract the initialization statement of a `for` and place it before an imagined `while`; the loop statement is simply the final statement of the execution body. The net effect is identical, except that error messages for a defective `for` may talk about a problem with `while`.

143

It is often helpful to bury an assignment in the test expression of a while-statement. We used this same technique with if-statements.

```
#define CR   0x0D;        /*  ASCII carriage return code */
    i = 0;
    while ((c = getchar()) != CR && i++ <= MAX_INPUT)
        process (c);
```

When the user presses Return or when `i` reaches `MAX_INPUT`, character reading and processing stop.

143A

```
    while ((c = getchar()) != CR)
        process (c);
```

Because the precedence of `=` is below the relational operators such as `!=`, the parentheses around the embedded assignment statement are required. Otherwise, the character from `getchar()` would be compared to a Return, and the truth value of the comparison, that is, 0 or a 1, would be stored in `c`.

A nasty bug can occur by writing

```
    if (c = calc (n) == 0)        /*  MISSING () */
```

```
        do_it (c);
```

The compiler finds no syntax error. However, if `calc` returns 0, perhaps signaling a result that should not be processed by `do_it`, the relational operator evaluates to 1, which becomes the value of `c`. Consequently, `do_it` is performed when it should not be, and on a spurious value of `c`.

SELF TEST   **144**

```
int i, n;

    n = i = 0;
    while (i < 3)
        n += 2 * i++;
```

What is the value of `n` after these statements?

SELF TEST   **144A**

```
int i, n, j;
    n = i = 0;
    while ((j = i++ * 2 + 1) != 5)
        n += j;
```

What is the value of `n` after these statements?

144B

The next program searches a string of characters. Since these are stored in arrays, which we have not studied, a "black box" function `get_ts` provides successive ASCII digits.

144C

```
/*  Count characters until a digit */

char test_string[80] = {"What is this exercise 4 anyway?"};

main()
{
int count;

    count = digit_search();
    printf ("%d characters\n", count);
}

digit_search()
```

```
/*  Return: count of characters preceding a digit.
            -1 if no digit in the characters.
    WRITE this function.
    INVOKE get_ts() to access each character.
*/
{


}


get_ts()
/*  Return: next character in test_string.
            binary 0 when no more available.
    Written for you.  Do not change it.
*/
{
static int index = 0;
int c;

    if (!(c = test_string[index++]))
        index = 0;
    return (c);
}
```

145

The break Statement

Getting a user's name with a while-statement has a potential defect: the user's name might overflow the memory set aside for storing it. In this event, chaos would result as characters were stored in memory whose role is unknown. Therefore, a sturdy program needs to watch the amount of input. This test may be done in the execution statements.

To stop the loop, the `break` operation is available. It may be placed as a statement inside the execution body of a `while` or a `for`. It forces termination of the loop.

145A

```
#define NAME_SIZE   40

    i = 0;
    while ((c = getchar()) != CR)
        {
```

```
        process (c);
        if (++i >= NAME_SIZE - 1)    /* prevent overflow */
           break;
        }
    process ('\0');
```

This loop stops when the user presses Return or the 39th character. The Return is not processed.

For reasons to be discussed later, the program initializes i to 0 instead of 1.

146

```
/* Process indefinite number of inputs */

int score[80] = {3, -1, 5, 7, 0, 10};

main()
{
int max, i;

    max = find_max();
    printf ("The maximum is %d.\n", max);
}


find_max()
/* Read successive scores until a 0 and
    Return: the maximum score (excluding the 0 unless
        it is the only integer read).
    WRITE this function, INVOKING get_ti to access integers.
*/


int ti_index = 0;    /* for get_ti() */
get_ti()
/* Return: next score.
            binary 0 when no more available.
    Written for you.  Do not change it.
*/
{
int i;

    i = score[ti_index++];
```

```
    if (i)
        ti_index++;
    if (ti_index >= 20)
        ti_index = 0;
    return (i);
}
```

147

An "infinite" loop does not specify in the program when it ends. It has the form

```
#define TRUE    1
    while (TRUE)
        do_it();
```

or

```
    for (/* ... */; ;/* ... */)   /* No test condition */
        do_it();
```

You can end an indefinite loop with a `break` or `return` statement.

One way to get a random number is to wait in an indefinite loop until a key is pressed (make sure your program calls for user input at this moment!), then store the loop count as the random seed.

The next screen illustrates the use of an indefinite `for` and the `break` statement to get a random number.

147A

```
/* Seed random number while waiting for key */

/* Just read this program then RUN it. */

unsigned int seed;

main()
{
    randomize();
    printf ("(The random seed is %d)", seed);
}

randomize()
/* Put a random number 0..99 in seed. */
```

```
{
int key;
unsigned i;

    puts ("Press A, B or C menu selection:");
    for (i = 0; ; i++)          /*  indefinite loop */
        if ((key = inkey()) != 0)
            {
            key = tolower (key);
            if (key >= 'a' && key <= 'c')
                {
                menu (key);
                break;
                }
            else
                puts ("Please press A, B or C.");
            }
    seed = i % 100;
}

menu (key)
int key;
{
/*   ... */
}
```

148

The do-while Statement

A while-statement evaluates its test expression first. Conceivably, the execution statements may never execute. Sometimes you want to start a process, insuring at least one iteration. The do-while statement is the answer; it evaluates the test after the execution statements.

```
#define CR   0x0D

do  {
    process (c = getchar());      /*  get key */
    } while (c != CR);            /*  loop while not CR */
```

Braces should be used even when there is only one simple execution statement. A semicolon always follows the test expression.

We need to get at least one key from the keyboard, so the do-while construction is appropriate.

As with the for- and while-statements, `break` may be used in a do-while statement. A more realistic input routine would be

```
int i, c;

    i = 0;
do  {
    process (c);
    if (++i >= MAX_INPUT)
        break;
    } while (c != CR);
```

Another example of the do-while statement is in the number guessing game at the beginning of this Workshop.

```
do  {
    mid = low + 1 + (high - low) / 2;
    printf ("\nIs it greater than %d? y/n:", mid - 1);
    if (toupper (getchar ()) == 'Y')
        low = mid;
    else
        high = mid - 1;
    } while (high - low);   /*  while there is a range */
```

The question must be asked at least once, and as long as `high` and `low` have a gap between them, the loop must be performed again.

SELF TEST

```
    a = n = 0;
do  {
    n++;
    a += 3;
    } while (a < 10);
```

What is the value of n?

```c
/*  Find highest digit in ASCII number */


char test_string[80] = {"52918"};

main()
{
int c;

    c = find_max();
    if (c)
        putchar (c);
    else
        puts ("Empty string");
}

find_max()
/*  Return: highest ASCII digit in a sequence.
    Return binary 0 if string is empty.
    You may assume the characters are all ASCII digits.
    WRITE this function. Use a do-while statement.
    INVOKE get_ts() to access each character.
*/
{

}

get_ts()
/*  Return: next character.
            binary 0 when no more available.
    Written for you.  Do not change it.
*/
{
static int index = 0;
int c;

    if (!(c = test_string[index++]))
        index = 0;
    return (c);
```

}

151

The switch Statement

Suppose a function receives a variable containing the user's choice from a menu of options. For each choice, the function should perform a block of statements.

When we want to do things based on which of several constants a variable equals, we can use the case feature, which in C is termed the switch statement.

151A

```
c = menu_choice;
switch (c)
    {
    case 'A':              /*  executed when c == A */
        write_text();
        store_text();
        break;             /*  break out of switch { } */
    case 'B':
        delete_file();
        break;
    case 'C':              /*  case  and  :  required */
        display_dir();
        break;
    default:               /*  performed when no match */
        error_choice();
        break;
    }
```

The construction is *fall-through:* execution starts at the matched constant value and continues until a `break` or `return`.

151B

If you wanted to display the directory after deleting a file, you could omit the `break` for case 'B'. The common error, however, is omitting a `break` that is needed. Put one at the end of each `case` paragraph.

151C

```
#define CR   0x0D
```

```
switch (c)
    {
    case 'A':
        write_text();
        break;
    case 'B':
        delete_file();
        break;
    case CR:                    /*  upon Return */
    case 'C':                   /*  or 'C' */
        display_dir();          /*  display directory */
        break;
    default:
        error_choice();
        break;
    }
```

The fall-through nature of a `switch` makes it easy to perform the same actions for two or more different values. Here, pressing Return as well as 'C' displays the directory.

152

When the `switch` variable does not equal any of the case values, the `default` paragraph is performed. The compiler does not insist on a `default` paragraph, but you usually want one, if only to catch an "impossible" error.

You may select a `case` by an expression consisting of constants combined by operators, if the compiler can compute the value. For example,

```
case 'A' + 1:
    do_it();
    break;
```

The compiler knows the value of these constants, so it can evaluate the expression.

152A

The `switch` statement may evaluate an entire expression, not merely a single variable.

```
switch (toupper (getchar()) + 1)
    {
```

```
case 'A':
/* ... */
```

Your compiler has a choice when it translates a `switch` into machine instructions. It may compile the same code that it would for a series of if-else statements, testing each case in turn. Or it may build a table in which the program looks up the case constant and an address for the corresponding code. At the level of C source code, you can ignore the technique used, but if you ever peek into the compiled machine instructions, you may find these switch tables.

SELF TEST   **153**

Which fragment is NOT correct?

A) `case 'A':`
B) `case ('B' + 1):`
C) `case (c == 0):`

153A

```
/*  Move North, South, East or West using switch */

#define TRUE     1
#define FALSE    0

int ns_coord, ew_coord; /*  N, E positive; S, W negative */

main()
{
int c;

    ns_coord = ew_coord = 0;

do   {
    printf ("\nYour coordinates are (%d, %d).\n",
            ns_coord, ew_coord);
    printf ("Press N, S, E, W, or Q to quit: ");
    c = toupper (getchar());
    } while (process (c));
}

process (key)
```

```
int key;
/* Change  ns_coord  or  ew_coord  based on key.
   Return: TRUE/FALSE  keep going or quit.
   WRITE this function with a switch statement.
*/
```

154

The continue Statement

A break statement terminates execution of a loop, as well as having a job in a switch.

An inverse to break is continue. It says, suspend the execution statements for this round and go to the "top" of the for, while, or do-while loop.

```
for (i = 0; i <= MAX; i++)
    {
    if (score (i) < PASSING)
        continue;
    praise (i);
    }
```

If score (i) is too low, control goes to the top of the for, incrementing i and giving no praise.

154A

The continue statement may also be used in do-while and while loops. Control skips to the test expression, which is at the top of the while or the bottom of the do-while.

The continue is used much less than break. Usually a series of if-else statements removes the need for continue. Occasionally, however, its use simplifies a complicated pattern of nested control statements.

SELF TEST   **154B**

```
for (i = 0; i <= MAX; i++)
    {
    if (!(i % 2))
        continue;
    process (i);
    }
```

This loop processes only
    A) odd numbers
    B) even numbers

The goto Statement

Within a function, unstructured programming is possible with the `goto` statement.

```
find_it()
{
int i, j;

    for (i = MIN_NUM; i <= MAX_NUM; i++)
        for (j = MIN_FAC; j < i; j++)
            if (i % j == 0)
                {
                printf ("%d divides %d", j, i);
                goto done;
                }
done:
    /*  (optional additional processing) */
    return;
}
```

A `goto` jumps to a label, which always has a colon. A `goto` and its target label must be in the same function, or you can count on disaster.

Any function that has a `goto` can be rewritten to eliminate it. The usual technique is to define a `flag`, initialize it to FALSE, then set it to TRUE where the jump would occur. At an appropriate point, the flag is tested and if true, a `break` from a loop made.

Exercise. Rewrite the above function without a `goto`.

CHAPTER 10
Storage and Scope of Variables

In an earlier chapter we introduced several basic types of data, namely, the plain `int` and integer varieties, including `char`, as well as floating types. This chapter studies other aspects of a data item, its degrees of permanence and visibility.

We have already seen local variables that are born and removed each time a function executes, and global data that exists during the life of the program. Now we will see how to control the visibility of an object, that is, what sections of a program know about it.

The extern Declaration

Another name for a global object is "external" object, which means external to functions. There are two kinds: external data, which is defined outside a function, and functions. Because a C function cannot be defined inside another one, all C functions are external objects.

Although an external object exists during the entire execution of a program, it is not necessarily known to all functions. A simple declaration

```
int salary;
```

outside all functions makes the external object known to any subsequent function in the source file. This is the case with the common single-pass compiler, which reads the source text once. By declaring external data before writing functions, you can make the data known to all functions in the file.

When a program consists of several source files, a means of communication is necessary to let the compiler know that an external object is defined in a file other than the one currently being compiled.

By the way, most of your programs so far have been built from at least two files. One "file" is the edit buffer you work in. The other file is the collection of library functions, such as `printf`, `getchar`, and `tolower`. Those functions had to be written like any others; the special things about the C Workshop library are that its source files were compiled in advance, and its object code is automatically made available to your program.

The `extern` declaration may be used to make external data known from another file (or from later in this file), and it may be used to make known functions that return other than `int`. Suppose your program is divided into two files, *whizbang.c* and *wb1.c*, and that you defined `salary` in *whizbang.c*. If you want to refer to this object in *wb1.c*, you can declare

```
extern int salary;
```

This statement, because of the key word `extern`, does not allocate memory for a new object. It merely lets the compiler know that an `int` of this name is defined elsewhere. Similarly, if in *whizbang.c* you defined `salary` near the end of the file but a function at the start referred to it, you could use an `extern` declaration at the beginning of the file.

The `extern` says that this statement is a type declaration, but the object is not actually created here. The term "declare" in C means specifying the type of an object. By contrast, when something is "defined," it is declared *and* allocated space. An `extern` statement is a declaration without a definition. To declare is to specify qualities; to define is to find room for the thing, too. Declare, qualities; define, fin' room.

You may declare `salary` as an `extern` as often as you wish, for example, once in every source file. An equivalent method, we will see later, is to `#include` a file of `extern` declarations at the front of every source file. In any event, the entire group of source files must have exactly one *definition* of `salary`.

The situation for external functions is slightly different than that for external data. Unlike data objects referred to before declaration, function invocations are acceptable at any time. However, the compiler assumes that the unknown function returns an `int`. If that is not the case, an `extern` declaration is needed to specify what type of object the function returns.

```
extern double fabs();
```

The scmicolon immediately following the parentheses lets the compiler know you are not writing out a function here, merely declaring it. Note, also, that you do not list parameters, even if the function has them.

You have seen this use of `extern` several times when a program declared a library function that returned something other than an `int`.

If an `extern` declaration is globally placed, that is, outside all functions, then the object will be known from the declaration through the end of the file.

It is also possible to write an `extern` within a function.

```
calc_pay (wage_rate)
double wage_rate;
{
int sum;
extern int salary;
    /* ... */
}
```

In this case, the external object `salary` is known only to the statements of this function.

The static Declaration

Within a function we have declared local variables, like `sum` in the code fragment above. This variable is created every time the function is executed and disappears when the function returns to its invoker. Suppose a function `calc_pay` requires an index that must survive from one execution to the next. How can you create it?

An unsatisfactory solution would be to define

```
int index;
```

as a global object prior to the function. However, the object will be known to the rest of the file. Furthermore, you would probably have to rename the variable

```
int calc_pay_fn_index;
```

in order to avoid name conflicts with other index variables. Although descriptive, this is rather tedious.

The solution is to declare the object within its function but as a `static` object.

```
calc_pay ()
{
static int p_index = 0;

}
```

This internal static object exists throughout the program; it is not destroyed and recreated. However, the name `p_index` is recognized only by statements in the function `calc_pay`.

It is possible to initialize global data in its definition; we discuss the rules later. An optional initialization has been written for `p_index` above, since you usually want to initialize a static variable.

The declaration

```
int static p_index;
```

is also acceptable to many compilers. That is, the basic data type and the storage class modifier may occur in either order.

The `static` declaration may be used outside a function body, too. The most common use is for a function itself.

```
static
bump_index()
{
/* ... */
}
```

An external static object is known only from its point of declaration through the end of the file in which it occurs. Normally, you cannot define two functions of the same name in different files; using `static` you can.

It is purely a matter of style whether to write `static` on its own line or in front of `bump_index`.

Similarly, you can define global but static data objects, like

```
static int stack_ptr;
```

which are known only from their declaration to the end of the file. For example, if your program needs a few software stacks (to be studied later), this technique can prevent the different stack pointers from being confused. Without the `static` storage modifier, your development system would complain during the linking stage that two or more objects of the same name exist.

The `extern` declaration tells a compiler about objects in other files. The `static` declaration tells a linker that objects of the same name in different files are distinct.

Local variables are either static or automatic. These are the ones that are born and die every time the function is executed. The keyword for this storage class is `auto`.

```
calc_pay (wage_rate)
double wage_rate;
{
auto int sum;          /*  auto made explicit, not required */
extern int salary;
    /* ... */
}
```

Since `auto` is assumed within a function unless an object is declared otherwise, the typical practice is to omit writing it. We have been using `auto` variables all along.

Automatic variables are typically allocated space on the hardware stack. Machine instructions at the beginning and end of the function manipulate stack pointers to reserve and remove the space these variables occupy. You can request that the compiler maintain certain automatic variables in processor registers instead.

```
bump()
{
register index;

}
```

The formal parameters of a function may also be declared with this storage class.

```
calc_next (step)
```

```
register int step;
{
}
```

A `register` declaration is nothing more than the programmer's notification to the compiler that this variable is heavily used. In practice, some restrictions limit the declaration from having any effect:

The particular compiler may or may not implement this feature; the C Workshop does not.

Only a few `register` variables per function can be implemented.

The variable must have a type that will fit into a register, for example, `int` but not `long`.

The program may not take the address of the variable, something you will learn to do with pointers.

When these restrictions prevent a `register` implementation, the compiler silently reduces the variable to a plain `auto`.

A quick compiler like the C Workshop is ideal for developing a program. Once the program is ready for production use, you may gain significant performance by recompiling it under a compiler that is specialized for optimizing the object code. A good optimizing compiler does not need `register` declarations.

SELF TEST   161

An `extern` statement is always a

A) declaration
B) definition

SELF TEST   161A

```
get_ts()
{
static int index = 0;
int c;  if (!(c = test_string[index++]))
          index = 0;
      return (c);
}
```

Earlier, we defined `index` as `static` because

A) The program is divided into two or more files
B) The index must be remembered from one invocation to the next
C) This is necessary to initialize the variable

```
/*  Declare a function returning a double */

/*  WRITE the extern statement needed here to compile
    the invocation of give_float() */

main()
{
int n;

    printf ("%d as a double is %f", n, give_float (n));
}

double
give_float (n)
int n;
{
    return ((double) n);
}
```

Braces and Blocks

So far every object has been either external to functions or within one. To a limited degree, C permits objects to be defined in nested levels inside a function.

Braces group the statements of a function. They also group compound statements, most commonly in control mechanisms like `if` or `while`. Statements enclosed in braces ({ }) make a block.

We saw local variables defined at the beginning of a function, right after its opening brace. Local variables may also be defined at the beginning of a block in most compilers. Even if no if-statements or other control structures are used, a block may be written with its own local variables.

Here is an example of nested and parallel blocks.

```
silly_func()
{
int fn_var;                /*  exists throughout function */

    fn_var = 65;
```

```
    {
    unsigned inner1;    /*  exists in block and inner block */
        inner1 = fn_var;
        {
        char inner1a;   /*  exists in inner block */
            inner1a = inner1;   /*  both exist at this time */
            putchar (inner1a);
        }
    }
    {
    unsigned inner2;    /*  exists in this block */
        inner2 = fn_var;
        printf ("Inner2 = %u", inner2);
    }
}
```

A local variable exists only within its block. In the above code, `fn_var` exists throughout the function, which is a kind of block. There are two parallel blocks in the function, one with `inner1` and the second having `inner2`. It is incorrect to write

```
    inner2 = inner1;
```

because they never exist at the same time.

The variable `inner1a` exists in the shortest-lived block, which is nested inside the first block. Here it is permissible to write

```
    inner1a = inner1;
```

because both variables are alive within the nested blocks.

A function is a block. Blocks are used frequently with control structures, too.

Other blocks like the ones just shown might be used, perhaps to duplicate names, which can be an aid or a source of confusion. However, such blocks cannot be counted on to conserve stack memory for local variables, because many compilers allocate stack space for all the blocks in a function at its beginning and free the space only after the function executes.

Initializing Data

When a program starts, global and static variables are set to zero unless you define the variable with initialization.

```
int number_base = 10;
int edit_flag = TRUE;
```

The semicolon is moved over to make room for an equals sign and the constant value.

This syntax is used for the elementary types of variables we have encountered so far.

The value may be computed in a constant expression.

```
int year = 52 * 7;
int hex_gap = 'A' - '9';
```

The initial value in a global or static variable is lost as soon as a statement in the program alters it. Automatic variables in a function behave differently. Since they are created every time the function executes, their initialization is merely a shorthand for an assignment.

```
count_down (ceiling)
int ceiling;
{
int max = 100;
    /* ... */
}
```

This amounts to the same thing as

```
count_down (ceiling)
int ceiling;
{
int max;

    max = 100;
    /* ... */
}
```

The second form is more explicit about what happens; some compilers, including the C Workshop, do not support the first form.

Unlike the initialization of global and static variables, this initialization is not limited to constant expressions. You may write

```
max = ceiling - 1;
```

or declare

```
int max = ceiling - 1;
```

However, you will get an error message if you write

```
static int max = ceiling - 1;
```

because the compiler must calculate a static initialization once before the program runs, something it cannot do if the expression has a variable.

For the same reason, a simple automatic declaration

```
int max;
```

does not insure zero nor any other value in `max`. Every time the function begins, memory is allocated for storing `max` during this execution of the function. The contents of this memory, which is somewhere on a stack, is unknown.

SELF TEST   **165**

```
#define MAX_ROW 24
```

Which global declaration is *not* correct?

A) `int eindex = 1;`
B) `int total_rows = MAX_ROW + 1;`
C) `int screen = total_rows * 80;`

CHAPTER 11
One-Dimensional Arrays

166

All data objects until now have been elementary data types, in the sense that an `int` is not made up of other C parts. This chapter begins a look at C data types that are combinations of other types.

166A

A collection of objects of the same type may be kept together as an array. The statement

```
int grade[10];
```

defines an array of integers `grade`. It has ten elements.

In C, arrays are always indexed from 0. The first grade is `grade[0]`; the last is `grade[9]`.

The subscript is enclosed in square brackets.

After the statements

```
grade[2] = 3;
grade[3] = 4;
grade[0] = grade[2] + grade[3] + 1;
```

`grade[0]` has the value 8.

The essential characteristics of a one-dimensional array are that 1) all its elements are the same kind of object, and 2) the objects are numbered sequentially from zero. The array `grade` is composed of `int`s; other arrays might be collections of `char`, `long` or other types. Later, we will see that the elements of an array may be complicated objects themselves, but they must be the same sort of object.

Initialized Arrays

A global array may be initialized in its definition. You enclose a list of values, separated by commas, in braces following an = sign. A semicolon concludes the definition.

```
int grade[] = {78, 91, 84, 63, -1};
```

Until changes are made, `grade[0]` has a value of 78, and so on. The compiler assumes the array has five elements. You may also specify an array size within the brackets and initialize. The three possibilities are the following:
1) The number of elements declared matches the number of initializers.

```
int grade[5] = {78, 91, 84, 63, -1};
```

2) The number of elements declared exceeds the number of initializers. The leftover elements are set to zero.

```
int grade[5] = {78, 91, 84, 63};
```

Here the value of the last element, `grade[4]`, is 0.
3) If there are more initializers than declared elements, this is an error.

```
int grade[2] = {78, 91, 84, 63, -1};   /*  SYNTAX ERROR */
```

Automatic arrays may be declared in a function.

```
get_scores()
{
int score[BUF_SIZE];
    /* ... */
}
```

However, an automatic array may not be initialized in its declaration.

SELF TEST   **167**
```
int a, grade[10];
```

```
grade[0] = 17;
grade[3] = 1;
a = grade[0] + grade[3];
```

What is the value of a?

SELF TEST   **168**

```
int a;
int grade[] = {17, 8, -5, 1};

    a = grade[0] + grade[3];
```

What is the value of a?

An array holds elements that are of interest as a group. Much of the work done on arrays consists of processing each element in turn. Loop statements are therefore common when processing arrays.

```
#define BUF_SIZE 30

int score[BUF_SIZE];
```

A typical fragment of code might be

```
int i;

    for (i = 0; i < BUF_SIZE; i++)
        score[i] = 0;
```

This loop initializes all the elements to zero. Notice that the index variable i starts at zero because C arrays are indexed from zero. If the array is BUF_SIZE elements large, the last element is score[BUF_SIZE - 1].

This code might appear in a program for two reasons. The array may be automatic; when the function containing it begins, the array contents are undefined. Or the array, whether automatic or global, might be re-used, in which case it must be initialized each time.

You may prefer to write the code in terms of the maximum index.

```
#define BUF_MAX 29

int score[BUF_MAX + 1];

int i;

    for (i = 0; i <= BUF_MAX; i++)
        score[i] = 0;
```

In either case, it is helpful to `#define` a symbolic name. In a real program, the declaration of `score` is likely to be far away from the loops that work on it, and the name `BUF_SIZE` makes the loop code easier to read.

Arrays often have a special value like 0 or -1 to mark the end of the active part of the array. As we will see, a string constant is stored in an array and ends with a null. In these cases, the loop may test for the final value.

```
#define EXCEPTION    (-1)
int i;

    for (i = 0; score[i] != EXCEPTION; i++)
        process (score[i]);
```

The loop usually examines the value of an element then processes it. The program may do less work by stuffing an assignment into a temporary variable during the test statement.

```
#define EXCEPTION    (-1)
int i, n;

    for (i = 0; (n = score[i]) != EXCEPTION; i++)
        process (n);
```

This code usually executes faster than the previous loop. Most compilers repeat a subscript calculation every time they see `score[i]`. This calculation consists of multiplying the index times the number of bytes occupied by a single element and adding the resulting offset to the starting address of the array. Then the program fetches the value stored there. By remembering the value, your program avoids repeating the work.

Because array elements are usually examined one after another in loops that increment or decrement an index variable, like `i` above, it would be good to have a way to remember the address of an element and simply add or subtract from the address to reference the next element. Later we will see how to do this with pointers. This will simplify many loops that you would otherwise write by manipulating array subscripts.

169

```
/*  Compute sum of elements of array */

#define COST_SIZE 5     /*  (do not change size) */
```

```
int cost[COST_SIZE] = { 13, 8, 4, 9, 27 };

main()
{
    printf ("Total costs are %d", sum());
}

sum()
/*  Return: sum of elements of the array cost
    WRITE this function.
*/
```

170

The preceding exercise used a fixed array size. The next exercise allocates an array of a certain size, but the array may hold a varying number of entries of interest to us. In this case we will use the value -1 to mark the end of the elements we have actually defined.

170A

```
/*  Compute sum of elements of array */

#define COST_SIZE 80

int cost[COST_SIZE] = { 13, 8, 4, 9, 27, -1 };

main()
{
    printf ("Total costs are %d", sum());
}

sum()
/*  Return: sum of elements of the array cost
    The array ends with -1.  Exclude it from the sum.
    WRITE this function.
*/
```

170B

With arrays and loops, short programs can perform large chores.

171

```
/*  Fill array of even numbers  */

#define MAX_EVEN    99
int even[MAX_EVEN + 1];

main()
{
    init_even();
}

init_even()
/*  WRITE this function to fill the array even[] with the
    first 100 positive even numbers.
*/
```

171A

A function cannot return an array nor accept one as a parameter. Later we will see how pointers are used to get around this limitation. But a single value in an array may be passed.

```
int score[CLASS_SIZE];

    i = 17;
    report (score[i]);
```

171B

String Arrays

The elements of an array may be characters.

```
char name[] = { 'B', 'e', 't', 't', 'y', 0};
```

A string is a special case of an array of characters. A character array can be initialized to a text string.

```
    char error_msg[] = {"Input error."};
```

This array has 13 members, not 12, because a string in double quotes always has an understood null (binary zero) at its end. C provides the symbol ' \0 ' to represent a null.

A tedious but equivalent statement would be

```
char error_msg[] = { 'I', 'n', 'p', 'u', 't', ' ',
        'e', 'r', 'r', 'o', 'r', '.', '\0' };    /* note null */
```

172

String array size follows the general rules.

```
char name[80] = {"Betty"};
```

The array has 80 elements, of which the first six (five letters and a null) have been initialized. A function might copy a longer name that would still fit, like "Bettina," into the array.

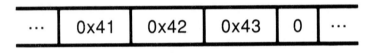

ASCII "ABC" in memory

SELF TEST   **172A**

```
int a;
char msg[] = {"Array hit me"};

    a = msg[0] + msg[12];
```

What is the value a in decimal?
(You may have to review the ASCII code.)

172B

```
/* Find highest digit in ASCII number using subscript */

char test_string[80] = {"52918"};

main()
{
int c;

    c = find_max();
    if (c)
        putchar (c);
    else
```

```
        puts ("Empty string");
}

find_max()
/*  Return: highest ASCII digit in a string of digits.
    Return binary 0 if string is empty.
    You may assume the characters are all ASCII digits.
    WRITE this function.
*/
```

173

```
/*  Return last character of a string */

char adv[2];
char msg[80] = {"The breeze felt like cheese"};

main()
{
    putchar (last_char());
}

last_char()
/*  Return: last non-null character in  msg
            0 if string is empty.
    WRITE this function.
*/
```

173A

A word of caution is in order regarding side effects in array indexes. It might seem logical to write

```
    dest[i++] = source[i];
```

but you cannot depend on the compiler to do what you want. Many compilers increment i while processing the left-hand side of the assignment. Consequently, the value used would actually be source[i+1] rather than the intended source[i]. It is better to write

```
    dest[i] = source[i];
    i++;
```

or use two indexes

```
    dest[j++] = source[i++];
```

An Arithmetic Quizmaster

We will use a random number generator and pull together some concepts to write an arithmetic quizmaster.

After the program, the text suggests several ways to improve and expand the quiz.

The quizmaster randomly generates two numbers and asks the user to multiply them and enter the answer. The quizmaster approves the right answer or displays the correct value if the response is incorrect. When the user enters Q instead of an answer, the quizmaster program quits.

Avoiding the temptation to write the program as one big function `main`, we break it down into five functions. This approach follows the guidelines of modular programming and makes it easier for you to modify the program.

The quizmaster process divides into three steps: start the quiz, play the game as long as desired, and wind up. Suppose we write

```
main()
{
    startup();
    while (play())
        ;
    windup();
}
```

This structure implies that `play` returns a value. It will return TRUE or FALSE, signaling to continue playing or quit.

```
play()
/*  Return: TRUE/FALSE keep asking questions.
*/
```

The flag from `play` reminds us to write some #defines.

```
#define TRUE    1
#define FALSE   0
```

Let's work on `play`. We must generate two numbers to be multiplied, display them, and get the response.

```
char response[30];
```

```
int op1, op2, answer;

    op1 = gen_random (RANGE);
    op2 = gen_random (RANGE);
    answer = op1 * op2;
    printf ("How much is %d  X   %d? ", op1, op2);
    gets (response);
```

This code calls on a function to generate random numbers.

In `play` we have referred to

```
#define RANGE   20
```

to set the range of the number we want, from 1 to 20.

Because we will refer to the product several times, we define `answer` and calculate it. Following that, the program displays the question in a `printf` statement and asks for a response.

The user enters a series of digits (or Q), so we store them in the character array `response`, using the library function `gets`. This function returns a non-integer object, so the program needs an `extern` declaration before referring to `gets`.

The array is fairly large in order to avoid overflow from a long response. Since `response` is a local data object, it is created and destroyed each time `play` is invoked.

Having obtained a response, we need to process it.

```
    if (toupper (response[0]) == 'Q')
        return (FALSE);
    if (atoi (response) == answer)
        puts ("Correct!");
    else
        printf ("No, the answer is %d\n", answer);
    return (TRUE);
```

Before looking at the number, we check the user's first character, `response[0]`, for Q. By applying the library function `toupper`, we accept q, too, so the user need not press the Shift key.

The library function `atoi` gives us an integer, and we compare it to the answer. We display encouragement or report the correct answer.

Notice that `play` returns TRUE or FALSE as required.

It is time to think about the random numbers. We can get the first random number while waiting for a key. The logical place to do this is in the `startup` function.

```
startup()
{
    puts ("A quiz on multiplication");
    puts ("Enter Q instead of an answer to quit.");
    puts ("Press key to start.");
    for (seed = 17; inkey() == 0; seed += 2)
        ;
    /*  bump seed by 2 to keep it odd */
}
```

The function displays instructions and waits for a key, counting for the seed of a random number generator. This variable is shared globally with the `gen_random` function.

We need two random numbers per question. Instead of waiting for keys, we use a random number generator. It should start with an odd seed, hence the special loop statement.

The random number generator uses a mathematical technique called the congruential method. Without going into details, we can say that a pseudo-random series of numbers should run as long as possible before it starts to repeat. Since each seed in reality determines the next one, once a seed repeats, so does the entire sequence. (The random numbers, however, are compressed into a smaller range where duplicates can and do occur.) The sequence should meet common tests for randomness. For example, the difference between successive numbers should itself be random.

The following function is satisfactory for our purposes.

```
gen_random (limit)
/*  Return: random value in 1..limit inclusive.
    Congruential method: new seed = 259 * seed mod 64K.
*/
unsigned limit; /*  results valid only for small values */
{
unsigned temp_seed;

    temp_seed = seed;
    temp_seed <<= 8;    /*  x   256 mod 64K */
    temp_seed += (seed * 3);
```

```
        seed = temp_seed;
        temp_seed = ((unsigned) 0xFFFF / limit);
            /*  new use for temp_seed */
        return (seed / temp_seed + 1);
}
```

Here the left shift operator << is used to multiply by 256 (2 to the 8th power). The function then adds three more to complete the multiplication by 259. The multiply by shift works because the object is declared unsigned, and it retains only the low-order 16 bits on our computer, which is just the multiplication modulus 64K that the method requires.

In the last two lines of the function, the meaning of temp_seed changes. We use it to hold a division intended to be performed before the final division in the return statement. A comment is made to note the altered meaning. An alternative would be to define another local variable.

177

```
/*  Arithmetic quizmaster */

/*  Just study and RUN this program. */

#define TRUE    1
#define FALSE   0
#define RANGE   20

extern unsigned char *gets();   /*  non-int library function */

unsigned seed;

main()
{
    startup();
    while (play())
        ;
    windup();
}

play()
/*  Return: TRUE/FALSE keep asking questions.
*/
{
```

```
char response[30];
int op1, op2, answer;

    op1 = gen_random (RANGE);
    op2 = gen_random (RANGE);
    answer = op1 * op2;

    printf ("\nHow much is %d  X  %d? ", op1, op2);
    gets (response);
    if (toupper (response[0]) == 'Q')
        return (FALSE);
    if (atoi (response) == answer)
        puts ("\nCorrect!");
    else
        printf ("\nNo, the answer is %d\n", answer);
    return (TRUE);
}

startup()
{
    puts ("A quiz on multiplication");
    puts ("Enter Q instead of an answer to quit.");
    puts ("Press key to start.");
    for (seed = 17; inkey() == 0; seed += 2)
        ;
    /* bump seed by 2 to keep it odd */
}

windup()
{
    puts ("It was fun quizzing you.");
}


gen_random (limit)
/* Return: random value in 1..limit inclusive.
   Congruential method: new seed = 259 * seed mod 64K.
*/
unsigned limit; /* results valid only for small values */
{
unsigned temp_seed;
```

```
temp_seed = seed;
temp_seed <<= 8;      /*  x   256 mod 64K */
temp_seed += (seed * 3);
seed = temp_seed;
temp_seed = ((unsigned) 0xFFFF / limit);
    /*  new use for temp_seed */
return (seed / temp_seed + 1);
}
```

179

See the end of this chapter in the book for some suggested modifications to the quizmaster program. If you do them, you can appreciate the value of modularized, top-down programming. What starts as a trivial `windup` function acquires some work to do. Keeping track of things is much easier when a problem is divided into small functions.

179A

The sizeof Operator

Suppose we initialize an array of gas mileages

```
int mpg[6] = {22, 14, 38, 29, 26, 41};
```

In order to run an index through this array

```
for (i = 0; i < num_elements; i++)
    /*  process mpg[i] */
```

we might want to set the limit in terms of a variable, here named `num_ele-ments`.

The solution is to use the `sizeof` operator.

179B

The `sizeof` operator is a unary operator, one of the rare operators that is spelled out instead of using a special symbol. It produces the number of bytes occupied by the object to which it is applied. A "byte" is not formally defined in C.

Here we use a ratio of `sizeof` terms to compute the size of the array.

```
num_elements = sizeof (mpg) / sizeof (mpg[0]);
```

The numerator is the size of `mpg` in an undefined unit termed a byte. By taking the size of the whole array and dividing by the size of one element, we get the number of elements in the array.

The precedence of `sizeof` is the same as `++` and the other unary operators.

SELF TEST   **180**

```
int an_array[10], n;

    num_elements = sizeof (an_array) / sizeof (an_array[0]);
```

What is the value of `num_elements`?

Exercise.   Write a program implementing a function `line_editor (max_length)` that accepts a line of input and puts it in a buffer. The user should be able to erase a character (destructive backspace) and to start the line over by pressing *Ctrl Y*. The line is done when the user presses Return, but characters beyond the maximum length are ignored. End the buffer input with a null instead of a Return.

The library function `inkey` is helpful for getting a key without immediately displaying it.

Save your work in a disk file. A later exercise uses it.

Exercise.   Here are several things you can do to modify the quizmaster program:

A) Change multiplication to addition.

B) Count right and wrong answers. In `windup` report totals for the session.

C) Change multiplication to subtraction. Avoid negative numbers by exchanging `op1` and `op2` when necessary.

D) If an answer is wrong, repeat the question up to N times.

E) Let the user specify the number range. Change RANGE to a variable, alter the references to it, ask the question in `startup` and convert the answer to an integer.

F) (Advanced; for later review.) After you learn about pointers to functions, let the user choose whether to be quizzed on addition, subtraction, or multiplication.

CHAPTER 12

Pointers

Every data item (except register variables and bit fields, which we will en-counter later) has an address in memory. This address is usually silent; when an expression refers to a variable by its name, like `max`, the value stored at the address is used.

```
int max;

   max += 10;
```

The program adds 10 to the value stored in the memory cell reserved for `max`.

The address of `max` might be 1078. That is, memory cell number 1078 is where the values for `max` are stored. If the value of `max` before the above statement were 13, then the situation would now be as follows:

Memory address	Contents of Memory
1078	23

Sometimes we want to refer explicitly to the address where `max` is stored. That is, we are interested in the 1078 before we are interested in the 23. In C we can declare another object to hold this address.

```
int *iptr;
```

The asterisk (*) in the declaration says that `iptr` holds an address, specifically, the address of an `int`. This is a new data type, the pointer.

182

We could store the address of `max` in `iptr`. The way we do this is by using the address operator, which is an ampersand (&).

```
iptr = &max;
```

After this statement, the value stored in `iptr` would be 1078.

182A

Of course, `iptr` is stored somewhere, perhaps in memory cell 8241. Then we have

Memory address	Contents of Memory
1078	23
8241	1078

Beware of extending this scheme carelessly. The value 23 is an integer, because we declared `max` to be `int`. The value 1078 stored in memory cell 8241 is not an integer. It is the value of `iptr`, which is a pointer. A pointer to an integer is not the same thing as an integer. Although the above diagram shows several numbers, they operate differently in C depending on their type, just as the treatment of a `char` and an `int` is different.

182B

In any case, we are now ready to fetch the value 23 indirectly through the pointer. The indirection operator, symbolized by an asterisk (*), fetches the value at the memory address noted in the pointer variable.

```
over_max = *iptr + 1;
```

Now the value of `over_max` is 24. The indirection operator is applied to a pointer. It says, get the address stored in the pointer variable, then fetch the value at that address.

182C

The * operator is the inverse of &. Thus,

```
iptr = &max;
n = *iptr;
```

assigns the same value to n as

```
n = max;
```

In other words, the value of *&max is simply the value of max.

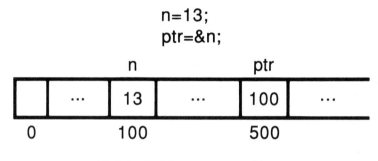

Pointer holds a memory address

Consider two sequences of statements.
First:

```
a = 3;
a_ptr = &a;
a++;
x = *a_ptr;
```

Second:

```
a = 3;
a_ptr = &a;
x = *a_ptr;
a++;
```

In the first case, both a and x have the value 4 after the statements execute. In the second example, the value of x is 3, while the value of a is 4.

True, a_ptr still points to a, but with the * operation, x has been assigned a value. Then a is incremented.

184

```
/*  Write pointer statements */

int max;
int *mptr;

main()
{
    set_indirect (27);
    printf ("The value stored in max is %d", max);
}

set_indirect (v)
/*  Set mptr to address max, and use the pointer
    to store the value v in max.
    WRITE this trivial two-statement function.
*/
int v;
```

SELF TEST   184A

```
int m, n;
int *iptr;

    m = 38;
    iptr = &m;
    n = *iptr;
```

What is the value of n?

SELF TEST   184B

```
    n = 10;
    iptr = &n;
    n = 11;
    m = *iptr;
```

What is the value of m?

SELF TEST   184C

```
int *l_ptr;
int c, d;
```

```
    c = 65;
    l_ptr = &c;
    d = *l_ptr + 1;
```
What is the value of d?

The address operator & is meaningful only when it applies to a variable with an address, or to an *lvalue*. It makes no sense to take the address of an expression.

```
    iptr = &(a + b);      /*  NONSENSE */
```
Nor can we take the address of a constant.

```
    iptr = &49;           /*  NONSENSE */
```
Nor can we assign the address of a register variable.

```
    register int n;
        iptr = &n;        /*  NOT ALLOWED */
```

A pointer to a character may be defined.

```
char *cptr;
char key;

    cptr = &key;
```

A pointer to an object is a different type of thing than the object pointed to. A character pointer is not a character. Furthermore, pointers to different data types are different types of pointers. A pointer to a character, we will see, behaves differently than a pointer to an integer. There are as many different kinds of pointers as there are underlying data types to which they may point. The variety of pointer data types is virtually infinite.

Notice that we are rarely interested in the numerical value of a pointer. The important thing is that we have assigned

```
    iptr = &max;
```

but the address, such as 1078, according to the numbering scheme in the particular computer chips is hardly ever of interest to us.

Aside: if you really want to know the memory address value, you can see it with a statement like

```
    printf ("The address is %u", iptr);
```

Note that this statement displays `iptr`, not `*iptr`. Incidentally, if the memory number exceeds the range of unsigned integers, the specification `%u` will not work.

As a convenience in the syntax of pointer declarations, we may combine them with declarations of objects of the same underlying type.

```
char c, *cptr;
```

This multiple declaration says that `c` is a `char`, and `cptr` is a pointer to a `char`.

The indirection operator `*` should not be used until a pointer has been assigned an address (with `&`, or by equating the pointer to an array or to another pointer). The following function is incorrect.

```
bad_func (i)
int i;
{
int *ptr;

    *ptr = i;    /*  WHERE IS THE VALUE OF i STORED?! */
    printf ("Your number is %d", *ptr);
}
```

A program containing this function may work or crash mysteriously. The value of `i` is stored in an unknown memory location. What you don't know will hurt you, someday.

186

Passing Pointers Between Functions

So far, the discussion of pointers has not demonstrated a practical use for them. Suppose we want to write a function `ordinal` that examines two integers and replaces the larger by 1 and the smaller by 0. It does no good to write

```
ordinal (i, j)
int i, j;
```

because the function receives copies of the values of `i` and `j`. No matter how it juggles them, the values in the invoker's locations will not change.

The solution is to pass pointers to the variables.

The problem may be clearer if we try some invocations.

```
invoker()
{
int a, b;

    ordinal (a, b);
}
```

We could make `ordinal` return the value of the larger integer, but this method tosses most of the work back to the invoking function.

We could work through global variables, but that would be sad programming indeed.

```
int g1, g2;

invoker()
{
int a, b;

    g1 = a;
    g2 = b;
    ordinal();
}
```

The solution is to pass pointers representing the addresses of the variables to be altered.

```
invoker()
{
int a, b;
    ordinal (&a, &b);
}
```

Here `ordinal` receives the addresses of the variables to be altered. This is how a C function grants another function access to locations.

```
ordinal (mptr, nptr)
int *mptr, *nptr;   /*  pointers to integer, not integers */
{

}
```

The function may compare values

```
    if (*mptr > *nptr)
```

```
    /* ... */
```

and assign values to the variables of its invoker.

```
    *mptr = 1;
```

188

```
/*  Reduce two integers to 1 and 0 using pointers */


main()
{
int a, b;

    a = 1610;
    b = 3199;
    ordinal (&a, &b);
    printf ("a and b reduce to %d and %d", a, b);
}

ordinal (
/*  Action: replace the greater integer by 1 and
            the lesser integer by 0.
            If equal, replace both by -1.
    WRITE this function.  DECLARE its pointer
    parameters and write statements to examine
    and replace values.
*/
```

Sort routines commonly pass pointers in this manner. The basics of sorting are to compare and exchange two values. The overall sort routine invokes a function to perform the swap on various pairs of values. The communication between them is by way of pointers.

188A

Elementary Pointer Arithmetic

Although programs occasionally assign the address of a simple integer variable to a pointer,

```
    iptr = &max;
```

by far the most common use of a pointer is to address an array element. Let a program declare an integer array and a pointer to integer. This may be done in a multiple declaration.

```
int score[MAX_SIZE], *iptr;
```

We may take the address of an element of the array, such as the first one.

```
    iptr = &score[0];
```

Now we can move through the array by performing arithmetic upon the value of the pointer.

The above expression applies two operators to a single operand, `score`. One operator is the array reference, `[]`. It is a binary operator that combines the name of an array and a subscript expression, here 0. The other operator is `&`.

As always in C code, we decide the order of evaluation using the precedence chart. According to it, the array reference has higher priority than the unary `&` operator. Therefore, the expression is calculated by referring to the location that stores `score[0]` then taking its address, which is assigned to `iptr`.

It is legal to add an integer to a pointer.

```
    iptr = iptr + 1;
```

After this statement executes, `*iptr` is the value of the next integer in memory, `score[1]`. Note that if you add one to a character pointer, the pointer addresses the next character in memory; pointer arithmetic is scaled to the underlying type.

A shorter way to write the statement is

```
    iptr += 1;
```

but as we know, this is equivalent to

```
    iptr++;
```

Putting it all together, here is a loop that examines every element of an array.

```
    for (iptr = &score[0]; iptr <= &score[MAX_SIZE - 1]; iptr++)
        process (*iptr);
```

The test expression is legal; it is permissible to compare the address value in a pointer to an address.

The initialization statement in this loop could be written

```
iptr = score;
```

because an array name `score` is simply the address of the zero-th element. However, the reverse would be invalid

```
score = iptr;        /*  INVALID */
```

because `score` points to a given location in memory; its address may not be changed. By itself, `score` is not an *lvalue*. It takes a reference to a specific element of the array to specify an *lvalue*.

```
score[0] = 83;  /*  assign value to lvalue */
```

The loop moves the pointer through the array. An alternative method is to keep the pointer where the array starts and add varying offsets to it.

```
for (iptr = score, i = 0; i < MAX_SIZE; i++)
    {
    n = *(iptr + i);     /*  iptr stationary, add offset */
    process (n);
    }
```

Each time through the loop, a different value of i is added to `iptr` and the corresponding value fetched indirectly. A look at the precedence chart shows that * outranks +. Therefore, the parentheses are necessary to enforce the desired order of evaluation.

SELF TEST 190

```
int salary[] = { 250, 275, 300, 325, 350 };
int *sptr, n;
    sptr = &salary[0];
    n = *(sptr + 2) - 20;
```

What is the value of n?

SELF TEST 190A

```
int class[] = {3, 6, 4, 1, 9, -1 }, *class_ptr, n;

    for (class_ptr = class, n = 0; *class_ptr != -1; class_ptr++)
        n += *class_ptr;
```

What is the value of n?

SELF TEST

```
char grade[] = {'A', 'A', 'B', 'C', 'C', 'D'};
char *front_ptr, *back_ptr;
    front_ptr = grade; back_ptr = &grade[5];
    while (*front_ptr != *back_ptr)
        {
        if (*front_ptr != *back_ptr)
            front_ptr++;
        if (*front_ptr != *back_ptr)
            back_ptr--;
        }
```

Now what is the value, in decimal, of `*front_ptr`?

```
/*  Scan an array for a character */

char cmd_line[80] = {"B:CW"};

main()
{
int flag;

    flag = check_colon();
    if (flag)
        puts ("Has a colon.");
    else
        puts ("Does not have a colon.");
}

check_colon()
/*  Return: TRUE/FALSE a colon is in the string.
    WRITE this function.
*/
```

```
/*  Convert string to lower case */

char test_string[80] = {"THE COUGHING GNU KNEW PHONETICS"};

main()
```

```
{
    string_to_lower();
    printf ("%s", test_string);
}

string_to_lower()
/*  WRITE this function so that it converts
    test_string[] entirely to lower case.
    Remember that ASCII 'A' = 0x41, 'a' = 0x61.
*/
```

192

A common bug is forgetting the * operator.

```
int c, *ptr;

    c = ptr;         /*  WRONG */

    c = *ptr;        /*  CORRECT */
```

192A

```
/*  Copy a string */

#define MAX_LINE 80

char source[MAX_LINE + 1] =
            {"The coughing gnu knew phonetics."};
char dest[MAX_LINE + 1];

main()
{
    string_copy();
    puts (dest);
}

string_copy()
/*  Copy the string in source to dest.  Copy through the
    terminal null inclusive.
    WRITE this function.
*/
```

Close Ties between Arrays and Pointers

The preceding exercise may have disturbed you, because we can hardly expect to keep strings in special global arrays reserved for the `string_copy` function. We have seen how to pass pointers; now we can do something similar with arrays.

```
main()
{
char dest[30], source[30];

    string_copy (dest, source);
}

string_copy (dest, source);
char *dest, *source;
{
/* ... */
}
```

An array as a whole cannot be passed to a function, but a pointer to the zero-th or other element of an array works fine.

In `main` above, the invocation passes two addresses. As we have seen, it could be written

```
    string_copy (&dest[0], &source[0]);
```

In the invoked function, the declaration of the formal parameters is given as pointers, since this is the C mechanism that holds addresses.

C notation for formal parameters becomes a little tricky here. It is also legal to write

```
string_copy (dest, source);
char dest[], source[];  /*  STILL POINTERS! */
{
/* ... */
}
```

Because C does not allow the passing of arrays, the compiler knows that the formal parameters `dest` and `source` must be pointers.

The payoff from this suggestive notation is that

```
    n = *(iptr + i);
```

may be written

```
    n = iptr[i];
```

even though `iptr` is a pointer, not an array. Usually, it is faster and more compact to dispense with indexes, but if you wish, you can write statements like

```
    dest[i] = source[i];
```

When you are manipulating a pointer and occasionally need to refer to an object three places ahead in the array, you can use the notation

```
    iptr[3];
```

rather than saving and restoring the value of the pointer.

In the `main` function above, the arrays were defined as local arrays of the function. Everything just stated applies whether these arrays are global or local data objects.

Function parameters are formal parameters; they are declarations, not definitions. Although you may declare a formal parameter as a pointer or an array with the same effect, definitions of local variables do not enjoy this luxury. Creating an array and creating a pointer are two different actions.

```
string_manip (str)
char str[];      /*  formal parameter: same as char *str */
{
char work[];
char *work_ptr; /*  TWO DIFFERENT KINDS OF OBJECTS */
    /* ... */
}
```

194

Now we can repeat the exercise for copying strings. This time, however, we make the function `string_copy` useful by giving it pointers to the arrays. The next screen has a program exercise to write

```
    string_copy (dptr, sptr)
```

to copy a string. The function will successively copy the values stored in source locations to dest locations. The pointers start at the beginning of the arrays, and indexes can be used to move through them.

We give the pointer arguments distinctive names, but since they are formal parameters, they could repeat the names dest and source.

A typical library function named strcpy does just that, so in effect you will be writing part of a C library.

195

```
/*  Copy a string by passing pointers */

#define MAX_LINE 80

char source[MAX_LINE + 1] =
         {"The coughing gnu knew phonetics."};
char dest[MAX_LINE + 1];

main()
{
    string_copy (dest, source);
    puts (dest);
}

string_copy (dest, source)
/*  Copy the string in source to dest.  Copy through the
    terminal null.
    WRITE this function.
*/
char *dest, *source;
```

195A

```
/*  Sweep through array using pointer */

int expense[80] = {384, 215, 21, -1}; /*  -1 signals end */

main()
{
int sum;

    sum = add_expense (expense);
    printf ("Total expenses were %d.\n", sum);
```

```
}

add_expense (expense)
/*  Return: sum of expenses, excluding the -1
    at the end of the array.
    WRITE this function.
*/
int *expense;
```

In the preceding exercise, suppose you wanted to refer back to the first element of the array after doing the sum. You might choose to remember the starting address in another pointer.

```
int *ptr;
```

To initialize it, you may write

```
    ptr = expense;
```

or

```
    ptr = &expense[0];
```

but *not*

```
    ptr = &expense;
```

The first statement works by simply copying one pointer value to another. It would also work if `expense` were actually an array, because an array name is like a pointer (except its value cannot be changed). The second statement works because `expense[0]` is the first integer of the array, and `&` takes its address. However, the last statement takes the address of the object `expense`. This is the address on the stack of the passed pointer, not the address of the array `expense`. Some compilers may issue a warning message about mismatched types: `&expense` is a suitable value for a pointer to a pointer to `int`, but `ptr` is merely a pointer to `int`.

Pointers of Different Types

It is important to realize that pointer arithmetic is *scaled*. The expression `iptr + i` depends on the underlying type. When `iptr` is a pointer to int, adding i makes iptr refer to the location that is (or should be) occupied i integers ahead in memory. In the C Workshop, for example, a char occupies one byte and an int occupies two bytes. The expression iptr + i is calculated by scaling i by a factor of two. If the program has a character pointer

```
char *cptr;
```

then this factor of two is not used.

Assignment works between two pointers of the same type.

```
iptr1 = iptr;
```

and

```
iptr = iptr1;
```

are both valid, although their effects are opposite.

When you write

```
cptr = iptr;
```

between pointers that address objects of different types, your compiler may silently accept the statement or issue a warning. You may use the cast mechanism to make the change of type explicit.

```
cptr = (char *) iptr;
```

The cast specifies the type in parentheses; the only difference between this cast and earlier ones is that its type is more complex than the elementary forms.

If you write

```
cptr = (char *) iptr + 1;
```

the precedence chart shows cast having higher priority than addition. Therefore, 1 is added to a character pointer. This is different than adding 1 to an integer pointer.

```
cptr = iptr + 1;
```

Note, however, that an increment operator has the same precedence as the cast.

```
cptr = (char *) iptr++;
```

This statement increments `iptr` as a pointer to integer, because the two unary operators associate from right to left.

SELF TEST   **198**

```
int *iptr, n;
```

   A) `(char *) (iptr + n);`
   B) `iptr + n;`
   C) `(char *) iptr + n;`

Two of these expressions evaluate to the same address.
Which one is different?

SELF TEST   **198A**

```
char an_array[10], *cptr;
int *iptr;

    cptr = an_array;
    iptr = (int *) cptr++;
```

After these statements, `cptr` points to
   A) `an_array[0]`
   B) `an_array[1]`
   C) `an_array[2]`

SELF TEST   **198B**

```
char an_array[10], *cptr;
int a;

    cptr = an_array;
    a = (int) (*cptr++);
```

After these statements, `cptr` points to
   A) `an_array[0]`
   B) `an_array[1]`
   C) `an_array[2]`

SELF TEST   **198C**

```
char an_array[10], *cptr;
int a;

    cptr = an_array;
    a = *((int *) (cptr++));
```

After these statements, `cptr` points to

   A) `an_array[0]`
   B) `an_array[1]`
   C) `an_array[2]`

SELF TEST   **199**

```
char *cptr;
int *iptr;

    cptr = ((char *) iptr)++;
    iptr++;
```

The two statements have
   A) the same
   B) different
effects incrementing `iptr`.

199A

More Pointer Arithmetic

Besides adding or subtracting an integer to a pointer using scaled arithmetic, C permits you to compare pointers, subtract one from another, and compare a pointer to null (0).

These operations enable programs to form test expressions that look at what has happened to pointers.

Subtracting pointers of the same type tells you how many objects of that type separate the two addresses. This number is, depending on your compiler, typically of `int` type.

```
#define MAX_SIZE 10

int *iptr1, *iptr2, n;
int score[MAX_SIZE];

    iptr2 = &score[MAX_SIZE - 1];
    iptr1 = &score[0];
    n = iptr2 - iptr1 + 1;
```

After these statements the value of n is `MAX_SIZE`. There are nine integer objects between the zero-th and ninth elements of the array.

The special value 0, or null pointer, may be assigned to a pointer. For example, suppose a function returns a pointer to character.

```
char *
calc_line()
{
}
```

The function may return the null value to indicate an exception condition. The invoking function may test the pointer for this value.

```
char *cptr;

    cptr = calc_line();
    if (cptr == 0)
        abort();
```

The null pointer is special. On most computers you should never read or write to memory address 0.

A string constant is an array of characters. Therefore, you may write

```
char *note;

    note = "Here's a pointer about string constants."
```

The compiler generates an array with the null-terminated characters in it. Assigning the array to the pointer means that the address of the zero-th element becomes the value of note.

200

```
/*  Report index of character */

#define EXCEPTION    (-1)

char cmd_line[80] = {"B:CW"};

main()
{
int pos;

    if ((pos = check_colon (cmd_line)) == EXCEPTION)
        puts ("Does not have a colon.");
    else
```

```
        printf ("Colon first occurs at position %d\n", pos);
}

check_colon (str)
/*  Return: index (from 0) of first colon in the string.
            -1 if no colon.
     WRITE this function.
     Hint: use a work pointer, then subtract  str  from it.
*/
char *str;
```

Incrementing a Pointer

We have already seen pointers incremented or decremented in expressions like iptr++. Often we want to use indirection (*) to read the value at the pointer address and increment the pointer. The syntax of these operations is worth some study.

Consider the statement

```
    n = *ptr++;
```

This statement applies two unary operators to a single object, ptr. The precedence chart says the operators have equal precedence, so we must use the associativity of this precedence level, which is right to left. Since ++ is to the right of *, we know that the increment applies to the pointer, not to the object to which it points. However, since ++ follows its operand ptr, the increment is applied to the pointer after the * operation is performed.

In other words, to step a pointer to the next location while fetching a value, you write

```
    n = *ptr++; /*  first fetch, then advance pointer */
    n = *++ptr; /*  advance pointer, then fetch value */
```

In both cases, ++ is to the right of * and therefore applies to the pointer itself. This question being settled, the position of ++ in relation to ptr determines whether it is applied before or after the expression is evaluated.

On the other hand, to increment the stored value:

```
    (*ptr)++;   /*  fetch, then increment stored value */
    ++*ptr;     /*  increment stored value, then fetch it */
```

The parentheses are required so that the increment operator ++, when it is to the right of *, is applied to the object *ptr rather than to the pointer. We must force * to apply to ptr.

No parentheses are needed to pre-increment then fetch the stored value. The operator to the right, *, applies to ptr, so ++ applies to the stored value. Since ++ precedes its operand, the stored value is incremented then fetched.

Note that writing

```
n = (*ptr)++;
```

fetches the stored value and assigns it to n, then performs the side effect of incrementing the stored value.

Similar remarks apply to --.

Once you are comfortable with the rule, it is more compact and efficient to write

```
c = *ptr++;
```

rather than

```
c = *ptr;
ptr++;
```

SELF TEST   202

```
int *ptr, a, b;
int list[] = {10, 20, 30, 40};
    ptr = list;
    a = *ptr++;
    b = *ptr;
```

What is the value of b?

SELF TEST   202A

```
int *ptr, a, b;
int list[] = {10, 20, 30, 40};

    ptr = list;
    a = *ptr++;
    b = *ptr;
```

What is the value of a?

SELF TEST   **203**
```
int *ptr, a, b;
int list[] = {10, 20, 30, 40};
    ptr = list;
    a = (*ptr)++;
    b = *ptr;
```
What is the value of b?

SELF TEST   **203A**

```
int *ptr, a, b;
int list[] = {10, 20, 30, 40};

    ptr = list;
    a = (*ptr)++;
```
What is the value of a?

SELF TEST   **203B**
```
int *ptr, a, b;
int list[] = {10, 20, 30, 40};
    ptr = list;
    a = ++*ptr;
```
What is the value of a?

SELF TEST   **203C**
```
int *ptr, a, b;
int list[] = {10, 20, 30, 40};

    ptr = list;
    a = ++*ptr;
    b = *ptr;
```
What is the value of b?

                                                                          203D

The next screen repeats the string copying program. This time you should write it using pointers, increment and indirection operators, but no indexes.

                                                                          203E
```
/*  Copy a string using pointer increment and indirection */
```

```
#define MAX_LINE 80

char source[MAX_LINE + 1] =
            {"The coughing gnu knew phonetics."};
char dest[MAX_LINE + 1];

main()
{
    string_copy (dest, source);
    puts (dest);
}

string_copy (dptr, sptr)
/*  Copy the string in source to dest.  Copy through the
    terminal null.
    WRITE this function using no indexes.  Use pointer
    increment and the indirection operator together.
*/
char *dptr, *sptr;
```

Exercise. Write a function `main` with two local variables that invokes a function `swap` to exchange their values.

Exercise. Write a function `do_factor (u, factor)` that finds all the factors of an unsigned integer and puts them in an array `factor`. It also returns the number of factors. Have `main` exercise the function and print some results. Allow enough room in the array; the largest number of factors we found was 118.

Exercise. Most books have an International Standard Book Number on the back cover. Ignoring hyphens, it consists of nine digits and a concluding check digit. In a valid ISBN, 10 times the first digit (from the left) plus 9 times the second digit and so on through 2 times the ninth digit, plus the check digit, is evenly divisible by 11. If the check digit has to be 10, the symbol X is used. Write a function that accepts a string consisting of the first nine digits and returns the ASCII check digit. Put this function in a program whose `main` function invokes it.

Exercise. Write a program which, when executed, displays its own source code.

CHAPTER 13
Structures

206

The most elaborate data declaration is the structure, which is a grouping of diverse elements. In some other languages, the construction is called a record.

206A

The template (also called a tag) gives the form of the record.

```
struct e_tag {
    int id_number;
    char pay_grade;
    char name[MAX_NAME+1];
    };
```

This template says that a structure of the form e_tag has three members: an integer id_number, a pay_grade character, and a character array holding the name.

The braces and semicolon are required. Within the braces is a list of data declarations for the members of the structure. We may choose the tag name. It is only a helpful convention to put _tag in it.

206B

To create a data item of e_tag:

```
struct e_tag worker;
```

This defines a single instance of the structure with its various members. Often you want to create an array, each of whose elements is a structure. This could be done:

```
struct e_tag employee[STAFF_SIZE];
```

If you will use the structure template only once, you may combine the template and the definition:

```
struct e_tag {
    int id_number;
    char pay_grade;
    char name[MAX_NAME+1];
    } employee[STAFF_SIZE];
```

207

Having created a structure, the next thing is to access its members. The period operator (.) does it.

```
int n;

    n = worker.id_number;
```

If we have an array of structures and want a member from one element of the array, we write

```
    n = employee[0].id_number;
```

The array index is applied to the whole structure, not to a member. Conversely, a statement may set the value of a member.

```
    employee[2].pay_grade = 'B';
```

207A

You may initialize a structure (except an automatic one) by writing the values of the members, separated by commas, within braces after an equal sign.

```
struct e_tag worker = { 2683, 'B', "Samuel A. Drew" };
```

An array of structures may be initialized by listing the individual structures, separated by commas.

```
struct employee[] = {
    { 2683, 'B', "Samuel A. Drew" },
```

```
    { 2684, 'A', "Gladys L. A. Drew" }
    };
```

SELF TEST   **208**

```
struct c_tag {
    int speed;
    int price;
    char name[MAX_NAME+1];
    } computer = { 83, 2100, "Multimodern 180"};
```

What is the value of 2 * computer.price?

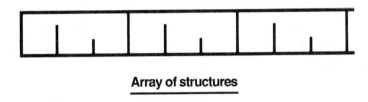

Array of structures

When all the elements of an array of structures are initialized explicitly and each member is a simple variable or string constant, most compilers do not require inner braces, just the outer braces.

The compiler assigns each structure enough memory to hold its members. Although the members usually follow each other consecutively in memory, you cannot use their sizes to determine their addresses. The reason is that many processors require or work better by having data objects aligned in memory. If an int takes up two bytes, the processor might want the integer to begin at an even byte address, that is, a word address. When a structure has members of byte and word size, some padding (wasted bytes) may be required to align the word or double word objects.

Normally, the C programmer can ignore alignment. However, in calculating total memory requirements, examining memory dumps, or following assembly language instructions, you may need to allow for it.

Pointers to Structures

We may define a pointer to a structure.

```
struct e_tag *eptr;
```

This defines `eptr` to be a pointer to an `e_tag` type of structure, rather than pointing to a character or integer.

To get the value of a member in the structure, we use the `->` operator.

```
eptr->id_number
```

refers to the `id_number` member of the structure to which the pointer currently points. It is simply an integer in this case.

```
int curr_id;
    eptr = &employee[2];        /*  point to third employee */
    curr_id = eptr->id_number;  /*  get his ID number */
```

Here we see another kind of pointer. Like all pointers, a pointer to a structure contains the address of the object pointed to. The difference is that the object is a structure rather than an integer or a character.

In fact, for every kind of structure, as defined by different templates, pointers to those kinds of structures are different objects. One of the practical differences between pointers of different types occurs when a pointer is incremented. In order to point to the next integer in memory, the address value of the pointer has a certain number of bytes added to it, for example, two. To increment a pointer to a structure, the compiled instructions add a number of bytes to its address value, perhaps 102 for example, depending on the space occupied by each instance of the structure.

Pointer to structures may be passed.

```
main()
{
    process (&employee);
}

process (eptr)
struct e_tag *eptr;
{
int m;
```

```
    m = eptr->id_number;
}
```

The invoking function, `main`, provides an address to the function that expects a pointer. The invoked function `process` has a formal parameter, a pointer to a structure of a certain type. The value of a pointer is passed, and through this mechanism, statements within `process` may access (and alter!) members of the structure.

```
    m = eptr->id_number;
```

The `->` operator accesses the member of the structure. It is logically equivalent to

```
    (*eptr).id_number;
```

because `eptr` points to a structure, and `*eptr` is the structure pointed to.

Note: Entire structures cannot be passed in "Kernighan and Ritchie" C, the original and still common version of C. ("K&R C" is the C described in a book by these authors; Ritchie was one of the inventors of the language.) New versions do allow structures to be passed to functions. Suppose you write a program using a compiler that passes a pointer whether you write

```
    process (employee);
```

or

```
    process (&employee);
```

Later, you might want to recompile the program with a compiler that accepts both structures and pointers to structures as function parameters. You may need to review your code for discrepancies.

Passing a structure requires making a copy of all its data; passing a pointer to a structure involves only a copy of the address at which the structure starts. However, when a pointer is passed, the invoked function has the power to change the actual data rather a copy of the values.

210

Like other pointers, structure pointers may be incremented and decremented.

```
    eptr++;
```

advances the pointer to the next structure in the array of structures. That is, when a pointer is incremented, the address is increased by the size of the object pointed to. This is true for all types of pointers: integer, character, and, as we have here, a structure pointer.

It is a coding error is to forget the * operator in the definition of a pointer to a structure.

```
struct e_tag *eptr;       /*  CORRECT */

struct e_tag eptr;        /*  WRONG */
```

A pointer to a structure is a different object than a pointer to a member of the structure.

```
struct n_tag {
    int id;
    char name[MAX_NAME+1];
    } roster[STAFF_SIZE];

struct n_tag *sptr;
int *iptr;
char *cptr;

    sptr = roster;
    iptr = &roster[0].id;
    cptr = &roster[0].name[0];
```

The addresses in sptr and iptr are the same after this initialization, but the pointers behave differently. Applying the increment operator, for example, sptr++ points to the next structure in the array, while iptr++ addresses one integer past the first id, which is a nonsense location somewhere in the first person's name array. Finally, cptr points to the first character of the first person's name, and successive increments cptr++ will scan the name.

SELF TEST   **211**

```
struct r_tag {               struct r_templ {
    int weight;                  int weight;
    int winner;                  int winner;
    } race[MAX_RACE + 1];        } race_array[MAX_RACE + 1];
```

Is the structure of data in these two declarations

A) different

B) the same

SELF TEST 212

```
struct e_tag {
    int id_number;
    char pay_grade;
    char name[MAX_NAME+1];
    } worker = {3174, 4, "John Prole"};

    number = worker.pay_grade + 2;
```

What is the value of number?

SELF TEST 212A

```
struct e_tag {
    int id_number;
    char pay_grade;
    char name[MAX_NAME+1];
    } worker = {3174, 2, "John Prole"};
struct e_tag *eptr;
    eptr = &worker;
    number = eptr->pay_grade + 3;
```

What is the value of number?

212B

```
/*  Access a member of a structure */

struct c_tag {
    int catalog;
    char key;
    char key1;
    char title[30];
    char composer[15];
    } composition =
    {543, 'd', 0, "Organ concerto", "Bach, J. S."};

main()
{
char key;

    key = fetch_key (composition);
```

```
        printf ("The key is %c", key);
}

fetch_key (cptr)
/*  Return: key of the composition.
    WRITE the declaration for cptr and the function.
*/
```

213

Using Structures and Pointers to Them

Suppose a statistician friend analyzes horse races. For each race he wants to keep some information. To begin, the weight of the winning jockey and the post position of his horse will be sufficient. You may hold this information in an array of structures.

```
struct r_tag {
    int weight;
    int post;
    };
struct r_tag race[MAX_RACE + 1];
```

An `r_tag` structure consists of two integers. In the array `race`, each element is one such structure. By convention, the array will end with a null race {0, 0}.

We will write a program searching the array to find a race meeting certain criteria.

The weight of the jockey in race `i` is

```
    race[i].weight
```

In practice, however, we use pointers. Instead of going through the array by stepping an index `i`, we define a pointer

```
struct r_tag *rptr;
    rptr = race;    /*  initialize the pointer */
```

and use

```
    rptr->weight
```

to get the weight. Writing `rptr++` would advance to the next race.

Actually, because we need to keep `rptr` as a mark of the beginning of the array, we use a work pointer to examine its elements.

```
struct r_tag *wptr;
    wptr = rptr;
```

Now we may step `wptr++` through the array. When we need to calculate the equivalent index,

```
    wptr - rptr
```

does the job. Note that the subtraction of pointers yields the number of races, not a distance in "bytes" or other things formally unknown to C.

A function that analyzes a race needs a pointer to that race, which can be provided with the invocation

```
    analyze (wptr);
```

where `wptr` has been stepped to the *i*-th race.

The function itself has the header

```
analyze (rptr)
struct r_tag *rptr;
```

Within `analyze`, the pointer notation is also used.

```
    rptr->weight
```

is the weight of the jockey in the race.

214

```
/*  Find first horse race meeting criteria */

#define TRUE     1
#define FALSE    0
#define EXCEPTION (-1)

struct r_tag {
    int weight;     /*  of winning jockey */
    int post;       /*  post position 1.. of winning horse */
    };
struct r_tag race[20] = {103,4, 104,1, 106,1, 112,3, 0,0};

main()
{
```

```
int i;

    i = find (race);
    if (i == EXCEPTION)
        puts ("No such race");
    else
        printf ("Race #%d", i);
}

find (rptr)
struct r_tag *rptr;    /*  gets pointer to whole array */
/*  Return: first race won by horse at inside (#1) where
        jockey weight is over 105.
    The races are numbered 0, 1, 2, ...
    Return EXCEPTION if no such race.
    WRITE this function, invoking  analyze. */



analyze (rptr)
struct r_tag *rptr;       /*  pointer to a race */
/*  Return: TRUE/FALSE winning horse was at inside
        and jockey weight was over 105.
    WRITE this function.
*/
```

SELF TEST   215

Suppose the terminal {0, 0} `race` element is not used.

```
struct r_tag race[MAX_RACE + 1];
```

Which statement sets `wptr` to the last element of `race`?
    A) `wptr = race + MAX_RACE;`
    B) `wptr = &race[MAX_RACE];`
    C) `wptr = race + (sizeof (race))/sizeof (struct r_tag) - 1;`
    D) All of the above

In the preceding program, we chose to declare the template `r_tag` separately from defining the array `race`. If we did not need the template for any other object, we could have combined them:

```
struct r_tag {
```

```
int weight;
int post;
}; race[] = {103, 4,  104, 1,  106, 1,  112, 3,  0, 0};
```

The function `find` in the program received a pointer to the whole array (actually, to its zero-th element).

```
struct r_tag *rptr;    /*  gets pointer to whole array */
```

In `main` it was sufficient to write

```
find (race);
```

to pass the address of the first element of the array.

Within `find`, it was necessary to pass `analyze` a pointer to a single structure. Something like

```
test = analyze (&race[i]);
```

would do it. Here it is necessary with many compilers and always good practice to specify `&`. If `race` were a simple array of integers, `race[i]` would be an integer, which would be passed. This is different from `&race[i]`, which is the address of the *i*-th race.

More likely, we write

```
test = analyze (wptr);
```

within a loop in which we are incrementing `wptr`. This is an example of the fact that C tends to rely heavily on pointers.

To test for the end of the array in `find`, something like

```
(wptr->weight == 0)
```

would work. If this condition becomes true without having discovered a race of the desired type, then `find` should return -1.

The reason pointers proved easier to work with lies in the fact that parameters were passed to functions. The argument to `find` is a pointer to an array, presumably because the program might process several arrays of races. Thereafter, we passed pointers down through all the function calls.

If there were only one global array `race`, then `find` would not need a parameter. An index could step through the array, for example,

```
for (i = 0; race[i].weight != 0; i++)
    /*  ... */;
```

The function `analyze` would be invoked with an index argument

```
test = analyze (i);
```

The preference is for pointers. First, it conforms with the general advantages of passing local variables.

Second, the repeated calculation of

```
race[i].weight
```

takes more computation than the pointer reference

```
rptr->weight
```

where we change `rptr` only when necessary.

A subscript calculation involves a multiplication to scale `i` to the size of each array element and an addition to add the offset to the memory base of the array. The pointer reference is simply an indirect memory fetch.

217

Nested Structures

A structure member may be another structure.

```
struct j_tag {        /*  jockey template */
   char name[MAX_NAME + 1];
   int weight;
   };

struct e_tag {
   int horse;
   struct j_tag jockey;
   } entrant[MAX_ENTRANT + 1];
```

The `entrant` array consists of structures composed of two members, a horse's number and a structure for the jockey. The latter structure has two members, a character string for the name and an integer for the jockey's weight.

You must let the compiler know about `j_tag` structures before defining an `e_tag` structure. You may define the `j_tag` structure before mentioning `e_tag` structures, or you may declare the `j_tag` template but define the actual objects later.

To access members in a nested structure, just put the . and -> operators together.

```
w1 = entrant[i].jockey.weight;
```

```
struct e_tag *eptr;
```

```
    eptr = &entrant[i];
    w2 = eptr->jockey.weight;
```

Here, w1 = w2, the weight of the jockey riding entrant i. The member operators are applied from left to right.

More common is the situation in which a member of a structure is a *pointer* to a structure.

```
struct e_tag {
    int horse;
    struct j_tag *jockey;
    } entrant[MAX_ENTRANT + 1];
```

After all, a jockey may ride several horses in an afternoon, so it saves memory if we simply point to the information on the jockey. Given an entry, you may refer to the weight of the jockey.

```
struct j_tag *jptr;
    w2 = eptr->jptr->weight;
```

SELF TEST   **218**

```
eptr = &entrant[0];
```

```
    (entrant[0].jockey.name[1] == eptr->jockey.name[6])
```

Suppose the first entrant's jockey's name is "Andy Anderson." Is the expression

A) true
B) false

                                                                                         218A

The typedef Declaration

Our study of data types began with elementary building blocks given to us by C: integer, character, and floating point. We combined them in arrays and structures and set pointers to them.

To attach helpful names to data types, C offers the `typedef` declaration.

```
typedef int POINTS;
```

The syntax begins with the key word `typedef`. The declaration follows, using our chosen name. This is not the name of a data object; rather, it is the parameter of the `typedef` substitution scheme, which works much like `#define`.

Now we can declare

```
POINTS max_score;
```

in place of

```
int max_score;
```

219

You may write

```
typedef struct r_tag    /*  (tag name optional but advised) */
   {
   int horse[10];
   char *jockey[10];
   } RACE;
```

after which you may define

```
RACE bel_mar[8];
```

instead of writing out

```
struct r_tag bel_mar[8];
```

The shorthand spares you from creating a tag name for the structure.

Perhaps the most common `typedef` is

```
FILE *fid;
```

This statement defines `fid` to be a pointer to an object of the form described in a `typedef` declaration using the name `FILE`. Most C compilers require a certain structure definition in any program that does file input or output. This structure contains necessary data about files, such as pointers to buffers used during disk reads and writes. Typically, the compiler writer uses a `typedef` to name this template `FILE`. You manipulate files with pointers to these structures, using declarations like the one above.

A `typedef` is like a `#define` except that the textual substitution is performed during compilation, not during preprocessing.

Like a `#define`, a `typedef` can improve the readability of a program. Changes to data types can be made quickly when transferring a program to a new environment, too. For example, a change of

```
typedef int POINTS;
```

to

```
typedef long POINTS;
```

and a recompilation of the program will adjust all the data declared with `POINTS`.

In practice, the `typedef` facility is used primarily for `FILE` and to help document large programming projects.

SELF TEST   **220**

```
typedef struct s_tag {
    char *name;
    int rank;
    int serial_number;
    } SOLDIER;
```

You could declare an array of 200 pointers to soldiers by writing
  A) `*SOLDIER a_company[200];`
  B) `SOLDIER *a_company[200];`
  C) `SOLDIER[200] *a_company;`

                                                                     220A

Unions

A union in C is just like a structure, except that all the members of a union originate at the same memory location. That is, they overlap. The member objects may be of different types and sizes; the compiler allocates enough space for the largest one and insures that each data type is aligned in memory as required.

Unions can hold different kinds of data at different times with economy of memory space. However, your program must keep track of what kind of information is stored in a union.

Structures and unions are defined and accessed in the same way. Both have a list of members in braces { } that are referred to with the . and -> operators. The compiler cannot initialize unions.

221

```
/*  Example of a union */

/*  PREDICT what this program will print.  Then Run
    the program. */

union {
    int i;
    char c;
    } example;

main()
{
    example.i = 0x41;    /*  (ASCII code for 'A') */
    printf ("What first had %c", example.i);

    example.c = 'B';
    printf (" now has %c.", example.i);

    /*  Note: we are displaying member .i */
}
```

221A

Here is a more useful example of unions.

A bookstore has a computerized record of its suppliers. Most of the publishers have ISBN publisher numbers. (ISBN stands for International Standard Book Number.) For our purposes, we will bend the truth and assume these are integers. Some smaller publishers, however, have not obtained an ISBN number. The bookstore identifies them with a three-character abbreviation.

A union is an appropriate tool to store the identifying number or mnemonic. We will nest a union inside the publisher structure; the union will hold either an ISBN integer or a character string for the publisher. In addition, the structure needs a flag that signals which data the union holds.

All you will do in this example is write some code to install initial data values.

222

```
/*  Write to publisher data record with union */

#define TRUE    1
#define FALSE   0

union c_tag {
    char abbr[4];
    int isbn;
    };

struct p_tag {
    char flag;        /*  TRUE/FALSE has ISBN/abbreviation */
    union c_tag pub_id;
    int payable;
    };
struct p_tag supplier[2];

main()
{
int i, p;

    init_supps (supplier);

    for (i = p = 0; i < 2; i++)
        p += supplier[i].payable;
    printf ("The total owed is %d\n", p);
    printf ("Supplier #2 code: %s", &supplier[1].pub_id.abbr[0]);
}

init_supps (sptr)
struct p_tag *sptr;
/*  WRITE code here to initialize the structure
    for the following publishers (in order listed):
    Simian & Shooter    ISBN 3845    2812
    Okeefenokee Press   "OKF"        119
```

*/

Besides managing space allocation in a union, the compiler obeys alignment requirements imposed by the processor.

Suppose you declare a union

```
union c_tag {
    char code;
    int isbn;
    };
```

The compiler reserves enough space for an integer, which we assume is one word, or two bytes, for this discussion. Some microprocessors require that a word begin on an even memory address (100 is valid; 101 is not). If necessary, the compiler will pad the union with a byte in order to meet this requirement.

223

Bit Fields

Bit fields, sometimes just called fields, are structure or union members with a specified width in bits. This is the most machine-dependent construction in C.

```
struct ser_tag {
    unsigned word_length : 2;
    unsigned : 1;
    unsigned parity : 2;
    unsigned baud_rate : 3;
    } int_14h_reg;
```

This structure has four members, each a field as indicated by the colon and the specified bit width.

Bits are allocated within a byte, word, or other unit of memory. If a tag member of a structure will not fit in the current memory unit, it goes into the next one. The compiler may work with one memory unit, such as a word, or it may respect boundaries implied by your type declaration. The above declaration using unsigned integers is kept word-aligned.

The compiler also is free to decide several other things:

Bits may be allocated from the least significant bit to the most significant (as in the C Workshop), or in the reverse order.

Once defined, fields are used like small integers. (Note that a signed integer bit field uses one bit for the sign.)

```
int_14h_reg.baud_rate = 7;
p = int_14h_reg.parity;
```

You cannot take the address of a bit field; the & operator is invalid. Nor can you create arrays of fields, although you may define arrays of structures that have bit field members.

A bit field need not be named, which spares a little effort when using a field merely to pad out a byte or word. A field declared with zero width says that additional fields go into the next byte or word.

```
struct bf_tag {
    int first : 3, : 4, third : 5, : 0;
    int fifth : 2;
    int : 0, seventh : 4;
} and_stream = { 2, 6, 1, 7 };
```

The unnamed : 4 causes four bits to be skipped before third is allocated. The : 0 moves to the next word, even though four bits are left. The second : 0 gives fifth the only named bit field in the second word. The whole collection of fields and_stream is initialized, values being supplied for the four named fields.

Bit fields may be useful in two situations. One is to communicate with the underlying hardware. The first example above in this section reflects the bits in the AL register when using the IBM PC BIOS interrupt 14 hex, which provides serial port communications.

Bit fields may also conserve memory. If you have eight flags that may be on or off, you might save space by packing them into a structure with bit fields filling a byte. On the other hand, it takes more object code to compute flagstaff.menu_flag than menu_flag.

If your compiler does not offer bit fields or you want a more portable program, you can still do what you want with bitwise operators and masks.

SELF TEST   **224**

```
struct ser_tag {
    unsigned word_length : 2;
```

```
    unsigned : 1;
    unsigned parity : 2;
    unsigned baud_rate : 3;
    } int_14h_reg = { 2, 3, 7 };
```
What is the (decimal) value in the byte of memory here?

Suppose the bookstore discussed above codes all its 17,576 publisher suppliers with three uppercase letters. There are 26 letters, so each letter could be represented in five bits, since two to the fifth power is 32. The following program is based on the structure

```
struct code_tag {
    unsigned let1 : 5;        /*  no arrays of bit fields */
    unsigned let2 : 5;
    unsigned let3 : 5;
    };
```

The code occupies one word, with a bit left over. We need to convert strings like "MIP" to this structure in order to store the code, and we need to expand a word that contains the three bit fields to a string with three uppercase letters and the conventional null.

225

```
/*  Pack three uppercase letters into 16 bits using fields */

/*  (Advanced exercise) */

#define MAX_FILE 10

/*  Macro instead of function converts 1..26 to 'A'..'Z' */
#define CODE_TO_LTR(L)  ((L) +'A'-1)

struct code_tag {
    unsigned let1 : 5;        /*  no arrays of bit fields */
    unsigned let2 : 5;
    unsigned let3 : 5;
    };

struct code_tag file[MAX_FILE + 1];

char test_code[] = {"ABC"};
```

```
main ()
{
char buffer[6];

    store_code (test_code, 3);
    load_code (buffer, 3);
    printf ("Code is: %s", buffer);
}

store_code (str, index)
/*  Convert and store three letters in a word of the array.
    WRITE this function.
*/
char *str;  /*  first three letters are the code */
int index;  /*  in  file  array */



ltr_to_code (letter)
/*  Return: 1 for 'A', .., 26 for 'Z'
    Useful when you write store_code().
*/
int letter;
{
    if (letter < 'A' || letter > 'Z')
    {
    puts ("Input must be uppercase letter");
    exit (1);
    }
    else
        return (letter - 'A' + 1);
}

load_code (buf, index)
/*  Expand three-letter code from a word of the array
*/
char *buf;  /*  fill first three letters, append 0 */
int index;  /*  in  file  array */
{
struct code_tag *ptr;
```

```
    ptr = &file[index];

/*  Bit fields cannot be arrays (although a word
    containing bit fields may be element of an array) */
/*  Employs macro with parameter, to be studied later */
    *buf++ = CODE_TO_LTR (ptr->let1);
    *buf++ = CODE_TO_LTR (ptr->let2);
    *buf++ = CODE_TO_LTR (ptr->let3);
    *buf = '\0';
}
```

Exercise. Define a structure that holds a pointer to a string, the screen coordinates from which to display it, and a direction indicator (left to right, backwards, up, or down). Write a function that accepts a pointer to such a structure and displays it. (The library function `setcur` is helpful.)

Exercise. Define a union that holds an `int` and a `double`. Embed it in a structure with a flag to indicate which is active. Write a function that displays the absolute value of the active value.

CHAPTER 14
Preprocessor Directives

228

We have seen how the `#define` statement makes programs easier to read. This chapter looks at more capabilities of `#define` as well as several other preprocessor directives. They all begin with the symbol **#**.

A `#define` statement may have parameters.

Before the compiler sees the text of your program, the preprocessor examines it, looking for lines beginning with the pound sign (#). It manipulates the program according to the key word that follows the pound sign. We have already encountered an example.

```
#define EXCEPTION (-1)
```

Some compilers require the directive to begin in the left column. Others, including the C Workshop, allow spaces first.

The #define Macro

The preprocessor inspects every identifier in the program before it goes to the compiler. If the identifier is the name of a `#define` macro, like **EXCEPTION** above, the definition text is substituted (`(-1)` in this example).

The term "macro" is a general one in computer science. A macro language is a specialized language for making substitutions in text. When substitutions can be made within substitutions, the situation can become extremely powerful, complex, and dangerous.

In recent years, a less precise use of "macro" has occurred in connection with application software like spreadsheets. Here, macros are more or less powerful languages for programming commands to the spreadsheet or whatever.

Back to C. Because the definition text of one macro may include the names of other macros, a good preprocessor checks the identifiers in a macro substitution for more substitutions; it keeps substituting until no more changes occur.

```
#define HEIGHT 25
#define WIDTH 80
#define SCREEN_SIZE (HEIGHT * WIDTH)
```

After all substitutions, the compiler sees (25 * 80) instead of SCREEN_SIZE. Since only constants are involved, an optimizing compiler can do the multiplication; your program refers to 2000 instead of repeatedly multiplying.

Note: Compile time refers to the execution of the compiler program that translates your source program into object code. Run time refers to the execution of your program. If you intend to execute your compiled program many times after you have written and debugged it, efficiency dictates that nothing be left for run time that may be performed at compile time.

The macro name may have parameters.

```
#define TRIPLE(n)  (3 * (n))
```

The parameters are enclosed in parentheses and must immediately follow the macro name; no spaces are allowed before the (. Subsequently, your program could use TRIPLE with a parameter.

```
    t = TRIPLE(m + 1);
```

which the preprocessor translates to

```
    t = (3 * (m + 1));
```

Parentheses are used heavily in defining macros in order to maintain the desired order of operations. For example, without parentheses around (n), the above substitution would produce

```
t = 3 * m + 1;
```

which is not your intention. Parentheses associate the * and + operators as desired. Even a simple definition like

```
#define SIZE   (MAX+1)
```

should have parentheses around it to insure that addition precedes a multiplication with which it may be combined. For example, the quantity

```
    SIZE * DIM
```

looks plain enough, but if the macros are

```
#define SIZE    MAX+1
#define DIM     3
```

then the expanded text is the unintended

```
    MAX+1*3
```

You may remember that the first real function you wrote in the C Workshop was a function to triple a number. Here a macro achieves the same result. Each method has its advantages. Macros are "in-line" code; they save the time expense of invoking a function and passing arguments. To a degree, they are independent of type. Note that the #define for TRIPLE works for floating point as well as integer numbers.

On the other hand, in-line code, repeated at every place it is substituted, tends to use up more memory. In addition, complicated macros are prone to errors, and the implementation of preprocessors is less uniform than compilers. For these reasons, we prefer to use macros with parameters sparingly.

Macros expand tokens and maintain the token unit. This means in practical terms that the expanded macro has white space around it.

The text inside a string or character constant is not examined for C macro expansion.

A #define is in effect from its definition to the end of the file, or until the same name is redefined, or until it is explicitly commanded to be forgotten by the directive

```
#undef TRIPLE
```

SELF TEST   **230**

```
#define QTRS_PER_BUCK  4
```

```
#define BUCKS_PER_CNOTE 100
#define QTRS_PER_CNOTE  (QTRS_PER_BUCK * BUCKS_PER_CNOTE)

    n = QTRS_PER_CNOTE;
```

What is the value of n?

SELF TEST   **231**

```
#define M(x, y)  ((x) < (y) ? (x) : (y))

    m = M(4, 7);
```

What is the value of m?

SELF TEST   **231A**

```
#define MAX_INDEX    10
#define SIZEA MAX_INDEX + 1
#define SIZEB (MAX_INDEX + 1)
```

Which statement comes closest to dividing the range in half?

```
    A) pivot_indexa = SIZEA / 2;
    B) pivot_indexb = SIZEB / 2;
```

It is even possible to change the appearance of C using macros. For example, you could write

```
#define EQ ==
#define NE !=
#define AND &&
```

and then write statements like

```
    if (a EQ b AND c NE d)
        process();
```

However, this writer does not know of one C programmer who uses such crutches.

Certain definitions appear in program after program.

```
#define TRUE 1
#define FALSE 0

#define EXCEPTION (-1)
#define EOF (-1)          /* end of file reported */
```

```
#define MAXINT  32767    /*  maximum integer in this compiler */
#define CR  0x0D          /*  Return key */
#define BLANK (' ')
```

and so on. The next section shows how we may centralize and re-use them.

The #include Directive

Virtually standard `#defines` are used in program after program. Programs large enough to divide into several source files need to use a common set of macro definitions, too. In both these instances, the macros may be written in one file, then incorporated into another one with the `#include` directive.

```
#include "cwstdio.h"
```

The quotation marks enclose the name of the file. Angle brackets may often be used instead

```
#include <cwstdio.h>
```

and in this case the compiler will search certain other directories for the file. For example, the C Workshop will search a directory specified by a parameter in the CW.PAR file (discussed in a later chapter).

The effect of `#include` is to read and process the file right away before proceeding to the next line after the directive. This directive may be nested: the file `cwstdio.h` might contain an `#include` directive of its own.

An included file is not limited to preprocessor directives; it may contain anything. However, directives never allocate memory for objects. If an included file had a statement

```
int key_queue[128];
```

then the array would be globally created every time the compiler processes another file with the `#include` directive. Most likely the linker will complain about multiply defined objects. It would be no problem, however, to have

```
extern int key_queue[];
```

in an included file. Structure templates are good candidates for included files, too.

As a matter of convention, included files of `#defines` and the like are called header files and are named with the file extension *.h*, because `#include` statements usually occur at the head of a file.

Conditional Directives

Sections of source code may be passed to the compiler or excluded from it by using the conditional directives.

```
#define PC_DOS TRUE

#if PC_DOS
    pc_display();
#else
    msdos_display();
#endif
```

The preprocessor evaluates the constant expression following `#if`. If the result is non-zero, the following lines are included. The `#else` (which is optional) and `#endif` directives work as you expect. Conditional directives may be nested.

As the example illustrates, conditional directives are useful when you want to maintain close variants of a program. The program can be recompiled for a generic MS-DOS computer by changing the PC_DOS definition and recompiling all affected source files. All the code is in common except the two functions `pc_display` and `msdos_display`.

Instead of evaluating an expression, a directive

```
#ifdef PC_DOS
```

merely checks to see if a macro named PC_DOS is currently defined. Conversely,

```
#ifndef PC_DOS
```

is effective only when the macro is not currently defined.

C compilers are not required to support nested comments. A simple way to remove a section of code during program development is to enclose it as follows.

```
#if 0
    ...
#endif
```

Assembler Directives

Some compilers support a directive that allows you to merge your own assembler code into a C program.

```
#asm
    mov bx,word ptr in_buf_ptr_
    mov al,[bx]
#endasm
```

This directive causes the assembler instructions to be placed into the program right at this point. If the compiler produces a source file for an assembler, the lines are simply copied. If the compiler produces object code, an assembler would be invoked at this point. (The C Workshop does not support `#asm`.) In any event, you need to understand how the compiler uses the stack and registers before you employ this technique. A later section of this book discusses these issues.

CHAPTER 15
Disk Files and Other Library Functions

Up to this point, programs have displayed information to the screen using the `puts` and `printf` functions. Input has been limited to the `getchar` function, which obtains keys from the keyboard.

This chapter discusses input and output to disk files and the console using more sophisticated functions.

C performs input and output by invoking functions. Every compiler comes with a library of these functions. The library is highly standard from one compiler to the next, and a C program written using them can be recompiled for different operating systems with only minor changes.

The library usually consists of a file of precompiled object code. The linker, after your command tells it which library or libraries to use, extracts the necessary functions as it discovers references to them in your program. In the C Workshop, this process is automatic.

A disk file is a collection of data stored on a magnetic disk or equivalent medium. The file has a name conforming to rules set by the operating system. For example, the MS-DOS system allows eight characters in the name proper and three in a file extension, like THISWORK.DOC.

As far as C is concerned, a file is a sequence of bytes one after another. A byte is an undefined entity, but the legitimate data types (characters, integers, long integers, arrays of these objects, pointers, and so forth) are made up of one or more bytes.

To use a disk file, your program does three things: 1) open the file, 2) process its data, and 3) close it. Processing, in general terms, consists of reading or writing file data. A write file *must* be closed to record the data on the disk. It is essential to close files you are reading, too, when you are done with them. The operating system and the library functions can keep track of only so many open files at once; reach its limit and your program may refuse to perform file operations.

When you invoke a function that opens a file, the function returns something to identify the file. Usually it is a pointer to a structure, although some compiler writers use integers instead. This is your "file handle." You write code to make a note of the handle, because subsequent file functions that read or write information require the file handle as a parameter.

Closing a file performs some housekeeping chores in the disk operating system. It also frees the file handle for re-use.

The FILE Structure

Most C compilers have a header file, `stdio.h`, which contains a `typedef` for a structure template named `FILE`. (The C Workshop header file is called `cwstdio.h`.) The standard library function that opens a file returns a pointer to `FILE`; other functions require this pointer as an argument telling them which file to read or write.

In this situation, you can use the disk file functions by following two steps:

First, write near the beginning of your program

```
#include "cwstdio.h"
```

or

```
#include <cwstdio.h>
```

as discussed earlier concerning the `#include` directive.

Second, declare your file handles

```
FILE *fid;
```

You normally assign file handles, for example,

```
    fid = fopen (filename, "r");
```

and pass them as function parameters, for example,

```
    c = getc (fid);
```

A File Is a Stream

Stream input and output (I/O) regard the file as a stream of characters or bytes. When you open a file, you specify whether you want to read it, write it, or append to it. (Some libraries offer additional options.) The first two modes start at the beginning of the file; the third starts at the end.

Every time you invoke a function to access a file opened for reading, you fetch the next one or several characters in the file. In order to go back or skip over characters, you invoke a function that alters a file position indicator. This indicator is maintained by functions in the I/O library.

Writing a stream file means outputting the characters in order from first to last. If you open a file for writing, you are creating it anew; an existing file of the same name will be deleted!

Appending is writing, except that when the file is opened, it is not deleted and writing begins after the last existing byte.

Frequently, stream functions deal with ASCII characters. That is, binary bytes in the range 80-FFh may have their high bit cleared during I/O. It depends on your compiler; some have two groups of functions, one for reading and writing text files and another set for binary data.

Stream I/O is sometimes called buffered I/O. Disk reads and writes cannot be physically performed by the single byte, so the operating system and the stream functions read blocks of data, then spoon it out to your program character by character. Similarly, write functions accumulate characters in a memory buffer and "flush" the buffer to the disk when it fills, or when you close the file.

Some older implementations of C treat files differently, either as a substitute for the stream method or a supplement to it. This method is called raw I/O, sometimes referred to as random I/O. With these functions you manage the file position indicator yourself, passing it as an argument to the I/O functions. Also, in some small systems, the library functions read and write only in fixed-size blocks, which means your program must do a lot of internal buffering and translating between fixed blocks and your program's needs for data.

Sometimes disk functions must report an error or end of file. The conventional definition for the latter is

```
#define EOF    (-1)
```

Disk functions return either -1 (EOF) or 0 (FALSE) upon error as noted in their documentation.

238

Using Stream I/O Functions

This discussion introduces you to the mechanics of input and output using a few stream functions as examples.

For a complete list and definition of each standard function, consult the chapter in the book devoted to the library.

The next screen is a simple program that writes the alphabet to a file.

238A

```
/*  Create a file containing the alphabet */

/*  Just study and RUN this program. */

#include "cwstdio.h"        /*  declares FILE */

extern FILE *open_file();   /*  function returns non-int */

main()
{
FILE *out_fid;  /*  pointer to file handle of output file */

    if ((out_fid = open_file()) == 0)
        {
        puts ("Unable to open output file.");
        return;
        }
    else
```

```
            {
            recite_abc (out_fid);
            if (fclose (out_fid) == EXCEPTION)
                puts ("Unable to close output file.");
            }
    }


FILE *
open_file()
/*  Return: file handle.
            Like fopen(), returns null ptr if error.
    Opens for writing.
*/
{
char filename[64];

    printf ("Enter name of output file: ");
    gets (filename);
    return (fopen (filename, "w"));
}


recite_abc (fid)
/*  Write the alphabet in uppercase to a file.
    Conclude with a newline.
*/
FILE *fid;       /*  file handle */
{
int c;

    for (c = 'A'; c <= 'Z'; c++)
        writec (c, fid);
    writec ('\n', fid);
}


writec (c, fid)
/*  Centralize error-checked file output here.
*/
int c;
FILE *fid;
{
    if (putc (c, fid) == EXCEPTION)
        {
```

```
        puts ("Unable to output character.");
        fclose (fid);
        exit (1);        /*  or other error handling */
        }
}
```

Now that you are not on a Program screen, you can press *F10* and use the editor to Get and view the disk file created by the preceding program. It should be a one-line file of the alphabet.

In `open_file` the library function

```
    fopen (filename, "w")
```

is invoked. You supply it with a filename string and a parameter indicating this file is for writing. The parameter is a string "w", "r" or "a" indicating write, read or append. When your program specifies "w," a file in the directory having the same name will first be deleted. Use "r" to open a file for reading and "a" to write at the end of an existing file. Note that these are string constants in double quotation marks, not character constants in single quotes.

The function `fopen` returns a file handle. If it is 0, the file could not be opened. Otherwise, your program henceforth refers to the file by its handle. The test for 0 is very important, because in many systems 0 is also the standard file handle for console input. The results may mystify you if you try to work with this file. Because the file handle is a pointer to a `FILE` object, the function return must be declared. An `extern` is also written ahead of the first invocation of the function.

To write the file, `recite_abc` generates characters and invokes `writec`, where we have centralized all writing to the file. It invokes the library function `putc`. (Note that console output is done with `putchar`.) This function returns -1 if an error occurs. In the event of an error, we have chosen simply to report to the console and give up, using another typical library function, `exit`, which immediately returns to the operating system.

After writing the alphabet, the program invokes `fclose` to close the file. Upon an error this function returns -1.

The reverse operation, reading a file, would be done similarly. The program would specify the "r" option when invoking `fopen`. The companion to `putc` is `getc`, whose argument is the file handle. It returns -1 upon error and probably does not need to be embedded in a program function.

When you write programs relying heavily on library functions, you can consult the chapter on the library for details. You may also use the Help key to look up specifications.

241

```
/*  Write buffer to file */

#include "cwstdio.h"

char buffer[] = {"The car buffer uses whacks."};

main()
{
FILE *out_fid;

    if ((out_fid = fopen ("CHARBUF.TXT", "w")) == 0)
        {
        puts ("Unable to open output file.");
        return;
        }
    else
        {
        write_buffer (out_fid, buffer);
        if (fclose (out_fid) == EXCEPTION)
            puts ("Unable to close output file.");
        }
}

write_buffer (fid, buffer)
/*  Write the buffer through a null to the file.
    WRITE this function.
    You may assume the buffer has a binary null.
*/
FILE *fid;
char *buffer;
```

Formatted Input and Output

In addition to handling data a character at a time, a number of functions deal with strings of characters according to formats. The function `printf`, which writes to the console, is an example of formatted output. There is a counterpart for files: `fprintf` takes a file handle as its first argument, then writes a character string to it according to the control specification and values supplied in the remaining arguments.

For input, a function `scanf` reads from the keyboard; a counterpart `fscanf` reads characters from a file, interpreting them as numbers of various types.

The next screen has an example of a program that uses formatted output and input.

242A

```
/*  Example of formatted output and input */

#include "cwstdio.h"

main()
{
    if (write_data())    /*  must successfully write... */
        read_data();     /*     ...before we read */
}


write_data()
/*  Return: TRUE/FALSE operation successful.
*/
{
FILE *fid;

    /*  Test of fopen is very important.  Otherwise, will
        later use fid = 0, which is a file handle for the
        keyboard.
    */
    if ((fid = fopen ("JUNKNUM.DAT", "w")) == 0)
        {
        puts ("Unable to open file for writing.");
        return FALSE;
```

```
            }
      else if (fprintf (fid, "%d\n", 0x1234) == EXCEPTION)
            {
            puts ("Error writing data.");
            return FALSE;
            }
      /*  write a second item */
      else if (fprintf (fid, "%d\n", 0x5678) == EXCEPTION)
            {
            puts ("Error writing data.");
            return FALSE;
            }
      else if (fclose (fid) == EXCEPTION)
            {
            puts ("Error closing write file.");
            return FALSE;
            }
      else
            return TRUE;
}


read_data()
{
int m, n;
FILE *fid;

      if ((fid = fopen ("JUNKNUM.DAT", "r")) == 0)
            {
            puts ("Unable to open file for reading.");
            return;
            }
      else if (fscanf (fid, "%d %d", &m, &n) != 2)
            {  /*  failed to read the two items */
            puts ("Error reading data.");
            return;
            }
      else    /*  to console */
            printf ("Test values are %x and %x\n", m, n);
      fclose (fid);
}
```

The crucial statement for writing data is

```
if (fprintf (fid, "%d\n", 0x1234) == EXCEPTION)
    /*  ... */
```

We need to separate the data items in the file. Here we have used a newline character, \n, which is convenient for reading later. The read statement is

```
else if (fscanf (fid, "%d %d", &m, &n) != 2)
    /*  ... */
```

Notice that this function requires *pointers* to the variables where you want the input data stored. The function fscanf reads a "field" at a time, generally defined as a sequence of characters that are not white space (space, tab, newline). To read multiple values, scanf reads across white space, including newlines, to fulfill the command of its control string argument. The moral is: when using formatted file I/O, plan the output to meet the needs of your input function.

244

Random Record Access

The functions discussed so far read or write a file from the beginning, byte by byte. Later, you might want to read or alter bytes at various positions in the file, such as 100th through 109th bytes. Fortunately, you need not read and discard all the preceding data. Instead, you can change the file position indicator.

Every file stream has an index, usually maintained by the operating system, specifying the next position to read or write. Like arrays in C, the first byte is at position 0. The lseek function alters this index, after which you may read or write according to how you have opened the file.

```
lseek (fid, offset, origin)
FILE *fid;       /*  the file handle */
long offset;     /*  note: long; amount to move indicator */
int origin;      /*  0 - move relative to origin of file
                     1 - relative to current position
                     2 - relative to end of file */
```

The lseek function takes three parameters: 1) the file handle; 2) an offset, which is a positive or negative *long* integer specifying how much to move the index; and 3) the origin, a code telling the system to apply the offset relative to the start (code 0), current position (code 1), or end of the file (code 2).

```
lseek (fid, 0L, 0);
```

would go back to the beginning of the file.

```
lseek (fid, 0L, 2);
```

prepares to append new data to the file. That is, the origin coded 2 is the byte immediately following the last existing byte of the file. Since lseek returns the new position indicator,

```
lpos = lseek (fid, 0L, 2);
```

would tell you the size of the file.

Notice that the offset is always a long integer and must be specified as such.

This method of random access to files is particularly common when the file consists of data records of fixed length. Databases are often organized this way. If a record is the *n*-th one and each record is a certain size, then a program can set the file position indicator and read the record.

245

Before you write a program using the lseek function, the next exercise reviews simple stream I/O. Its real purpose is to create a data file with which to practice.

The data is highly stylized. A record will consist of 37 bytes. The first record will be 37 uppercase 'A's, the second 'B's, and so on through 26 records.

245A

```
/*  Create file of records */

#include "cwstdio.h"

#define RECORD_SIZE 37

main()
{
int l, i;
```

```
FILE *fid;

    create_data ();
    if (!(fid = fopen ("SAMPLE.DAT", "r")))
        {
        puts ("Unable to open the file");
        return;
        }

    for (l = 0; l < 26; l++)      /*  view the result */
        {
        for (i = 0; i < RECORD_SIZE; i++)
            putchar (getc (fid));
        putchar ('\n');
        }
}

create_data ()
/*  Write a file SAMPLE.DAT of 37 A's, 37 B's, .. 37 Z's.
    WRITE this function.
*/
```

246

If you are satisfied that the proper file now exists on the disk, you are ready to access it randomly.

246A

```
/*  Read random record from a file */

#include "cwstdio.h"

#define RECORD_SIZE 37

main ()
{
char buffer[RECORD_SIZE + 1];
int fid;

    if (!(fid = fopen ("SAMPLE.DAT", "r")))
        {
        puts ("Unable to open SAMPLE.DAT");
        return;
```

```
        }
     read_record (12, buffer, fid);
     printf
         ("To repeat, the 13th letter of the alphabet is \n%s",
         buffer);
     fclose (fid);
}

read_record (n, buffer, fid)
/*  Read the nth record (numbered from 0) into the buffer.
    Append a null to it.
    WRITE this function.  Reminder: lseek expects a long offset.
*/
int n;
char *buffer;
FILE *fid;
```

Before going on, you might want to delete the file SAMPLE.DAT from the disk. You could leave the C Workshop and issue a Delete command, or you can write and run a two-line program using the `remove()` function.

File Functions and the Newline

When a program displays lines over preceding ones, treatment of the newline may be the problem.

This quirk of file output concerns the newline character, symbolized \n. Operating systems treat newline codes differently. The MS-DOS console moves the cursor down a row but not to the left edge when it sees an ASCII code 0x0A, which is the usual value for newline. The code for carriage return, 0x0D, pushes the cursor back to the left edge. The Unix operating system performs both actions when it sees a newline 0x0A.

If a file output function converted a newline \n into a pair of bytes, 0x0D-0x0A, this would cause confusion. On the other hand, MS-DOS needs to receive the expanded pair.

A common solution, used in the C Workshop, works as follows. Functions that output to the standard console (`printf`, `putchar`, `puts`, and `putc` and `fputs` when the "file" is standard output or standard error) expand a newline \n to a 0x0D-0x0A pair. Functions that write to files or strings (`fprintf`, `sprintf`, `fputs`, and `putc` and `fputs` to files other than standard output) write 0x0A for a newline.

Console, String and Miscellaneous Functions

Some functions perform input from the keyboard and output to the screen. By regarding the keyboard as a stream that can only be read and the screen as a stream that can only be written to, several of these functions work analogously to the file functions.

However, it is sometimes convenient to check the keyboard and see whether a key is ready. The screen, too, is not really a sequential stream but a two-dimensional space. Functions to position the cursor and clear the entire screen are helpful. These functions are not as standardized as the stream functions.

In addition, most compiler libraries contain functions that manipulate character strings and perform other common operations.

248

Interlude: A Circular Buffer

Before moving on to advanced use of pointers, you can warm up with this exercise on a circular buffer. It uses pointers and has a "real-time" flavor by using a C Workshop function that reads the system clock.

Exercise. The C Workshop library function

```
time (&hour, &min, &sec, &hund)
```

reads the time from the operating system and places the results in the specified locations. Note that you pass *pointers* to the variables where the time is to be stored.

Write a function `timeout` that accepts a time, reads the current time, and updates data if a specified delay has passed:

```
timeout (n, hptr, mptr, sptr)
/*  If  n  seconds have elapsed
        post new time in specified locations and return TRUE
```

```
        Else return FALSE
        Must read hundredths of a second, but just ignore them.
*/
int n;   /*  assume n < 60 */
int *hptr, *mptr, *sptr;
```

Save your code for the next exercise.

A circular buffer or *queue* accepts input and reports output in first come, first serve order. The idea is implemented using an array and pointers that advance normally in the array except when they reach its end; there they are reset to the beginning.

Two pointers are used. One may be called the `put_ptr`, which notes where the next input item goes, after which it is bumped as described above. The `take_ptr` notes the next place from which to take an item, after which it, too, is advanced.

When the pointers are equal, there is nothing to take. Conceivably, so much input could flood in that the `put_ptr` would lap the `take_ptr`. We assume that the array, or circular buffer, is big enough to avoid overflow.

Exercise. Complete a program that accepts keys pressed by the user and buffers them in a queue. Every five seconds, read the keys out of the queue, displaying them on the screen.

Use the timeout function from the previous exercise. You will also need the library function `inkey`.

To test your program, run it and type quickly. You should see nothing until the buffer is dumped every five seconds.

```
/*  Run a circular buffer for keys */

#define TRUE     1
#define FALSE    0

#define BUF_SIZE     100
char circ_buf[BUF_SIZE];
char *put_ptr, *take_ptr;     /*  next spot to put, take key */

main()
{
int hour, min, sec;
int hund;
int n, key;
```

```
    puts ("Press keys.  Press Ctrl-Break to quit.");
    n = 5;
    put_ptr = take_ptr = circ_buf;
    time (&hour, &min, &sec, &hund);    /*  initialize */

    while (TRUE)
        {
        if (key = inkey())
            buffer_key();

        if (timeout (n, &hour, &min, &sec))
            /*  dump the queued keys */
            while ((key = extract_key()))
                putchar (key);       /*  Ctrl-Break quits */
        }
    }

buffer_key (key)
/*  Add the key to the circular buffer
*/
int key;
{
    *put_ptr++ = key;
    if (put_ptr - circ_buf >= BUF_SIZE)
        put_ptr = circ_buf;      /*  round the bend */
}

extract_key ()
/*  Return: next key or 0 if none
    WRITE this function.
*/

timeout (n, hptr, mptr, sptr)
/*  Use what you wrote for previous exercise. */
```

Exercise. Write a program that gets a filename from the user (using the library function gets) and displays the file on the screen.

Exercise. The most common letters in English text and their percentages are E (12.7), T (9.8), A (7.9), O (7.7), I (7.0) and N (7.0). Are these the most frequent letters in your C programs? Write a program that prompts the user for a filename, reads the file, and counts the letter frequencies. Display the frequencies and the total count; remember that the screen does not have 26 lines. (After you do this exercise, you might want to think about how to display the letters in descending order of frequency.)

Exercise. The default tab stop in the Workshop editor is four spaces. Many editors default to eight spaces. Write a program that reads an input file and writes an output file with expanded spaces. Ask the user for the input and output filenames. Then convert every group of four blanks into eight blanks. Five blanks would become nine blanks.

Exercise. Write the reverse program for the above exercise. It should compact eight blanks into four.

Exercise. Write a function box that clears the screen and draws a box on the screen. The arguments are the row and column of the top left and bottom right corners and the character to draw with. Use a C Workshop library function to position the cursor. Let main invoke box and then move the cursor somewhere else and request the user to press a key.

In main or box, you should check that the second point is below and to the right of the first point.

Exercise. Write a program that accepts the month, date and year from the user and says what day of the week it falls on. To use the scanf function, display instructions telling the user to put space between the month, date, and year. If he enters a two-digit year, assume he means the twentieth century.

If the month is January or February, set jf to 1, otherwise 0. Then after the integer calculation

```
l = year - jf;
o = month + 12 * jf + 1;
p1 = 1/400;
p2 = 1/100;
p3 = (5 * l) / 4;
p4 = (13 * o) / 5;
a = p4 + p3 - p2 + p1 + date - 1;
a = a - (7 * (a / 7));
```

the variable a is 0 for Sunday, 1 for Monday, etc. This method works for the Gregorian calendar after 1752.

Exercise. John Conway invented an experiment called Life. Life exists on a world consisting of a grid of cells. The user creates live cells in a desired pattern. The program then calculates successive generations according to these rules:

1. A live cell survives if and only if it has two or three neighbors that are alive.

2. A dead cell that has exactly three live neighbors comes alive.

The grid is assumed to be connected at the edges; that is, a neighbor of a cell in the first row is the cell at the same column in the bottom row, and similarly all around the edge of the grid.

Program Life on a grid of 20 rows of 80 columns each. Give the user instructions (in the remaining area at the bottom of the screen) and let him move the cursor using the 2, 4, 6, and 8 keys. Wherever he wants to create a live cell, he presses the Space bar. After he presses Return, calculate and display the second generation. Calculate each succeeding generation when the user presses Return. Quit upon Escape.

Use `inkey` to get keys from the user and other C Workshop library functions to clear the screen and position the cursor.

Exercise. An expert on artificial intelligence declares, "A good compiler should compile the comments, not the source code." He argues that the purpose of a programming language is to state human intentions in a form people can understand; the compiler should translate the program into machine instructions.

As a modest beginning on this project, write a program that reads a C source file and outputs a file consisting of only the comments. Replace /* and */ by blanks. Because people occasionally start a comment but forget to close it, detect and report this situation.

CHAPTER 16
Advanced Use of Pointers

In this chapter we will study arrays of pointers, pointers to pointers, multi-dimensional arrays, and pointers to functions. When you want to make C dance, you will find these techniques essential.

253A

Arrays of Pointers

Suppose your statistician friend wants to analyze craps games using C. The experiments consist of trial games. Each trial ends when the shooter wins or loses.

Here is a short course in craps: A pair of dice is thrown and shows a number from 2 to 12. The shooter's first throw wins with a natural (7 or ll), loses with a craps (2, 3, or 12), or establishes a point (any other number). After establishing a point, the shooter throws the dice until the point appears again, which is a win, or 7 comes up, which is a loss.

The program on the next screen has nothing to do with pointers. It simply gives you computerized craps.

253B

```
/*  Play craps */

/*  No work.  Just run and play if you wish.
    No wagering in states where prohibited by law.
```

```
*/

#define TRUE 1
#define FALSE 0

unsigned seed = 17;

main()
{

    while (TRUE)
        {
        puts ("Let's play craps.  Press key (q to quit):");
        if (get_key() == 'q')
            return;
        else
            play();
        }
}

play()
/*  Return: TRUE/FALSE won/lost.
*/
{
int dice, point;

    putchar ('\n');

/*  first throw */
    if ((dice = throw()) == 7 || dice == 11)
        {
        printf ("%d - A natural.  You win.\n\n", dice);
        return (TRUE);
        }
    else if (dice == 2 || dice == 3 || dice == 12)
        {
        printf ("%d - Sorry, you crapped out.\n\n", dice);
        return (FALSE);
        }
    else
        {
        point = dice;
```

```
            printf ("%d is your point.\n", point);
            }

/*  throw until make point or lose */
    do  {
        puts ("Press a key.\n");
        get_key();
        dice = throw();
        printf ("%d - ", dice);
        if (dice == point)
            {
            puts (" You win.\n");
            return (TRUE);
            }
        else if (dice == 7)
            {
            puts ("Sorry, you lose.\n");
            return (FALSE);
            }
        else
            puts ("C'mon baby");
        } while (TRUE);
}


throw()
/*  Return: dice throw
    Adds two dice to mimic distribution 1..12
*/
{
    return (gen_random (6) + gen_random (6));
}


gen_random (limit)
unsigned limit; /*  use only small values */
{
unsigned temp_seed;

    temp_seed = seed;
    temp_seed <<= 8;     /*  x 256 mod 64K */
    temp_seed += (seed * 3);
    seed = temp_seed;
    temp_seed = ((unsigned) 0xFFFF / limit);
```

```
        /*  new use for temp_seed */
    return (seed / temp_seed + 1);
}

get_key()
/*  Return: key pressed
    Reseed the random generator at same time
*/
{
int key;

    for (seed += 2; !(key = inkey()); seed += 2)
        ;
    return (key);
}
```

256

A craps trial consists of a sequence of integers; we will add the convention that a 0 is appended after the last throw of the dice. One trial can conveniently be stored in an integer array. To conserve space, the elements of the array could be characters.

SELF TEST   **256A**
```
char trial[] = {6, 12, 4, 3, 8, 7, 0};
```

In this game did the shooter

A) win
B) lose

256B

The problem is how to store a collection of trials. A two-dimensional array (to be encountered later) is inconvenient, since the length of the trials varies. For example, if we allotted 30 tosses to each game, an occasional game would not fit, while most would waste the majority of their space.

One solution is to store each trial in its own array of exactly the right size, and to store pointers to the trials in a master list or array. The overhead is the space occupied by the game pointers in the master list (and some nulls to mark ends of sequences). In a typical microcomputer implementation, a pointer occupies two bytes.

The definition of the master list is

```
int *trial[MAX_TRIAL + 1];
```

This definition establishes an array of **MAX_TRIAL + 1** trials, each of which is a pointer to an integer. Once you set such a pointer to the first throw of a trial, you can read the rest of the trial by incrementing the pointer.

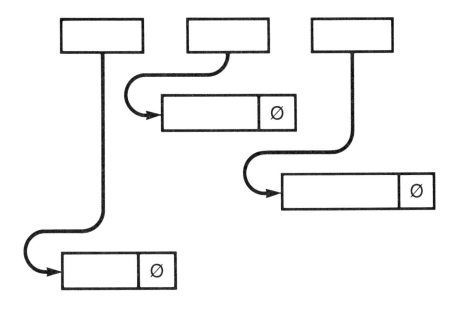

Array of pointers

You parse declarations like expressions, using the precedence and associativity of operators. The operator [ ] has precedence over *, so it associates with `trial`, which is therefore an array. What is it an array of? Pointers to integers.

By convention, the last pointer is a null. So

```
      if (trial[i + 1] == 0)
          /*  trial[i] points to the last real trial */  ;
```

SELF TEST   258

Which statement sets **k** to the second throw of the third trial?

```
A) k = *trial[2] + 1;
B) k = *(trial[2] + 1);
C) k = *trial[3] + 2;
D) k = *(trial[3] + 2);
```

258A

```
int *trial[MAX_TRIAL + 1];
```

With this definition, `trial[i]` is a pointer to an integer. Applying the
`*` operator fetches the integer pointed to, `*trial[i]`. No parentheses are
required because the precedence of `[ ]` is higher than `*`. First, the *i*-th pointer
in the array `trial` is addressed, then the integer to which it points.

The trials addressed by the various `trial[i]` may be scattered all over
the computer's memory. Once we set a pointer to the start of a trial, we may
increment it and move through the trial, an array of integers terminated by 0.

In other words, `trial[i]` is a pointer to an integer, a special integer as
it happens: the 0-th element of an array of integers. The array `trial[]` is
an array of array addresses.

258B

```
/*  Find first game with a 12 thrown */

#define EXCEPTION   (-1)

int game_0[] = {4, 8, 5, 7, 0};
int game_1[] = {6, 12, 6, 0};
int game_2[] = {5, 9, 6, 12, 5, 0};
int *trial[] = {game_0, game_1, game_2, 0};
    /*  these are the pointers */

main()
{
int first;
```

```
    first = find_12 (trial);
    printf ("A 12 first thrown in game %d", first);
}

find_12 (ip_array)
/*  Return: index of first game in which a 12 was thrown.
          or EXCEPTION if no 12 thrown in any game. */
int *ip_array[];          /*  array of integer pointers */
/*  WRITE this function.  Suggested strategy:
        Pick up each pointer in turn.  For each one,
        step through the game until find a 12 or a 0.
*/
```

Pointers to Pointers

You may have noticed something odd about the previous program. The working function `find_12` has a parameter

```
find_12 (ip_array)
int *ip_array[];
```

However, we know that arrays cannot be passed in C. The formal parameter written in array notation is really equivalent to

```
int **ip_array;
```

The parameter is a pointer to a pointer. The function receives a pointer to an array element that is a pointer. It needs this information, because to examine the second game, it must access the next pointer, not the next integer of the first game.

Initializing Pointer Arrays

The preceding program showed how we can initialize an array of pointers.

```
int *trial[] = {game_0, game_1, game_2, 0};
```

An equivalent definition is

```
int *trial[] = {&game_0[0], &game_1[0], &game_2[0], 0};
```

When the compiler sees the array name without a subscript, it simply compiles the starting address of the array.

260

Probably the most common use of arrays of pointers is to hold character strings. Initialization of these is simple. For example, you could initialize a table listing the days of the week as follows:

```
char *german_day[7] = {
    "Sonntag", "Montag", "Dienstag", "Mittwoch",
    "Donnerstag", "Freitag", "Samstag"};
```

Each string constant causes the compiler to generate the string with a null and put a pointer to it in the array german_day. The C Workshop compiler does not require the element count [7], while other compilers may need a count even when you explicitly initialize.

If you specify an array size in brackets, then provide fewer initializations, the array is created at your defined size and the first elements are initialized per your specifications.

260A

```
/*  Display days of the week */

char *german_day[7] = {
    "Sonntag", "Montag", "Dienstag", "Mittwoch",
    "Donnerstag", "Freitag", "Samstag"};

char *english_day[7] = {
    "Sunday", "Monday", "Tuesday", "Wednesday",
    "Thursday", "Friday", "Saturday"};

main()
{
    printf ("\nThe days of the week in German are\n");
    display_days (german_day);
    printf ("\nThe days of the week in English are\n");
    display_days (english_day);
}

display_days (week_ptr)
/*  Display the names of the days in a column.
```

```
        WRITE this function.
*/
char **week_ptr;      /*  pointer to character pointer */
```

Allocating Space

In a production environment, it would be tedious to initialize the dice game structures with initialization statements. Most likely, you would store the data in a disk file as a single long string of integers or characters. You would read the file in sequence. Upon reading a 0, you would conclude a game and start a new one.

There are at least two ways to do this. One is to reserve a large array of integers and set pointers into this array.

```
int universe[4000]          /*  or whatever size */
int *trial[MAX_TRIAL + 1], *work_ptr;

    work_ptr = universe;    /*  start here */
```

At appropriate moments, you set

```
    trial[i] = work_ptr;    /*  point to first throw of game */
```

Another way to obtain memory is to allocate it. When your program loads for execution, its instructions and the global data you have defined occupy memory. In addition, a program may request space during execution. This space generally comes from one of two places. It may come from an area called the heap, which is assigned to your program and allocated to specific objects when you invoke a suitable library function. Since you can release this memory back to the heap, you can reuse space in different phases of your program.

Alternatively, your program may be able to obtain memory from the operating system, which tells the function what additional memory your program can safely use. If your program does not need allocated memory after awhile, it can release the space back to the system. This courtesy may be important on a multitasking computer.

Particularly in a multitasking computer, the memory blocks granted upon successive requests will be scattered all over the place. In the dice example, each craps game could be allocated a block of memory cells. The different games will be located in no particular order in memory. The master array of pointers is the vital device that keeps track of the starting address of each array.

Most C compilers have functions for requesting and freeing space. Typically, the function `malloc (n)` returns a pointer to a contiguous space of `n` characters. The function returns 0 if space is unavailable. The C Workshop provides a simpler function called `sbrk`.

The `malloc` function allows you to release a memory block back to the system at any time. The `sbrk` function is less flexible. Given a positive parameter, it assigns you a block of memory from the heap. A negative parameter releases memory back to the heap. All the allocation and deallocation occurs by moving an indicator at the edge of the heap. Therefore, a deallocation returns the most recently allocated memory to the heap.

262

Command Line Variables argc and argv

A common instance of an array of pointers is `argv`. The variables `argc` and `argv` give a C program access to parameters that the user entered on the operating system's command line. For example, if the user command is

```
edit oldfile.c newfile.c
```

the program *edit* needs to know the file names.

When the C program begins at `main`, it may obtain these two parameters.

262A

```
main (argc, argv)
int argc;
char *argv[];
```

The value of `argc` is the number of arguments on the command line. White space separates each argument from the others. The program's name is an argument, so `argc` is at least one.

The variable `argv` is an array of character pointers to the command line arguments. The pointer `argv[0]` points to the program name (most MS-DOS compilers do not support this), `argv[1]` is the first argument after the program name, and so forth.

The compiler attaches some code, called the root or prologue, to your program which executes before `main`. This code analyzes the command line information and builds an array of pointers. For example, it stores the string "oldfile" somewhere in memory then puts its address in `argv[1]`.

Because arrays cannot be passed as parameters to functions, what `main` receives for `argv` is actually a pointer. In other words, `argv` is a pointer to pointers.

As formal parameters to `main`, the declarations

```
char *argv[];    /*  array of pointers */
char **argv;     /*  pointer to first pointer in list */
```

are equivalent.

Because it is a pointer, `argv` can be incremented.

When you write `*++argv` at the start of `main`, it is therefore a pointer to the first command line option. When processing the command line switches, this technique may be used instead of incrementing `i` in the expression `*argv[i]`.

SELF TEST   263

A user starts a program by the command

```
edit oldfile.c newfile.c
```

Which expression is a pointer to the last argument, `newfile`?

    A) `argv[3]`
    B) `*argv[2]`
    C) `argv[2]`

SELF TEST   263A

Which statement scans the second argument (after the program name) on the command line?

```
int c;
```
    A) `while (c = *argv[2]++)`
       `;`

    B) `while (c = **argv[2]++)`
       `;`

    C) `while (c = (*argv[2])++)`
       `;`

You might wonder, which is correct:

```
main()
```

or

```
main (argc, argv)
int argc;
char *argv[];
```

The answer is that both forms work. If your program pays no attention to the command line, the short form is acceptable, but the complete form will work, too. The prologue makes the two parameters available to `main` and also destroys them after `main` executes. In C unlike most other languages, the invoking function does this bookkeeping.

A typical convention in programs that accept command line switches is to begin genuine options with a hyphen. File names do not begin with a hyphen. For example, a program might be started

```
edit oldfile newfile -A
```

where the option specifies, according to the rules of the program `edit`, that the output will be written as an ASCII file.

264

In the C Workshop, a program has no name and is not started with a command line. However, you can press the Run function key again to see a Run menu. Select "Compile only." Then write a disk file, which should have a .COM extension, for example, SAMPLE.COM. You may execute SAMPLE outside the C Workshop or within it (select "Run .COM program from disk"). In both cases you may use command line options.

The next screen asks you to complete a program that lists which command line arguments begin with a hyphen. To run and test the program, you should use the "Compile only" option, write the result as a disk program, then run it from the disk with some test options, like

```
sample sourcefile -A -B destfile
```

264A

```
/*   Count command line options beginning with hyphen */
```

```
#define OPTION_CNT   10
#define EXCEPTION    -1

int option[OPTION_CNT];

main (argc, argv)
int argc;
char **argv;
{
int *iptr, i;

    list_options (argc, argv, option);
    printf ("The arguments representing options are ");
    for (i = 0, iptr = option;
        *iptr != EXCEPTION && i < OPTION_CNT; i++, iptr++)
            printf ("%d  ", *iptr);
}

list_options (argc, argv, list)
/*  List the command line argument numbers that start '-'
        in the specified list array.  End the list with -1.
    WRITE this function.
    When you are ready to compile:
        Press the function key twice to get the menu.
        Select the Compile only option.
        When the program compiles,
            go to the menu again and Write a disk file.
        Go to the menu once more and Run program from disk.
*/
```

Exercise. An earlier exercise asked you to write a function to input a line with some editing facilities. If you saved the program, you can use it to write the skeleton of a simple editor. Write a program that prompts for text and stores each line in a character array. Also create an array of line pointers and store the address of each line in it. Place a limit of 80 characters on the length of a line and a limit of 40 lines. Tell the user that typing a line beginning ".q" (no quote marks) signals the end of input. (Internally, it helps if you write a null over the period to mark the end of the text.) Then display the entire text again, using the array of line pointers.

Multi-Dimensional Arrays

C notation for multi-dimensional arrays puts each subscript in its own brackets.

```
int coord [10][10];

    coord [i][j] = 4;
```

The definition creates a 10 by 10 array whose subscripts range from [0][0] to [9][9]. The array is stored by rows:

```
    coord [0][0]    coord [0][1]    ... coord [0][9]
    coord [1][0]    coord [1][1]    ... coord [1][9]
        ...
    coord [9][0]    coord [9][1]    ... coord [9][9]
```

A three-dimensional array similarly is stored with the rightmost subscript varying, then the middle subscript, and finally the left subscript.

Suppose you want to track the character displayed at each cell on a typical computer screen of 25 by 80 lines. You may define

```
#define MAX_ROW 24
#define MAX_COL 79
```

because indexes may range from 0 to **MAX_** . . . You define the array itself

```
char screen[MAX_ROW + 1][MAX_COL + 1];
```

The way we have defined it, the memory representation sweeps across the columns of each row in turn.

A nested for-loop that covers the screen might be

```
    for (row = 0; row <= MAX_ROW; row++)
        for (col = 0; col <= MAX_COL; col++)
            ; /* process screen[row][col] */
```

The C compiler sees computer memory as a linear sequence, and it maps the cells of a multi-dimensional array into this memory. When we say that the rightmost subscript varies most rapidly, this means that the compiler, after setting the subscripts to 0, counts each successive cell by incrementing the rightmost subscript to its maximum. Then the compiler adds one to the next subscript from the right and resets the rightmost subscript to 0. It repeats the process until all the subscripts reach their maximum.

Because the compiler follows this rule, it is possible to mix array and pointer notation. For example,

```
screen[row][col]
```

may also be referred to as

```
*(screen[row] + col)
```

For C, `screen` in the expression simply refers to the address of the array, regardless of its dimension. In our two-dimensional array, `screen[row]` is the starting address of the specified row. Because the rightmost subscript varies most rapidly, the next cells are counted off by `col`. We may add `col` to the address of the row, then apply the indirection operator to access the value there.

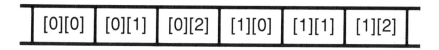

Storage of a 2 by 3 array

It is sometimes useful to regard a two-dimensional array as one-dimensional with a pointer to the array.

```
char screen[MAX_ROW + 1][MAX_COL + 1];  /* screen image */
char *cptr;
```

We may process every cell with a single loop.

```
    cptr = screen;
    for (i = 0; i < (MAX_ROW + 1) * (MAX_COL + 1); i++, cptr++)
        *cptr = ' ';    /* initialize to blank screen */
```

A global multi-dimensional array may be initialized when it is defined.

```
int coord [3][2] = {
    {17, 23},  {0, -2} , {9, 5}
    };
```

The overall braces enclose a list of the rows, each of which is itself a braced pair of elements. Here, `coord[0][1]` has the value 23.

Many compilers permit you to omit the inner braces. The compiler would assign values in the order of the subscript increase. This method is similar to initializing arrays of structures without the inner braces.

SELF TEST   268

The element stored in a 5 x 5 x 5 array immediately after

```
humidity[i][j][k]
```

could *never* be

```
A) humidity[i][j + 1][0]
B) humidity[i][j][k + 1]
C) humidity[i][j + 1][k]
D) humidity[i + 1][0][0]
```

SELF TEST   268A

```
int table [3][4] = {
    {{3, -1, 5, 8} , {2, 1, 19, 4}, {9, 6, 7, 40}
    };
```

What is the value of `table[1][2]`?

                                                                                                 268B

```
/*  Lookup in a two-dimensional array */

int coords[4][2] = {{8, 1}, {3, 17}, {-1, 10}, {0, 39}};

main()
{
int v, i, j;

    i = 2; j = 0;
    v = lookup (i, j);
    printf ("The value is %d", v);
}

lookup (i, j)
/*  Return: the value at coords[i][j].
    i and j are assumed to be legal.
```

```
    WRITE this simple function.
*/
```

To pass an array to a function, you actually pass a pointer.

```
main ()
{
    examine (coord);
}

examine (table)
int table[] [2];
{
}
```

The leftmost subscript, or the row, need not be specified in the function declaration. The compiler can calculate the address of any array element if it knows that each row has two elements.

```
/*  Scan a two-dimensional array */

int coord [2] [3] = {{17, 23, 0}, {0, -2, 1}};

main ()
{
int sparsity;

    sparsity = zero_scan (coord, 1);
    printf ("Has %d zero entries", sparsity);
}

zero_scan (array, max_row)
/*  Return: the number of 0 entries in an array.
    The array is assumed to have 3 columns.
    The maximum row subscript is passed as an argument.
    WRITE this function.
*/
int array[] [3];
int max_row;     /*  maximum row subscript (start from 0) */
```

270

Good programming practice in the previous exercise would replace the magic numbers for the dimension sizes by #defines.

```
#define MAX_ROW 1
#define MAX_COL 2

int coord[MAX_ROW + 1][MAX_COL + 1];
```

In a real application, the array would be built from input obtained by an instrument or from a disk file. Still, the function zero_scan can only process an array with rows of size MAX_COL + 1, which is a constant. The program would have to be recompiled for an array with a different width.

270A

Suppose we want to generalize the sparsity scan exercise so that it accepts arrays of any size. One way is to work with a pointer to the array.

```
zero_scan (array, max_row, max_col)
int *array, max_row, max_col;
{
}
```

To access element [2][4] the program itself calculates

```
offset = 2 * (max_col + 1) + 4;
```

Then we can write

```
n = array[offset];
```

or

```
n = *(array + offset);
```

270B

We use max_row only as a bound for the scanning, not to calculate the subscript. We changed the column size to a variable. Since we cannot put a variable subscript into an array declaration, we must do work that the compiler did before. We make array a pointer to the beginning of the array and use a working pointer to meander through it.

271

```
/*  Scan two-dimensional arrays of varying size */

int coord [2][3] = {{17, 23, 0}, {0, -2, 1}};

main ()
{
int sparsity;

    sparsity = zero_scan (coord, 1, 2);
    printf ("Has %d zero entries", sparsity);
}

zero_scan (array, max_row, max_col)
/*  Return: the number of 0 entries in an array.
    WRITE this function.
*/
int *array,
    max_row, max_col;    /*  maximum subscripts (start from 0) */
```

271A

An identity array has 1's along its diagonal and zero everywhere else. It is a square array, with the same number of rows and columns.

271B

```
/*  Test whether a two-dimensional array is identity */

#define TRUE    1
#define FALSE   0

int two_dim_a[3][3] = { 1, 0, 0, 0, 1, 0, 0, 0, 1 };
int two_dim_b[3][3] = { 1, 0, 0, 0, 1, 0, 0, 0, 0 };

main ()
{
    if (is_identity (two_dim_a, 3))
        puts ("This is an identity array");
    else
        puts ("This is not an identity array");

    if (is_identity (two_dim_b, 3))
```

```
          puts ("This is an identity array");
    else
          puts ("This is not an identity array");
}

is_identity (array, size)
/*  Return: TRUE/FALSE an identity array.
    Array is square of specified size.
    Assume: an array of integers.
    WRITE this function.
*/
int *array;        /*  pass the array address */
                   /*  function must calculate subscript */
int size;          /*  number of elements in each dimension */
```

The difference in processing labor between array subscripts and pointers is especially pronounced in multidimensional arrays. Consider two ways of initializing a 20 by 20 integer array.

```
    for (i = 0; i <= 19; i++)          /*  subscripts */
        for (j = 0; j <= 19; j++)
            an_array[i][j] = 1000;

    end_ptr = &an_array[19][19];     /*  pointer */
    for (iptr = an_array; iptr <= end_ptr; iptr++)
        *iptr = 1000;
```

For the moment, forget about the extra code managing nested for-loops and consider only the assignment statement. A typical 8086 system might require the following instructions (worded in English).

Move array address to secondary register
Move *i* to accumulator
Multiply accumulator by byte length of a row
Add accumulator to secondary register
Move *j* to accumulator
Double accumulator to scale *j*
Add accumulator to secondary register
Move 1000 to accumulator
Store accumulator in memory addressed by secondary register

On the other hand, the pointer statement is simply

Move pointer to secondary register

Move 1000 to accumulator

Store accumulator in memory addressed by secondary register

In this Workshop, the index method takes three times as many instructions and uses a multiply instruction, which takes several times as many processor cycles as most instructions.

When the work to be done requires knowing the two indexes of the array, you may not be able to use a pointer (or you might use both).

Exercise. Write a program to test comparative speeds of initializing a global two-dimensional array. Let `main` prompt the user for a key and execute `two_dim_init` and then, after getting another key, `one_dim_init` for comparison. Make the array a 50 by 50 character array. If the loops execute too fast for you to time them, add an outer loop in each function that goes through the initializing loop(s) 40 times. On one computer, execution speed varied by a difference of 2.8 times.

273

Pointers to Functions

The variety of pointers equals the diversity of objects to which they point. There are integer pointers, character pointers, pointers to integer pointers, etc.

A pointer can even point to a function. A function occupies a certain part of memory. The expression

```
&toupper
```

produces the starting address of the function `toupper()`.

A pointer to a function needs its own declaration.

```
int (*fptr)();
```

This declaration tells us that `fptr` is a pointer to a function returning an integer. Now you can write

```
fptr = &toupper;
```

Of course, later in the program we might want to reassign the pointer.

```
fptr = &tolower;
```

Since `*fptr` is the function, we can use it by providing the function parameter(s).

```
menu_choice = (*fptr) (key);
```

The function referenced at the moment, `toupper` or `tolower` in our example, will be invoked with the input `key`.

Suppose we perform an elaborate calculation which sometimes doubles but at other times triples the input parameter. We can pass this decision in the form of a pointer to a function.

A program exercise follows this discussion. Let the fancy calculation be performed in `fancy`. We give it two parameters: the input number and the function to use in the calculation.

```
fancy (n, scaler)
int n;
int (*scaler)();      /*  declare pointer to function */
{
}
```

The declaration

```
int (*scaler)();
```

says that `scaler` is a pointer to a function that returns an integer. Just as `[]` is used to indicate an array, so `()` indicates a function. The first parentheses are needed; writing

```
int *scaler();
```

would declare `scaler` to be a function returning a pointer to an integer, since `()` has precedence above `*`.

That is, to parse the declaration of a function pointer, we note that the parentheses force `*` to apply to `scaler`; it is a pointer. What does it point to? The `()` tell us it points to a function, an `int` function.

Within `fancy` we would write statements like

```
n = (*scaler)(i);
```

This applies the `*` pointer operation to access the specific function that `scaler` points to; the argument for this function is `i`.

To invoke `fancy`, we supply a pointer to a function.

```
extern int double_it();
```

```
main()
{
int a, b;
    b = fancy (a, double_it);
}
```

Thus, main provides fancy with the value a and a pointer to double_it. Just as the compiler does not need & before an array name in a function call, we can also write double_it without the & sign.

The extern declaration tells the compiler what double_it is before it compiles main. With some compilers, we could alternatively include within main a declaration

```
    int double_it();
```

275

```
/*  Scale number using a pointer to a function */

extern int double_it(), triple_it();  /*  declare before main
*/

main()
{
int a, b, c;

    a = 10;
/*  PUT statements here invoking  fancy  to calculate
    b = 2 * a + 7  and  c = 3 * a + 7. */


    printf ("b = %d, c = %d", b , c);
}

double_it (n)
/*  Return: 2 * n.  WRITE this function. */

triple_it (n)
/*  Return: 3 * n.  WRITE this function. */

fancy (n, scaler)
/*  Return: scaled n plus 7.
    WRITE this function using the function pointer.
```

```
*/
```

One of the most frequent uses of a pointer to functions occurs in sorting
routines. Many C libraries have a sort function, one of whose inputs is a
pointer to a function. Through this mechanism you provide the sort routine
with a function that compares two objects and returns an integer indicating
whether the first element is smaller, equal to, or larger than the second element. You select the kind of comparison you want. It could be numeric,
reporting that 234 is less than 1023, or it might be lexical (dictionary order),
in which case "anniversary" is less than "announce." The library programmer can write and compile the sort routine without knowing how two elements will be compared.

276

```
/*  Analyze arbitrary function using pointer */

/*  The object of this exercise is to analyze the
    behavior of an arbitrary function.  You write
    a routine that accepts a pointer to the function
    as an argument and searches for the minimum value
    assumed by the function over the integers [0..9].
*/

poly1 (i)    /*  Sample function to analyze */
int i;
{
    return (i * i - 3 * i);
}

main()
{
int n;

    n = find_min (poly1);
    printf ("The minimum of  poly1  over [0..9] is %d", n);
}

find_min (fn)
/*  Return: minimum value assumed by  fn  over the integer
    range [0..9] inclusive.
```

```
        WRITE this function.  Assume  fn  returns integer values
        over the specified range.
*/
```

277

The next program analyzes `double` functions instead of integer functions.

If a mathematical function is continuous over an interval, and it has a positive value at one endpoint and a negative value at the other endpoint of the interval, then it has a root in the interval. Speaking very roughly, a continuous function is like a string, so it has to cross the x-axis somewhere between the two endpoints.

The converse is not true: if the two endpoints are both positive, the function might still have a root. However, we will ignore this fact and assume there is no root.

Once we know there is a root in an interval, we will find it by repeatedly dividing the interval in half and applying the endpoint test to determine which interval.

As usual with floating point, we cannot require that the function value be exactly zero. Instead, we specify a small quantity `eps` ("epsilon") and accept a root if the difference between the function at two endpoints

```
    diff = fabs (fn_l - fn_r);
```

is less than `eps`. The library function `fabs` returns the absolute value.

277A

```
/*  Find approximate root of a function by bisection */

#include "cwstdio.h"

#define NO_ROOT   0  /*  no root here PER sign test */
#define HAS_ROOT  1  /*  within the interval */
#define LROOT     2  /*  left boundary is a root */
#define RROOT     3

extern double poly(), find_root();  /*  non-int fns */

main()
```

```
{
double left, right; /*  interval to search */
double x, (*fn)(), eps;

    left = -10.0;   right = 10.0;
    fn = &poly;
    eps = 1.0e-7;   /*  accept this value as effectively 0 */

    if (root_exist (left, right, fn, eps) == NO_ROOT)
        puts ("Endpoints do not indicate a root");
    else
        {
        x = find_root (left, right, fn, eps);
        printf ("Has root near %f where fn = %20.12f",
            x, (*fn)(x));
        }
}

double
find_root (left, right, fn, eps)
/*  Assumed: a root exists in this interval.
    Return: root.
    WRITE this function.
    Hint: use report from root_exist to reduce interval.
    Another hint: put  inkey();  somewhere in the loop so
        you can press Ctrl-Brk in case of an endless loop.
*/
double left, right, /*  interval to search for root */
    (*fn)(),        /*  ptr to function being analyzed */
    eps;            /*  precision */
{
double mid, l, r, x;
int flag;           /*  report from root_exist */


root_exist (l, r, fn, eps)
/*  Return: LROOT, RROOT, HAS_ROOT, or NO_ROOT
    Strictly, speaking, use in "small" intervals
*/
double l, r, (*fn)(), eps;
{
double fn_l, fn_r, diff;
```

```
    fn_l = (*fn)(l);
    fn_r = (*fn)(r);
    diff = fabs (fn_l - fn_r);

    if (fn_l == 0.0 || diff < eps)
        return LROOT;
    else if (fn_r == 0.0)
        return RROOT;
    else if (fn_l < 0.00 && fn_r > 0.00)
        return HAS_ROOT;
    else if (fn_l > 0.00 && fn_r < 0.00)
        return HAS_ROOT;
    else
        return NO_ROOT; /*  PER endpoint test */
}

double
poly (x)
double x;
{
    return (2.0 * x * x * x + (.3 * x) - 2.0);
}
```

Exercise. Write a function `hex_dump` that displays lines consisting of a starting address, 16 byte values in ASCII hexadecimal and the ASCII character equivalent of the bytes (displaying '.' for nonprintable values). Invoke the function from `main`, supplying two arguments: a pointer to a function that returns the next byte value to be displayed, or -1 if there are no more bytes to be read, and the starting address.

If you write in topdown fashion, the function `hex_dump` should invoke a function to display a line of data, which invokes additional functions to display an address or a byte of data.

For a test version, write a function to get the bytes from a sample array in your program. Then extend it to read from a disk file.

Exercise. Modify the craps program to allow betting. Add `startup()` to start the player with some money, and write functions to do the bookkeeping and keep the player informed. Make sure the player has enough money to make his bet. Stop the game if the player loses all his money.

CHAPTER 17

Lists, Stacks, and Trees

In computer science, the term "data structures" refers to general schemes for connecting data objects to each other. This idea is independent of any particular language. In this chapter we will see how the facilities of C may be used to create and manipulate some of these data structures.

The Linked List—A Self-Referencing Structure

A teacher wants to record and analyze the scores of his students on a test. He would like to enter the scores in the classroom with his nifty portable computer as the students turn in the exams (and his grading program scores them). Later he can look up scores, print them in student ID number order, etc.

A linked list is one possible way to arrange the data, and C structures are ideal for linked lists. Each element of a linked list contains information (for example, the score) and a pointer to the next item on the list. The links, not the sequential storage order, define the order of the list.

```
struct ll_tag {
    int student;
```

```
  int score;
  struct ll_tag *next;
  } test[MAX_STUDENT + 1];
```

This structure array has three members to each element: the student ID number, the score, and a pointer. The pointer will hold the address of another element in the array.

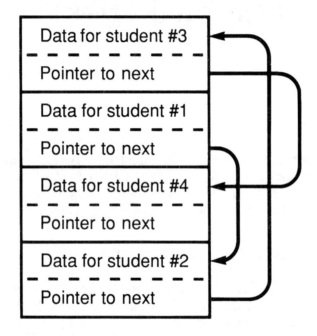

```
struct ll_tag *tptr;
    tptr = test;
    tptr = tptr->next;
```

These statements establish a pointer to type `ll_tag`, initialize it to the start of the array, and advance the pointer to the next linked item. Because `tptr->next` is also a pointer, it may be assigned to `tptr`.

The object `tptr->score` is the score, and `tptr->student` is the student ID number.

The links may be arranged as desired. After all the test papers are in, one way to arrange the links would be to point to the next higher student number. Then we will have

```
tptr->next->student > tptr->student;   /*  TRUE */
```

That is, the student ID number of the next linked entry, `tptr->next`, is greater than the student ID number of the current test paper.

There is a boundary condition. At the end of the list, we put

```
tptr->next = 0;
```

to indicate the end.

283

```
/*  Fetch values from a linked list */

#define EXCEPTION   (-1)

struct ll_tag {
    int student;
    int score;
    struct ll_tag *next;    /*  pointer holds link */
    } test[20] = {
    1, 90, 0,  5, 87, 0,  4, 93, 0,  2, 76, 0,  3, 45, 0};

main()
{
struct ll_tag *tptr;
int s;

    init_links();

    s = get_score (2);
    printf ("The score for student #2 is %d", s);
}

init_links()
/*  These statements initialize links in the data. */
{
struct ll_tag *tptr;
    tptr = test;
    tptr->next = &test[3]; tptr++; tptr->next = 0; tptr++;
```

```
    tptr->next = &test[1]; tptr++; tptr->next = &test[4]; tptr++;
    tptr->next = &test[2];
}

get_score (n)
/*  Return: the score for student #n,
        or EXCEPTION if there is no student #n score.
    WRITE this function.
    Hint: run a work ptr through the list, looking for the
    desired student number and returning the score, else
    using the link to move the pointer to the next list item. */
int n;
```

In the program `main` built the initial links by hand, so to speak.

Assuming the data is in a disk file, we could first allocate memory for the array `test`, initialize a pointer there, and read in the data. As we read the data, we would establish and maintain the links in student number order.

If the compiler has memory allocation functions, you could obtain the memory for each element of the array as it is read. One benefit is that the program need not know in advance how big an array it will read. When you deal with a linked list, array elements may be scattered all over memory.

We could read the data at least two different ways. If the output format has been designed appropriately, we may use `fscanf` from the library to read student ID numbers and scores. Or we may define a union

```
union in_tag
    {
    int datum;
    unsigned char byte[2];
    } input;
```

We could read bytes into input with statements like

```
    input.byte[0] = ...
    input.byte[1] = ...
    a_student = input.datum;
```

Linked lists are useful for sorting and other rearrangements of data. This is especially true if the data are of variable length. Each item can have a pointer to the name of a student, for example, instead of the actual name array. When a student drops the class, a maintenance function jumps the link from the previous student to the following student (and ignores or frees the space where the name was stored).

Other Data Structures

Once an array is established, the only way to add an element after the i-th element is to push the others forward to make room. A list is a more flexible arrangement because we may insert items by adjusting the links of the two structures between which the new item goes.

A C structure is the natural mechanism for a list, because even if we merely want to link integers, we need to associate two different objects, the integer and the pointer to the next integer.

A list may have two link pointers per item, one pointing to the preceding structure and one for the next structure. This is called a doubly linked list.

A circular list links the last item back to the first one instead of stopping with a null link.

```
struct ll_tag {
    int student;
    int score;
    struct ll_tag *next;
    struct ll_tag *previous;
    } test[MAX_TESTS + 1];
```

If test is to be a circular linked list and we assume the array is full, then

```
test[MAX_TESTS].next = &test[0];
```

SELF TEST   **285**
```
struct ll_tag {
    int student;
    int score;
    struct ll_tag *next;
    struct ll_tag *previous;    /*  doubly linked list */
    } test[MAX_TESTS + 1];      /*  assume full */
```

In this full, circular list, test[0].previous is
   A) &test[MAX_TESTS + 1]
   B) &test[MAX_TESTS]
   C) &test[1]

The Stack Structure

One of the most important data structures in computers is the stack. It is an array maintained according to the following rules:

To add an item to the stack, store it at the next free element. This is called a push.

To remove an item from the stack, take it from the current end of the stack. This is called popping the stack.

In other words, the last element into the array is the first one to come out. Although there may be ways to access other elements in the stack, pushing and popping are the defining ways to handle stack data.

The terms pushing and popping assume that we envision a stack array vertically.

Every stack has an associated stack pointer. Stacks are easy to maintain in C. For example,

```
#define MAX_STACK       99
char stack[MAX_STACK + 1];
int sp;
```

This defines a stack of characters. To initialize the stack,

```
    sp = 0;
```

Nothing needs to be done to the actual data space; only the pointer is important.

To push a character onto the stack,

```
    stack[sp++] = 'X';
```

and to pop a character off the stack,

```
    c = stack[--sp];
```

The stack pointer is incremented after pushing and decremented before popping. The alternative choice is to increment before pushing and decrement after popping. In the latter case, we say that the stack has a pre-increment push and a post-decrement pop.

We might also initialize the stack pointer at the other end of the available space.

```
    sp = MAX_STACK;
```

In this case, a push must decrement the stack pointer and a pop increment it.

A stack may be an array of any kind of objects: characters, integers, or elaborate structures. (It could even contain objects of varying size; such a stack would require a more complicated scheme to maintain its stack pointer.)

We will use a stack to evaluate an expression in postfix notation, sometimes called reverse Polish notation. This notation places the operator immediately following its operands. For example, 3 + 5 is written as 3 5 +. The infix expression

(2 * 7) + (21 / 3)

becomes

2 7 * 21 3 / +

Postfix notation eliminates parentheses.

Instead of evaluating arithmetic expressions, we will evaluate combinations of propositions. A proposition has the value *T* or *F* (we also accept lowercase *t* and *f*), and the operators are +, ⋆, and ~. The + operator is a logical *or*: pq+ is true if p or q or both are true. The ⋆ operator is a logical *and*: pq⋆ is true if and only if both p and q are true. The ~ operator ("not") simply flips the truth value of its single operand.

Our goal is to accept data like

Postfix sequence: t f + f * t f ~ * +

We want to evaluate whether it is true, false or an invalid sequence. The algorithm reads each input symbol in turn and applies the following rules.

If the symbol is an operand, push it.

If the symbol is a binary operator, pop two operands and apply the operator. Push the result.

If the symbol is a unary operator, pop an operand, apply the operator, and push the result.

When the input is exhausted, pop the result.

For example, while evaluating the above expression, a movie of the stack looks like this, reading from left to right.

```
            f T
    f   f   t t t T
t t T T F F F F F T
```

Here we have used lower and uppercase merely to distinguish incoming symbols from intermediate results.

The following program implements a stack-based evaluator of postfix propositions.

288

```c
/*  Evaluate propositions written in postfix notation */

#define EOF (-1)
#define EXCEPTION (-1)

char sample_input[30] = {"tf+f*tf~*+"};

#define STACK_SIZE      40
char stack[STACK_SIZE];
int sp = 0;                 /*  stack pointer */

main()
{
    switch (evaluate())
        {
        case 'T':
            puts ("Proposition is true");
            break;
        case 'F':
            puts ("Proposition is false");
            break;
        case EXCEPTION:
            puts ("Missing operator");
            break;
        default:
            puts ("Input not valid postfix sequence");
            break;
        }
}

evaluate()
/*  Return: 'T', 'F' or EXCEPTION for unused operands.
*/
{
int reg1, reg2, c;
```

```
while ((c = read_op()) != EOF)
    {
    switch (c)
        {
        /*  push valid operands */
        case 'T':
        case 'F':
            push (c);
            break;

        case '*':        /*  propositional AND */
            /*  MUST pop two operands */
            reg1 = pop(); reg2 = pop();
            if (reg1 == 'T' && reg2 == 'T')
                push ('T');
            else
                push ('F');
            break;

        case '+':        /*  propositional OR */
        /*  WRITE this case. */


            break;

        case '~':
            if (pop() == 'T')
                push ('F');
            else
                push ('T');
            break;

        default:
            printf ("Input %c ignored\n", c);
            break;
        }
    }

/*  report result */
    if (sp != 1)
        return EXCEPTION;
```

```
    else
        return (pop());
}

push (c)
{
    if (sp < STACK_SIZE)
        stack[sp++] = c;
    else
        {
        puts ("Stack overflow");
        exit();
        }
}

pop()
{
    if (sp > 0)
        return (stack[--sp]);
    else
        {
        puts ("Stack underflow");
        exit();
        }
}

read_op()
/*  Return: the next input operand or operator
            converted to uppercase.
    Isolate input function for later modification.
*/
{
int c;       /*  integer so can read EOF */
static int index = 0;

    if (c = sample_input[index++])
        return (toupper(c));
    else
        {
        index = 0;
        return (EOF);
        }
```

}

The program should be able to survive badly formed input strings. That is why the push and pop operations are segregated into their own functions, checking for stack overflow and underflow. The program also checks to see that one and only one result is on the stack at the end.

The check for underflow examines the value of the stack pointer. Another technique is to push a special BOS_MARK (bottom of stack mark) at the start and then to test for this mark. This technique simplifies the code. In this example, the mark could be a null. However, you must be sure that the mark is unique. A stack of integers, for example, might legitimately contain the null value.

The stack pointer need not be an integer index into the stack array. It may be a pointer (in the C sense) instead. You might want to rewrite the program using a BOS_MARK and a definition

```
char *sp_ptr;
```

(however, the Soft Tutor will no longer work).

The Binary Tree

We return to C structures and use them to represent another important data type in computers, the binary tree. A binary tree consists of nodes. Each node, besides holding data, may have a left subnode and a right subnode.

The node which is not a subnode is the root, here holding the letter E (see diagram). Nodes that have no subnodes are leaves, here A, C, and G. The left subtree of a node begins with the left subnode as a root. For example, the left subtree of E is the tree with root at B and extending to A, D and C.

One way to store a tree is to define an array of structures, each element representing a node. The data type might be

```
struct t_tag {
    int value;  /*  purpose is to hold data! */
    struct t_tag *left_node;    /*  pointer */
    struct t_tag *right_node;
    };
```

Typically, the nodes are entered into the next available element in the array; the definition of the subnode pointers defines the tree relationships.

The diagram was built by successively inputting the letters E, D, F, A, G, B, and C. They were inserted into the tree so that each left subnode is alphabetically prior to its mother node and each right subnode is alphabetically later than its mother node.

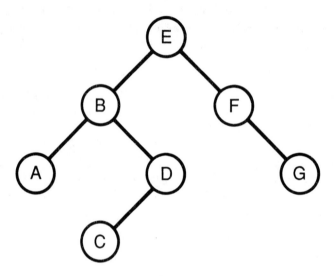

To traverse a tree, a program visits each node systematically, perhaps outputting it when visited in order to list the whole tree. There are several ways to traverse a tree. Given a tree built like our example, symmetric traversal will list the letters in alphabetical order.

Roughly stated, symmetric traversal starts at a root, processes the left subtree, visits the root, then processes the right subtree. "Process a subtree" means to apply the same idea to it. Later we will study recursion and handle algorithms defined in terms of themselves easily. For now, our algorithm will traverse the tree using a stack.

set the root at the root of the entire tree
x:

if the root has a left subnode
 push the root (remember where to come back)
 root = left subnode (process the earlier values)
 go to x
else
y:
 output the root (done processing earlier values)
 if the root has a right subnode
  root = right subnode (process later values)
  go to x
 else if stack is not empty
  root = pop from stack (after left, root, and right)
  go to y
 else
  done

This pseudocode expresses slightly more precisely the idea of symmetric traversal. Now we must translate it into C. Notice that algorithms stated in pseudocode tend to have `goto`'s and labels that we want to eliminate while writing good C code.

293

```
/*  Traverse tree using a stack */

/*  Just study and run this program */

#define TRUE        1
#define BOS_MARK    0              /*  bottom of stack mark */

struct t_tag {
    int value;
    struct t_tag *left_node;    /*  pointer */
    struct t_tag *right_node;
    };

extern struct t_tag sample[];
    /*  permits self-reference initializing */
    /*  C Workshop does not need, some compilers do */
```

```
struct t_tag sample[30] = {
    {'E', &sample[1], &sample[2]},
    {'B', &sample[3], &sample[4]},
    {'F', 0, &sample[5]},
    {'A', 0, 0},
    {'D', &sample[6], 0},
    {'G', 0, 0},
    {'C', 0, 0}};
/*  Allocate 30 cells, but initialize only first few */

struct t_tag *stack[80];
int sp = 0;

main()
{
    traverse (sample);
}

traverse (tree)
/*  Traverse tree in symmetric order.
    Display each node when visited.
*/
struct t_tag *tree;
{
struct t_tag *root, *t;

    stack[sp++] = BOS_MARK;
    root = tree;
    while (TRUE)
        {
        if (t = root->left_node)
            {
            stack[sp++] = root;  /*  remember where we are */
            root = t;            /*  traverse left subtree */
            }
        else
            {
            while (TRUE)
                {
                printf ("%c ", root->value);
                if (t = root->right_node)
                    {
```

```
                        root = t;
                        break;  /*  resume left tree traversal */
                        }
                else if ((root = stack[--sp]) == BOS_MARK)
                        return;
                }
            }
        }
}
```

The program is worth several comments. First, we assume the algorithm is embedded deep within a larger system. Therefore, we expect the tree to be well formed. Without error checking, stack pushing and popping remain simple statements.

In order to enter test data into `sample`, we put an `extern` declaration ahead of it. The reason is that while the compiler is processing the declaration of `sample`, it does not want to see "sample" in the initialization data. But by preceding the declaration with the `extern` (and the definition of the structure tag), we can initialize the tree.

The program treads on thin ice using a bottom of stack mark. The algorithm never pushes a null root, so we have used a null pointer as the BOS_-MARK. This simplifies the test for completion of the task.

Exercise. Rewrite the program so that `traverse` receives a pointer to an output function when visiting a root. Use this function pointer to remove the `printf` statement from `traverse`.

Exercise. Write a function that inserts a letter into the tree, maintaining the alphabetical relationships. Force the input letter to uppercase. Use a simple scheme to allocate space from the array: an index points to the next available cell and is incremented each time one is used. From `main` add 'X' then 'L' to the tree. Test your work by traversing and displaying the tree.

CHAPTER 18
Sorting and Other Applications

Sorting data into desired order and searching data for a specific item are workhorse chores for computers. Many hours of human experiment and thought have gone into devising efficient methods.

Recursion and scaling are also common techniques in programming.

Our purpose in this chapter is to see how we can express these techniques in C. First we will write a simple sort and a binary search of integers. Then we will sort small and large records. We conclude with a look at recursion and an arithmetical method called scaling.

The Bubble Sort

Suppose you execute a benchmark program on a number of computers, time how long each system takes to execute it, and record the results in tenths of seconds. That is, 281 means the elapsed time was 28.1 seconds. You have an array of these results and want to sort them in ascending order.

The bubble sort, or exchange sort, makes repeated passes over the array. Each element is compared to the next element and their order reversed if necessary. A program exercise follows this discussion.

```
if (array[i] > array[i + 1])
    {
    temp = array[i];
```

```
array[i] = array[i + 1];
array[i + 1] = temp;
flag = TRUE;     /*  an exchange was made */
}
```

This is the basic comparison and exchange embedded within a loop.

297

The name "bubble sort" expresses the fact that on the first pass the largest element is guaranteed to bubble up to the end of the array. On each pass, the next largest element is so guaranteed.

The `flag` tells whether any exchanges were made during the pass over the array. When no elements are swapped, we are done.

You can invoke a function

```
sort (array, size)
```

to do the work. Note that `sort` gets a pointer to the array.

The range of the loop is from element 0 through the next to last element, since each element is compared with the following one.

297A

```
/*  Sort array of integers */

int elapsed[] = {121, 43, 435, 28900, 106, 254, 381};

main()
{
int i;

    sort (elapsed, sizeof (elapsed)/sizeof (elapsed[0]));
    for (i = 0; i < 7; i++)
        printf ("%d  ", elapsed[i]);
}

sort (array, size)
/*  Sorts integer array in ascending numerical order.
    WRITE this function. */
int *array;     /*  pointer to array to sort */
int size;       /*  number of elements in the array */
```

A Binary Search

Once you have sorted the array, someone can give you a timing and ask you to find its relative position by determining its index in the array. The fastest timing is element 0.

You could search a small array from its beginning until a larger element than the supplied value is found. There is a faster method for searching large, sorted arrays.

A binary search picks an approximate midpoint of the array. If the desired value is not there, examine the upper or lower partial array the same way. Continue until the value is found or no more array is left (e.g., the upper bound has become less than the lower bound).

One complication is the policy for handling duplicate values. We specify that we want the first occurrence. Once you find the value, you must backtrack (being careful not to back right out of the array!) so long as the value is duplicated.

298A

```
/*  Binary search of integer array */

#define EXCEPTION    (-1)

int elapsed[20] = {43, 106, 121, 254, 381, 435, 28900};

main()
{
int i;

    i = search (elapsed, 7, 254);
    if (i != EXCEPTION)
        printf ("Value occurs first at position %d", i);
    else
        puts ("Not found in array");
}

search (array, size, value)
/*  Return: index of first occurrence of value
            or EXCEPTION if value not found.
```

```
      WRITE this binary search function.
*/
int *array, size, value;
```

Sorting Records

You sorted an array of elapsed benchmark times for several computers. The problem is that no record was kept of which machine took which time! Most real-life sorting is done on structures, not numbers. Keeping it simple, we might have a code for each machine associated with its elapsed time.

```
struct b_tag {
    int mach_code;
    int elapsed;
    };
struct b_tag bench[7];
```

The data now consists of an array of structures. We need to compare and swap them.

The basics of bubble sorting are the same: comparing two elements and swapping them if necessary. To compare two elements, compare their elapsed times; to swap them, swap the entire structures.

We should organize the task in modules from the top down. Let us write a sort function and subordinate functions to compare and swap elements. Another decision faces us, too: shall we tailor the code to our particular structure and array, or shall we be more general? C provides the facilities to write a clear, concise routine to sort any array of any kind of structure.

The essential tool is the pointer to a function. When we invoke the sort routine from main, we will give it pointers to the compare and swap functions. The comparison function will return an integer code indicating the result, which is all the sort needs. We can re-use the sort routine, changing only the comparison and swap functions and the invocation of the sort.

```
sort (array, size, compare, swap)
struct b_tag *array;
int size;
int (*compare)(), (*swap)();
{ }
```

The declarations of the parameters specify that `compare` and `swap` are pointers to functions that return integers. The parentheses are necessary (look at the precedence chart if you do not see why).

We have specified that `array` points to a certain kind of structure, but with most compilers, `sort` will accept any pointer. To be completely correct, you would use a `cast` or assignment in the invoking function; this would cast a `struct b_tag` pointer to a character pointer.

The identifiers `compare` and `swap` are formal parameters. It is necessary to write specific functions for our data.

```
bmrk_compare (array, i, j)
struct b_tag *bench;
int i ,j;
{ }
```

Although the program would compile if we simply used the name `compare`, the distinguishing name `bmrk_compare` will remind us how we are applying the sort routine.

We will have statements in `bmrk_compare` like

```
    if (array[i].elapsed > array[j].elapsed)
        return (1);
```

To invoke `bmrk_compare` from `sort`, we can write

```
    (*compare) (array, i, i + 1);
```

300

```
/*  Sort array of structures */

struct b_tag {
    int mach_code;
    int elapsed;
    };

struct b_tag bench[] = {10, 121,  20, 43,  30, 435,  40, 28900,
    50, 106,  60, 254,  70, 381};
extern int bmrk_compare(), bmrk_swap();
        /*  for one-pass compiler */

main()
{
```

```
int i;

    sort (bench, sizeof (bench)/sizeof (bench[0]),
            bmrk_compare, bmrk_swap);
    for (i = 0; i < 7; i++)
        printf (" %d", bench[i].elapsed);
}

bmrk_compare (array, i, j)        /*  WRITE this function */
struct b_tag *array;
int i, j;
/*  Return: 1 if elapsed time for i-th element
    >= for j-th element, else 0.
*/

bmrk_swap (array, i, j)           /*  WRITE this function */
struct b_tag *array;
int i, j;
/*  Swap the i-th and j-th elements of the array.
*/


sort (array, size, compare, swap)    /*  WRITE this function */
struct b_tag *array;
int (*compare)(), (*swap)();
int size;
```

If the compiler and linker are strict, we can pass a character pointer to sort using a cast.

```
main()
{
struct b_tag bench;

    sort ((char *) &bench, ...
}
```

In a full development system, the sort routine could be compiled and put into a library. Many compiler packages do in fact supply such a routine, obviously without knowing what programs it will be linked into.

Sorting Large Structures

We sorted a small structure containing only two integers. The benchmark data for each machine might be more extensive, including the brand name of the machine, its price, codes for the software, date of the test, and so on. When the structures are large, it is not desirable to swap them over and over. Instead, let us build an array of pointers to the structures. We can sort the pointers, then use them to display the structures or write the structures in sorted order into a new array.

For convenience in illustrating the idea, we will use the same structure.

```
struct b_tag {
    int mach_code;
    int elapsed;
/*  in real life, would have more elements here */
    };
```

In `main` we define an array of pointers.

```
struct b_tag *bench_ptr[7];
```

We initialize the array by pointing `bench_ptr[0]` to the address of the first structure, and so on.

```
    for (i = 0; i < 7; i++)
        bench_ptr[i] = &bench[i];
```

The function `sort` has a declaration to inform it what objects it is getting.

```
sort (bptr, size)
struct b_tag **bptr;
int size;        /*  count of elements in pointer array */
{
int flag, i;
struct b_tag *temp;
```

The routine `sort` gets a pointer to a `b_tag` pointer, that is, the address of the first pointer. The function cannot simply receive the address of the first structure; it would have no access to the other ones. The `**` accepts the address of a pointer. The effect of the `struct b_tag` is to inform `sort` what kind of underlying pointers these are, so it can calculate references to

members using the -> operator. The object `temp` holds one of these
pointers to a `b_tag` structure.

Within `sort`,

```
bptr[i]->elapsed
```

gets the elapsed time for the structure pointed to by the *i*-th pointer in the
array `bptr`. When necessary, we will have statements like

```
temp = bptr[i];
```

which assigns to `temp` the *i*-th pointer in the array. This statement is where
we benefit from economy of action. Instead of swapping entire structures,
we move only pointers. The structure may be hundreds of bytes long; the
pointer to it is only two or four bytes.

For now, we will simply perform the comparisons and swaps within
`sort`.

303

```
/*  Sort structures via pointers to them */

struct b_tag {
    int mach_code;
    int elapsed;
/*  In real life, more elements would be here */
    };

struct b_tag bench[20] = {10, 121,  20, 43,  30, 435,  40,
28900,
    50, 106,  60, 254,  70, 381};

main()
{
int i;
struct b_tag *bench_ptr[20];

    for (i = 0; i < 7; i++)
        bench_ptr[i] = &bench[i];
    sort (bench_ptr, 7);
    for (i = 0; i < 7; i++)
        printf (" %d", bench_ptr[i]->elapsed);
}
```

```
sort (bptr, size)
/*  WRITE this function.
    Declare parameters here.  bptr is a pointer to a pointer.
*/
```

In the previous exercise we lost generality in the sort routine. If we want to maintain the general case, `sort` must invoke, through pointers, functions that compare and swap. Whatever the underlying data objects, the comparison function need only return an integer. In addition, the invoker of `sort` may pass the address of the array to be sorted. So long as the sort function does not use this address but merely passes it to the comparison and swap functions, the exact pointer type is irrelevant. That is, by convention we may give `sort`

```
char *array;
```

then write the comparison and swap functions to receive pointers to `char` and if necessary cast them into the correct type of pointer.

304

Recursion

A recursive function is one that invokes itself, either directly or indirectly through another function. The statement

```
    n = recurs (n) + 1;
```

is legal inside the function `recurs` itself.

Recursive functions make it possible to solve some problems with very little programming.

Suppose, for example, that we want to add up the first n even numbers. (We ignore that the mathematician Gauss discovered a formula for this problem while he was still in grammar school.)

If we have the answer for n $-$ 1, then we know the answer is
*(answer for n - 1) + (2 * n)* ·

We had better get the answer for n equal to 1 right away in order to have a place to start (or rather, to stop postponing the problem). The answer is obviously 2.

```
sum_of_even (n)
/*  Return: sum of first n even numbers.
*/
int n;
{
    if (n == 1)
        return (2);
    else
        return (sum_of_even (n - 1) + (2 * n));
}
```

Let us turn to another problem. In arithmetic, the factorial of a number *n* is the product *1 x 2 x ... x n*. It is written with an exclamation point. For example,

3! = 3 x 2 x 1 = 6

Obviously, *n! = n x (n-1)!*, and this is the basis for calculating factorials recursively.

```
factorial (n)
/* Returns n! */
```

Let the function invoke itself to calculate *(n-1)!*. The function checks two cases. If n == 1, simply return 1. Otherwise, the function invokes itself to perform the calculation

```
    factorial (n) = n * factorial (n-1);
```

By convention, *0! = 1*. You must take this special case into account.

305

```
/*  Calculate factorial recursively */

/*  Note: factorials grow explosively.  Integers
    can only hold the factorial of n <= 7.
    For long integers the limit is 13.
*/

extern long factorial();

main()
{
long f, n;
```

```
    n = 7L;
    f = factorial (n);
    printf ("%ld! = %ld\n", n, f);   /*  format long display */
}

long
factorial (n)
/*  Return: n!.  You may assume n >= 0L.
    WRITE this function recursively.
*/
long n;
```

```
whats_this (str)
char *str;   /*  pointer to ASCIIZ string (ends with null) */
{
    if (*str)    return (1 + whats_this (++str));
    else         return 1;
}
```

This function returns:

A) the length of a string excluding the null

B) the length of a string including the null

C) nothing because it crashes the computer

The Tower of Hanoi

The recipe for calculating a factorial is comparatively easy to grasp as a whole. A puzzle whose details quickly get beyond us is the Tower of Hanoi (named centuries before the Vietnam war).

The tower has three poles. Pole A has a stack of disks, each one smaller in diameter than the one below it. The problem calls for moving the stack from pole A to pole B, subject to two rules: only one disk may be moved at a time, and a disk may not be placed on top of a smaller disk.

If there are only two disks, the solution is easy. Move the small disk from pole A to C. Move the large disk from A to B. Move the small disk from C to B.

You can use a deck of cards, with an ace representing a disk of diameter 1, a deuce a disk of diameter 2, and so on, to experiment with solutions for three or four disks. As it turns out, the solution for a pile of n disks requires two to the *n*-th power minus one moves. This number grows very rapidly.

Our challenge is to write a program that automatically generates the correct moves to solve a Tower of Hanoi.

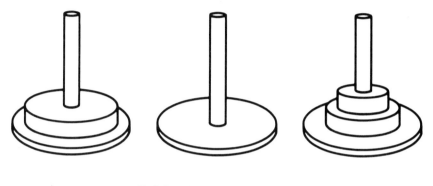

Solving the Tower of Hanoi

One solution is a recursive routine. To solve a three-disk Tower of Hanoi, for example, we might notice that it is a tower of two disks plus a disk underneath. We know how to move a tower of two disks. We move it from the source pole, to C, the spare pole. Now we move the largest disk to B, the target pole. Finally, we regard C as the source pole, use A for a spare, and move the two-disk tower on C to the target B, on top of the largest disk.

Abstractly, the solution mirrors the details of the solution of the two-disk tower. That is, move all but one disk from source to spare pole, move the bottom disk to the target, then reverse the roles of source and spare and move the rest to the target.

Using pseudocode, we can state the solution in an algorithm.

```
main()
{
    tower (n, pole_a, pole_b)
```

```
}

tower (n, source, target)
{
    if n == 1
        move the disk from source to target
    else
        tower (n-1, source, spare)
        move (source, target)
        tower (n-1, spare, target)
}


move (source, target)
{  move (top) disk from source to target  }
```

The routine `tower` invokes itself. This makes it recursive. Like all recursive routines, it needs a boundary condition to stop the recursion. When n is 1, `n-1` is zero, and there is no tower to move, only a simple move of one disk.

We translated from English into algorithmic pseudolanguage, but we have not made a single statement that encompasses the whole solution, a recipe analogous to "compute the factorial of n by multiplying together all the integers from 1 to n." This is the power of recursion, which solves a problem by repeatedly solving part of the problem and applying the method again to solve the remaining part.

Now we do the C coding. A program exercise follows this discussion. The code for the recursion is actually quite short, while the code for a fancy display of the poles on the screen would be quite detailed. Therefore, we will rely on the user to make the moves, perhaps with playing cards. We will merely display directions to move a disk from one pole to another.

Most of the pseudocode of the algorithm translates easily into C. We will refer to the poles as the ASCII letters 'A', 'B' and 'C.' To display a pole, we simply display the value of the source, target or spare variable.

We should add some input, such as getting the number of disks in the tower and waiting for the user to hit the Space bar after each move.

We should also pass three variables, not two: source, target, and spare. (The alternative is a routine that deduces the spare pole from knowledge of the source and target.)

In main we invoke tower with A as source, B as target, and C as spare.

```
tower (num_disks, 'A', 'B', 'C');
```

Within tower, we can switch the poles when tower invokes itself with an invocation like

```
tower (num_disks - 1, source, spare, target);
```

Notice how parameter position reassigns the poles. That is, the invoked tower gets a middle parameter for its target, namely, the value of spare in the invoking instance of the function.

309

```
/*  Tower of Hanoi puzzle with recursion */

int num_disks;

extern move_disk ();      /*  (Written for you) */
/*
Tells user to move a disk.
Pass two parameters:
int source,      take disk from pole letter 'A', 'B' or 'C'
    target;      and put it here
*/


main()
{
    puts ("How many disks? (1 - 9): ");
    num_disks = getchar() - '0';
    puts ("\nPress space bar after each move completed.\n ");

/*  WRITE invocation of tower() here */

}

tower (n, source, target, spare)
int n;
```

```
int source, target, spare;   /*  pole letters 'A', 'B', 'C' */
/*  WRITE recursively.
*/
```

Although it is not an exercise in this Workshop, you might consider how to display the successive steps of a solution to a Tower of Hanoi instead of making the user do it.

Essentially, more elaborate data structures are required. For example, notice that so far we have not kept track of which disks are on which poles! We might number the disks from 1 to n, small diameter to large. Each pole could be an integer array.

Regarding display, two general approaches are possible. One is to redisplay the poles horizontally after each move, showing the disks merely by their diameter numbers. This technique is relatively easy to implement on a display or printer.

```
Pole A: 5 4 3 2
Pole B:
Pole C: 1
```

A more elaborate approach would draw a picture with character graphics (building a disk, for example, as a row of **x**'s). A move would be shown by lifting a row of **x**'s up, shifting it over the appropriate pole, and settling it down.

310

The next screen has a program with functions that invoke each other.

310A

```
/*  Functions that invoke each other */

/*  RUN this program as is.
    Difficult question: Can you describe what these
    functions do to the starting number?
*/

main()
{
int n;
```

```
        n = co_recur1 (50); printf ("%d\t", n);
        n = co_recur1 (49); printf ("%d\t", n);
        n = co_recur1 (48); printf ("%d\t", n);
        n = co_recur1 (47); printf ("%d\t", n);
        n = co_recur1 (46); printf ("%d\t", n);
        n = co_recur1 (45); printf ("%d\t", n);
        n = co_recur1 (44); printf ("%d\t", n);
        n = co_recur1 (43); printf ("%d\t", n);
        n = co_recur1 (42); printf ("%d\t", n);
}

co_recur1 (m)
int m;
{
    if (m > 3)
        m = co_recur2 (m - 3);
    else
        return (m);
}

co_recur2 (n)
int n;
{
    if (n > 5)
        n = co_recur1 (n - 5);
    else
        return (n);
}
```

311

The function names in the previous program refer to the fact that they demonstrate co-recursion, a situation in which function A invokes function B and vice versa.

C Is Recursive

The C language has inherent support for recursion. The key feature is the passing of parameters by value. Each time one function invokes another (perhaps itself), it copies the values of the specified parameters and gives them to the invoked function, which stores these values in new memory locations.

Compare this with a typical Basic program with global variables like A, B and C. If a GOSUB calls a routine after storing a value in A and the invoked subroutine changes A, the old value in A is lost.

Recursion is a memory-intensive method of programming, and usually slower than the alternative. Every time a recursive call is made, the parameters are duplicated, along with a return address in the invoking function. These invocations pile up to a grand depth until the boundary condition is met. Then the nested functions unravel in reverse order.

A portion of memory, the stack, holds all the nested information. If the stack area is not large enough, the program will crash.

The alternative to recursion is iteration, which simply means some kind of loop. For example, it probably occurred to you to calculate the factorial of n in a function executed once.

```
factorial (n);
int n;
{
int fac;

for (fac = i = 1;  i <= n;  i++)
        fac *= i;
    return (fac);
}
```

Iteration takes up less stack space and runs faster than recursion.

Recursion is helpful when it is difficult to state an iterative solution. It is a useful technique when experimenting with different approaches to solving a problem. Although recursion has some overhead costs in time and space, these may be negligible for a particular program.

Finally, we have studied recursion because it exemplifies a style of thinking that turns up throughout computer science.

Scaling Integer Arithmetic

Numbers represented inside a computer have two limits: the range from the minimum to the maximum, and the fineness of distinction between two numbers. If an integer is represented by 16 bits, the range is 65,535 and the fineness is one part in 65,536. Similarly, floating point formats have a range (expressed by the largest and smallest positive values that can be represented) and a precision (the number of significant places).

Numerical analysis studies the consequences of these facts. Most of it is concerned with floating point formats, but here we discuss some ways of working with integers.

Sixteen bits can handle a large range of the units of things we are working with, by trading off fineness. Even though the annual profits of IBM are several billion dollars, we can represent them in an integer, provided we need to measure no finer than a million dollars.

On the other hand, a day is 86,400 seconds, so merely keeping a computer clock accurate to the second requires more than 16 bits. For example, you can store the hour, minute, and second each in an integer.

More abstractly, suppose you have two unsigned integers and need to display their product, but your compiler does not support unsigned longs. You can allocate two unsigned integers to represent the more and less significant halves of the product.

Using $e = 256$ (two to the eighth power), an unsigned integer may be represented mathematically as

$$e * fh + fl$$

where fh and fl are the high and low bytes of the number. Then

$$(e*f1h + f1l) * (e*f2h + f2l)$$
$$= e*e*f1h*f2h + e*(f1h*f2l + f1l*f2h) + f1l*f2l$$

where $f1h$ is the high byte of the first factor and so on.

In many situations, scaled integer arithmetic is preferable to floating point math. Scaled integers economize on hardware (numeric coprocessors) or software (an extensive library of floating point functions). They run fast. They do not display phony precision, and they do not raise the problems of propagated errors that floating point math does.

Exercise. Write a general `sort` function whose arguments are the address of an array of pointers to the underlying data elements, the number of elements in the array, and pointers to comparison and swap functions. These functions require parameters giving the address of the pointer array and i and

j as usual. Write these functions to operate on the array of pointers
`*bench_ptr[]`.

Exercise. Earlier while studying trees we wrote a program to conduct a
symmetric traversal of a tree. That program used iteration and a stack.
Rewrite the program so that `traverse` is recursive.

Exercise. A timer chip in a computer generates an interrupt 18 times a
second, causing a function to be executed that updates global variables for
the hour (0 .. 23), minute, second, and tick (0 .. 17). Write a function
`do_tick` that updates these variables. Write some test data in `main`, invoke `do_tick`, and display the time to check your function.

Exercise. Rewrite `main` of the previous exercise to emulate 65000 ticks,
displaying the time every 4713 ticks.

Exercise. Write a program that accepts two unsigned 16-bit factors and
stores the result in `unsigned answer[2]`. Then have `main` display the
result by printing the `answer` array in hexadecimal. For the display, you
will need a function that displays an unsigned integer in exactly four hex
digits.

Hint: Write the second part of the above equation on a piece of paper just
like an ordinary multiplication problem. You will see which eight-bit frag-
ments to add. Remember to carry overflows past eight bits.

This exercise is a good workout for the `&` and shift operators.

Once you understand the idea, you can see how to take a compiler that
supports 32-bit `long` integers and multiply them to get 64-bit results.

314

```
/*  Independent project */

/*  WRITE an interesting program. */
```

CHAPTER 19

Enlarging Your Horizons

This chapter discusses combining C and assembly language, managing large programs, and using other C development systems.

Combining C and Assembly Language

Many programs written primarily in C can benefit when a few functions are coded in assembly language. The two principal reasons are faster speed and custom interfaces to certain parts of the computer. Some of the video routines in this C Workshop, for example, are written in assembly language.

Block-structured languages like C pass arguments between functions on the stack. Programs written entirely in assembly language tend to pass subroutine parameters through registers in the processor. The main concept in mixing C and assembly language is the stack frame.

Your assembly language code should go inside a function, either comprising the whole function or occurring in line in the middle of a C function. In both cases you need to respect the stack frame and register conventions of your compiler.

In what follows, we assume that the hardware stack grows downward in memory. The 8086 family of processors works this way, for example. A *push* instruction pre-decrements the stack pointer by two and stores the pushed data at the word addressed by the stack pointer.

When a statement invokes a function

```
d. = compute (a, b c);
```

the compiled code pushes the parameters onto the stack then calls the function (which pushes a return address onto the stack).

```
push c_
push b_
push a_
call compute_
```

Most but not all C compilers push arguments from right to left, so the first argument is immediately above the return address pushed by the *call* instruction. If the compiler produces assembly code, C names are typically modified by adding a trailing underscore.

Every function has a few instructions called a prologue. They set up a frame pointer. It is a register that, with offsets added and subtracted from it, can access the parameters and the function's local variables. In the 8086 microprocessor, this is the BP register. The parameters are on the stack, so the frame pointer must point into the stack at the correct spot for this execution of the function. The prologue might push the caller's frame pointer to preserve it, move the stack pointer into the frame pointer, and subtract a value from the stack pointer in order to allocate space for local variables.

```
push bp      ;preserve caller's frame pointer
mov bp,sp    ;set this function's frame pointer
sub sp,4     ;two local words
```

If this function invokes another, it will pass arguments below all its own parameters and allocated local variables.

Arguments and local variables are accessed relative to the frame pointer. A map of the stack frame might be

```
Third argument
Second argument
First argument
Return address
```

Caller's frame ptr   ;address is in BP
First local
Second local

Assuming that the return address is one word, the first argument is 4 bytes above BP, and the first declared local is 2 bytes below it.

```
mov ax,[bp+4]      ;load first argument
add ax,ax          ;double it
mov [bp-2],ax      ;store in first declared local variable
```

At the logical end of the function (where all return statements must jump), an epilogue undoes the work of the prologue.

```
mov sp,bp          ;wipe out locals
pop bp             ;restore caller's frame pointer
ret                ;stack pointer is at return address
```

If the function returns a value, it is in a designated register or registers. The caller then adjusts the stack pointer.

```
call compute_
add sp,6           ;remove three words of parameters
```

In this respect C is unlike other languages: the calling code, not the epilogue of the called function, removes parameters from the stack.

The size of various elements may affect your assembly language arithmetic. If the program is compiled using long calls between functions (a segment and an offset in the 8086), then the return address takes up four bytes. Consequently, the passed parameters start at BP+6 in the above scheme.

A long integer might occupy four bytes. Parameters to its right have bigger offsets from the frame pointer, and the invoker will add a larger number to the stack pointer to remove the parameters from the stack.

Each compiler implements the general idea in its own way. There are always a stack frame and a frame pointer.

Assembly language requires the programmer to attend to more details than C. Some details that may concern you include the following:

A) If the compiler uses register variables, perhaps in the SI and DI registers, you must protect them, too.

B) When you call the operating system, you must protect registers that the system might destroy, such as the SI, DI and BP registers.

C) Large programs must respect the conventions of the compiler regarding the various data and code segments.

Managing Large Programs

When a program becomes too big for your editor, or you find yourself waiting for a long compilation every time you change a single line, it is time to divide the program into two or more files. Also, if you are part of a programming team, each member will be responsible for sections of the program kept in separate files.

We will suggest one strategy for coordinating source files. Suppose you are writing a program called "masterpiece," which we will abbreviate mp. The strategy depends on keeping shared definitions in a single file, which might be called mpdef.h. It would contain #defines for values used in more than one module. Structure templates go in mpdef.h, too.

```
struct xx_tag {
    int part_code;
    char name[20];
    };
```

Also in this file are extern declarations for functions that return something other than an integer.

```
extern char key_processor();
extern unsigned compute_range();
```

Another file, perhaps called mpext.c, consists of extern statements for the global data objects of the program.

```
extern int seg_code;
extern char in_buf[];
```

For every global data definition in some other file, there is a corresponding extern declaration.

Like the standard header file, these two files create no objects. You write

```
#include "mpdef.h"
#include "mpext.c"
```

at the beginning of each of the other files.

Although you could scatter definitions that create the global data objects throughout various files, most should probably go into a separate file, perhaps called mpglob.c. This file is not #included anywhere. If you did include it, you would get a link error for trying to create several objects of the same name. It is simply compiled like other program files. This file, obviously, need not include mpext.c.

The rest of the program files contain functions and private data. If an object is used only by the functions in one file, or if you need a #define symbol only among a couple of functions in a file, then you can define and declare these things in the file. The rest of the program will not know they exist.

You compile each file as you write or alter it. To create a new executable version, you link all the object modules together. Study the options in your compiler and linker for details. When you change a file, you need recompile only that one file, except when you change an included file; then you need to recompile each file that includes it. In any case, the linker must put the whole program together again.

Some systems have a facility called make. Once you set it up with a map of file dependencies, make will look at the time stamp on files, automatically recompile altered and affected files, and relink the program. This facility may be supplied with the compiler package or the operating system, or it is built as a batch file, sometimes called a submit file.

Names become more important in large programs. Global names should be long and descriptive. Define keybd_buffer not kbuf (if your system distinguishes among names with this many characters). Local names within functions that might conflict with global labels should be shorter and more generic, like ptr or kptr.

Using Other C Development Systems

The C Workshop provides a complete, self-contained programming environment. It is ideal for learning C, writing and testing individual functions, creating small and moderate size programs, prototyping ideas, and writing portions of a large program.

One day you will want to use another development system. This section discusses how to make the transition.

First, suppose you want to take a small program and put it under a conventional development system. The system has several parts: an editor, a compiler, usually an assembler, a linker, one or more header files, and one or more libraries. Different vendors may supply the various parts, and you can put together your own system by choosing the editor you like, such as the C Workshop editor.

You use the editor, compiler, and linker by entering commands to the operating system. With the editor you create a disk file containing the program source text. Typically, your program has the line

```
#include "stdio.h"
```

near the beginning. You do not have to write the header file; it comes with the operating system or the compiler, and it supplies #defines and structure templates for input and output. (In the C Workshop, the header file is cwstdio.h.)

Having written your program with the editor, you compile it. The compiler may produce an assembly language source program, after which the assembler is automatically or manually executed to produce an object code file. These files typically have an extension like *.obj* or *.o*.

The linker processes the object code into an executable module with an extension like *.exe* or *.com*. It combines your object code with library functions, too. A library file is a form of object code file. Every compiler system comes with at least one library containing typical input and output functions like getchar.

Finally, you execute the program, again with a command from the operating system (typically, the name of your program, followed by any parameters your program accepts from the argv mechanism).

Compilers differ in their error messages. If you assign the address of a character to an integer pointer, one compiler may say nothing, while another may issue a warning statement.

Development systems also have different libraries. A function in one library may not occur in another. When an error message tells you a function is not defined, you write your own version of the function.

Worse, a function of the same name may perform slightly differently in different libraries. For example, some versions of `puts` do not automatically add a newline to the display of the string.

CHAPTER 20
The Library

This chapter discusses each function in the C Workshop library. Functions dealing with file input and output act in a standard way; virtually all other C compilers are compatible with the C Workshop in this respect.

Bytes read or written to a file are taken "as is;" no distinction is made between text and binary bytes. End of file means the physical end. Some programs build text files with a mark *1A* hex signifying the end of the text. If you do not want that character and characters that may follow it (perhaps written to fill out a disk sector), you must test for it.

The functions are listed in alphabetical order.

```
atoi (cptr)
/*  Return: integer value represented by ASCII string
             0 if no valid characters found
*/
char *cptr; /*  pointer to the string */
```

Scan a string representing an integer and return the value represented.

Accept introductory white space, a plus or minus sign and digits 0..9. Stop when a null or invalid character is read.

```
cls()
/*  Clear screen and home cursor to upper left corner
```

```
*/
```

This function assumes the industry standard ROM BIOS as found in the IBM Personal Computer, for example. However, it is not a standard C library function.

```
date (month, day, year)
/* Fill in the specified integers with the system date
*/
int *month, *day, *year;    /* MUST be pointers */
```

The arguments are *pointers* to the locations where you want the information stored. After invoking the function, the following line will print the date.

```
printf ("%d/%d/%d\n", month, day, year);
```

```
exit (errorlevel)
/* Exit to the operating system with the specified number
*/
int errorlevel; /*  0 for no error, else error severity */
```

Immediately stops program execution.

The batch file IF command in the operating system can use the errorlevel number. For example, if you wrote a program LFFILT that removes line feeds from a file, a batch file might be

LFFILT SRCFILE.DAT NOLFFILE.DAT
IF NOT ERRORLEVEL 1 DEL SRCFILE.DAT

```
double
fabs (d)
/*  Return: absolute value of argument
*/
double d;   /*  must be a double */
```

Because the function returns a `double` rather than an `int`, a declaration should be used.

```
extern double fabs();
```

```
fclose (fid)
/*  Return: -1 if error closing file
    Close the file whose file handle is  fid
*/
FILE *fid;  /*  typedef FILE is in CWSTDIO.H */
```

A write file must be closed; a read file should also be closed to release the file handle. The operating system can maintain only a limited number of handles simultaneously.

```
char *
fgets (buffer, size, fid)
/*  Return: 0 if error or end of file
            pointer to buffer if no error
    Read a string from a file into a buffer
*/
char *buffer;   /*  place the string here */
int size;       /*  read up to size-1 characters */
FILE *fid;
```

The function builds a string by reading from the file. It stops when it reads `size` $-$ 1 characters, a carriage return or a line feed. The carriage return or line feed is placed into the buffer. A null is appended to the string.

Because the function returns a pointer, not an `int`, you need to let the compiler know with a statement like

```
    extern char *fgets();
```

This statement is in CWSTDIO.H.

```
FILE *
fopen (filename, mode)
/*  Return: file handle, or 0 if error
    Open the file
*/
char *filename; /*  path allowed */
int mode;       /*  string, not character: "r", "w", "a" */
```

The file may be specified with drive and path.

The mode "r" is for reading the file.

The mode "w" deletes an existing file of the same name and creates a file for writing.

The mode "a" opens an existing file for writing after the existing data in the file. If the file does not exist, it is created.

```
fprintf (fid, format, arg1, arg2, ...)
/*  Return: -1 if error writing
    Format the output and write it to the file
*/
FILE *fid;
char *format;   /*  the format string */
```

The format string is expanded using the conversion specifications and the arguments, then written to the file. For details of formatting, see `printf`.

```
fputs (buffer, fid)
/*  Return: -1 if error
    Write the null-terminated string to the file
*/
char *buffer;   /*  pointer to the string */
FILE *fid;
```

The concluding null is not written. No characters are appended to the string.

```
fscanf (fid, format, arg1, arg2, ...)
/*  Read from the file according to specification.
    Return: number of successful conversions
            0 if none
            -1 if end of file reached before conversions done
*/
FILE *fid;
char *format;
```

Characters are input from the file, interpreted according to the format specification, and stored in the addresses indicated by the pointer arguments. For details, see `scanf`.

```
getc (fid)
/*  Return: integer containing byte read from file
            -1 upon error or end of file
    Read a character from the file
*/
FILE *fid;
```

The byte is never sign extended.

```
getchar ()
/*  Return: integer with console input character
            -1 upon error
*/
```

The function waits for the next console input character, then returns it. The character is displayed; to avoid display, write a loop with `inkey`.

```
char *
gets (buffer)
/*  Return: the buffer pointer or 0 if error
    Read a string from the standard input device
    Terminate with null
*/
char *buffer;   /*  put the string here */
```

The function reads characters until a carriage return is read. The return is not put into the string.

```
inbyte (port)
/*  Return: the byte value read at the port
*/
unsigned port;  /*  the 16-bit port address */
```

```
inkey()
/*  Return: character available from keyboard
            0 if none
*/
```

The function checks whether a character is available.

If a key with an extended ASCII code has been pressed, the returned value is the extended code plus 100 hex.

```
inword (port)
/*  Return: the word value read at the port
*/
unsigned port;  /*  the 16-bit port address */
```

```
isalpha (c)
/*  Return: TRUE/FALSE  c  is 'A'..'Z' or 'a'..'z'
*/
int c;
```

```
isdigit (c)
/*  Return: TRUE/FALSE  c  is '0'..'9'
*/
int c;
```

```
isspace (c)
/*  Return: TRUE/FALSE  c  is white space or not
    White space is tab, line feed, vertical tab,
        form feed, carriage return, or a blank
*/
int c;
```

```
longjmp (0, errorcode)
/*  Jump across functions to code following setjmp
    Both parameters are required
*/
```

```
int errorcode;   /*  the setjmp return value */
```

Control transfers to the code following `setjmp`. This is the only way in C to jump across functions. It is usually used for error recovery.

For example, somewhere deep in your program you might write

```
if (readfile() == FALSE)
    longjmp (0, DISK_RD_ERR);
```

while in `main()` you might have

```
error = setjmp();
if (error)
    {
    printf ("Fatal error %d", error);
    exit (1);
    }
```

The first time, `setjmp` returns 0 and nothing happens. If `longjmp` comes back to this point, the nonzero error code allows the program to terminate gracefully.

The first parameter is a dummy value; it is required but ignored. The error code cannot be 0; if it is, it is changed to 1.

```
long
lseek (fid, offset, origin)
/*  Return: long integer value of file position pointer
            -1L if error
    Set the file position pointer for the next file access
*/
FILE *fid;
long offset;     /*  amount to shift the position pointer */
int origin;      /*  0 start of file, 1 current, 2 end */
```

The origin code specifies the point from which to shift the pointer. Offset specifies the amount. For example, if origin is 2, end of file and offset is -1L, the next file access will read or write the last byte in the file. If offset is 0 and origin is 2, the returned long integer is the size of the file in bytes.

Regardless of the size of the file, the offset must be specified as a `long`.

```
move (dest, source, count)
/*  Copy a block of memory
*/
char *dest, *source;
int count;
```

The function moves count bytes starting from source to dest. The source and destination areas may overlap.

```
outbyte (port, byte)
/*  Return: the byte value
    Output the byte to the specified port
*/
unsigned port;  /*  the port address */
```

```
outword (port, word)
/*  Return: the word value
    Output the word to the specified port
*/
unsigned port;  /*  the port address */
```

```
printf (format, arg1, arg2, ...)
/*  Format the output and send it to the standard output device
*/
char *format;  /*  the format string */
```

The format string is output after conversion specifications introduced by a percent sign (%) have been converted, using the values provided by arg1, arg2, etc.

The conversion character that goes with the percent sign governs output according to the following list. The examples assume that the argument is a variable of the appropriate type with value 65.

c   ASCII character represented by the code: A
d   Decimal notation: 65
e   Floating point with exponent: 6.500000e+001
E   Same as e with uppercase: 6.500000E+001

f   Fixed point notation of floating point: `65.000000`

g   Narrower of format `e` or `f`

G   Narrower of format `E` or `f`

o   Octal notation: `101`

s   The argument points to a string to be output

u   Unsigned decimal notation: `65`

x   Hexadecimal notation: `41`

b   Binary notation (C Workshop only): `1000001`

To output the percent sign itself, write `%%`.

In addition to elementary forms like `%d`, a conversion specification may optionally have a number of other parts. The syntax is as follows:

% [-] [0] [w] [.p] [l] x

Most of these options utilize a field width, a number of places within which the value is formatted.

A minus sign left justifies the output within the output field; otherwise, the default is right justified.

The leading 0 pads the output field to its width with zeros instead of the default spaces.

The number *w* specifies the minimum field width; spaces or zeros will be used to pad as necessary. An asterisk takes the next integer argument passed to `printf` to be the width, allowing for variable field width.

The number *p* after the decimal point specifies the output precision. For floating point numbers, this means the number of decimal digits to the right of the decimal point. For a string, it means the maximum number of characters of the string to display. An asterisk takes the next integer argument passed to `printf` to be the precision. The default precision is 6. In no case can more than 79 digits be output in the `%f` format.

An *l* indicates that the data item for `%d`, `%o`, `%u` or `%x` specification is a long integer. The C Workshop also accepts an *L*.

The *x* is one of the above basic conversion codes.

If the character after the percent sign does not fit the above syntax, it is simply output.

Here are some examples.

```
printf ("%5d", 372) outputs two spaces then 372
printf ("%05d", 372) outputs 00372
printf ("%-5d", 372) outputs 372 then two spaces
printf ("%4s", "Truncation") outputs Trun
```

To repeat, the arguments must be of the appropiate type: `int` for character or integer format, `long` if the `l` modifier is present, and `float` or `double` for the floating point formats.

The `printf` function builds up the display string in a buffer that is 255 bytes long. Exceeding this limit will cause the program to crash.

The number of arguments following the format string must match the number of conversion specifications.

```
putc (c, fid)
/*  Return: -1 if error
    Output character to the specified file
*/
char c;
FILE *fid;
```

```
putchar (c)
/*  Return: -1 if error
    Output character to the standard output device
*/
```

The character `c` may be an ASCII character. On computers having a BIOS ROM compatible with the IBM Personal Computer, graphics characters in the range 128..255 may be displayed, too.

```
puts (str)
/*  Output string to the standard output until a null is seen
    Then output a carriage return and line feed
*/
char *str;  /*  pointer to string to display */
```

```
remove (filename)
/*  Return: -1 if unsuccessful
    Delete the file
*/
char *filename;
```

This function deletes the file from the disk. The filename may have a drive and path; it must end with a null.

```
    remove ("\\cw\\exer\\temp.c");   /*  \\ in string to get \ */
```

```
rename (currname, newname)
/*  Return: -1 on error, otherwise 0
    Rename the file
*/
char *currname, *newname;
```

The current filename may include a drive and directory specification. The new name must imply or specify the same drive. Because the directories may be different, this function can move a file to another directory.

```
char *
sbrk (bytes)
/*  Return: pointer to next free byte upon entry (not exit)
            0 if unable to perform allocation
*/
int bytes;  /*  amount to request or release */
```

Data memory is organized with defined data at the bottom and the stack at the top. The area in between is the heap. The function `sbrk` tracks the boundary between memory previously allocated from the heap and available memory.

To obtain memory from the heap, the parameter should be a positive integer. The return is the address at which the granted memory starts; `sbrk (0)` reports this address without allocating any memory.

If the parameter is a negative integer, the indicated number of bytes are released by reducing the starting address for the next allocation. Nothing is done and 0 is returned if the amount released exceeds what has been allocated.

If this boundary would be within 1000 bytes of the stack pointer value, 0 is returned.

A declaration of the non-integer return is needed.

```
extern char *sbrk();
```

```
scanf (format, arg1, arg2, ...)
/*  Read standard input according to specification.
    Return: number of successful conversions
            0 if none
            -1 if end of file reached before conversions done
*/
```

Bytes received from the standard input device are interpreted according to the format string. The data are stored in the addresses supplied by the arguments. Therefore, the arguments *must* be pointers to appropriate variables (integers, floats, etc.).

The key parts of the format string are the percent conversion specifiers, similar to `printf`. They are interpreted in sequence. White space (blank, tab, carriage return, line feed) between the specifiers has no effect, with one exception for `%c`. Other text in the format string is expected to be matched exactly in the input stream.

For example,

```
int pay_grade;
float salary;
    scanf ("%d%f", &pay_grade, &salary);
```

would accept input like

```
    12   1083.20
```

storing 12 into pay_grade, 1083.20 into salary, and reporting that two items were input.

A group of non-white space characters in the input stream is interpreted according to the current format specification, which has the syntax

% [*] [w] [l] x

An asterisk tells `scanf` to read and parse the input stream but discard the result rather than store it per the next argument.

A field width *w* specifies how many non-white space characters to scan to complete the input field. The conversion character *x* interprets the field as follows:

d — A decimal integer, possibly signed.

e or f — A floating point number.

o — An octal integer.

s — A string. Remember that the field ends at white space, so at most one "word" may be input. A null is appended to the string and the result stored in the buffer addressed by the argument. You must be sure the buffer is large enough.

x — A hexadecimal integer.

c — A character. This is the only specification that pays attention to white space. The next one or *w* characters from input are stored at the buffer addressed by the character pointer argument. If a space precedes the percent sign in the specification, leading white space is skipped first; otherwise, the white space characters are counted in the input.

For example,

```
scanf (" %4c", buffer);
```

will skip white space then store four characters (the second through fourth could be white space) in the buffer. But with

```
scanf ("%4c", buffer);
```

the next four characters, any or all possibly being white space, would be scanned and stored.

Note that %c does not append a null to what it stores.

The optional l in the syntax specifies that a %d, %o or %x is a long, or that a %e or %f is a double. The corresponding arguments must be pointers to long or double storage locations.

```
setcur (row, col)
/*  Position the cursor at specified row and column
*/
int row, col;
```

The upper left corner is (0, 0), the bottom right of a 25-line screen is (24, 79). If either coordinate is invalid, nothing happens.

This function is not standard in C libraries.

```
setjmp (0)
/*  Mark target spot for longjmp() calls
    The 0 must be present
    Returns the value passed to it by longjmp
*/
```

The setjmp function marks a spot, generally in main, to which a subsequent execution of longjmp will jump.

The function returns 0 when it is called; it returns the error code from longjmp when longjmp comes back to it.

The setjmp function must occur in a function that is still executing when longjmp is invoked; that is why setjmp is usually placed in main.

```
sprintf (buffer, format, arg1, arg2, ...)
/*  Return: -1 if error writing
    Format the output and write it in the buffer
*/
char *buffer;   /*  store the output here */
char *format;   /*  the format string */
```

The format string is expanded using the conversion specifications and arguments, then written in the buffer with the usual null appended. For details of formatting, see printf.

```
sscanf (str, format, arg1, arg2, ...)
/*  Read from the string according to specification.
    Return: number of successful conversions
            0 if none
            -1 if null reached before conversions done
*/
char *str;  /*  read from this string */
char *format;
```

Characters are read from the string, interpreted according to the format specification, and stored in the addresses indicated by the pointer arguments. For details, see `scanf`.

```
strcmp (str1, str2)
/*  Return: 0 if the strings are identical through the nulls
            a positive integer if str1 is greater than str2
            a negative integer if str1 is less than str2
*/
char *str1, *str2;
```

The comparison is lexicographic, that is, dictionary style: the first position at which the strings differ decides which is greater. "Not clear" is greater than "Not abundantly clear" because 'c' is greater than 'a' at the fourth position.

```
strcpy (dest, source)
/*  Copy the source string to the destination array
    Copy through the null
*/
char *dest, *source;
```

The destination area should be entirely separate from the source string.

```
strlen (str)
/*  Return: length of the string, excluding the null
*/
char *str;
```

```
time (hour, min, sec, hundredth)
/*  Fill in the specified integers with the system time
*/
int *hour, *min, *sec, *hundredth;  /*  MUST be pointers */
```

Note that the arguments are pointers. After invoking `time`, the time may be printed by writing

```
    printf ("%d:%02d:%02d.%02d\n", hour, min, sec, hundredth);
```

tolower (c)
```
/*  Return: c, converted to lowercase if it is 'A'..'Z'
*/
int c;
```

toupper (c)
```
/*  Return: c, converted to uppercase if it is 'a'..'z'
*/
int c;
```

ungetc (c, fid)
```
/*  Shove character back to file
    Return: the character
*/
char c;
FILE *fid;
```

The specified character will be returned by the next invocation of `getc`, `getchar`, or `fgets`. You must use this function right after `getc`, with no intervening disk operations on the file. Only one invocation of `ungetc` is effective at a time; each invocation destroys the effect of the previous invocation, even if the file handles are different.

user_call (array, arg_cnt, arg1, .., argn)
```
/*  Return: AX register contents, or DX:AX for longs
*/
char *array;    /*  address of array holding the code */
int arg_cnt;    /*  number of arguments */
int arg1;       /*  ... */
```

This function provides a way to patch object code into a C Workshop .COM program. It is not a standard C library function; you should be familiar with assembly language programming.

Your routine is contained in the array. It must consist of 8086 machine language code, usually created by use of an assembler or debugging tool. You can initialize the array in your C program, or you might read a file.

Invoke `user_call` by passing the address of the code, the argument count, and the arguments, which are assumed to be word-sized.

The object code must be a valid routine respecting C conventions. It must protect the BP register and end with a RET instruction.

For example,

```
char triple[] = {
    0x55, 0x8B, 0xEC, 0x8B, 0x46, 0x4, 0x3, 0xC0, 0x3,
    0x46, 0x4, 0x5D, 0xC3 };

main()
{
int i;

    printf ("Enter a number:");
    scanf ("%d", &i);

    i = user_call (&triple, 1, i);
    printf ("\n%d is your number tripled", i);
}
```

The sample machine language code was assembled from the following routine:

push bp	;protect caller's BP
mov bp,sp	;set frame pointer
mov ax,[bp+4]	;first arg is above the invoker's RET
	;(a second one would be at [bp+6])
add ax,ax	;times 2
add ax,[bp+4]	;now times 3 is in AX for return value
pop bp	;restore BP
ret	;near return

CHAPTER 21

Advanced Use of the C Workshop

The first part of this chapter explains editing features that are helpful when you write your own programs and other documents. The chapter also discusses how to start the C Workshop quickly, change the standard allocation of memory areas for the C Workshop, enjoy faster screen display, and customize colors. The last part specifies some features of the compiler.

The Editing Keys

The basic editing keys are the function keys shown in the menu at the bottom of the editing screen. You perform other editing commands using various key combinations. The default command keys are shown on a Help screen. These keys generally follow two industry standards: first, operations labeled by the cursor keys, like *PgDn*, and second, control key combinations popularized by the WordStar program (for example, *Ctrl-R* to scroll back a screen). Consequently, two different key commands will often execute the same operation.

See the section on configuring the Computer Workshop if you want to change the default command keys. Besides the cursor pad and control key combinations, you may assign commands to function keys pressed in combination with the Shift, Alt and Control keys.

Program Text or Word Processing

A Set option toggles between program text and word processing. When you edit a program, you normally want a return character at the end of every line, so the editor puts one there when you press *PgUp* or some other key that moves off a line. In word processing, however, you press Return only to signal the end of a paragraph. Otherwise, the editor marks the end of the line with an invisible "soft" carriage return. This is a word wrapped line.

When you insert enough text in a line to make it overflow, a soft return will be inserted, even while programming.

In the default system setup, carriage returns are invisible while programming; they are displayed as ~ marks in word processing. An option on the Set menu changes these symbols.

Editing Commands

A number of commands make it easy to move around the text and manipulate it. Use the Help key to look up the default keys for these commands. Some of the commands deserve additional comment.

Backspace
The left arrow moves the cursor back one space. The backspace or rubout key erases, too.

Home
The first time you press this key, the cursor moves to the left edge. If you press the key again before pressing another key, the cursor moves to the top of the screen.

End
The first time you press the key, the cursor moves to the last character on the line. The second consecutive key press moves the cursor to the beginning of the bottom line on the screen.

Insert

Normally, when you press a letter, it overwrites the letter under the cursor. Pressing the insert key causes existing text to be pushed forward as you insert characters. New lines are created as needed, too. The word INSERT appears in the lower right corner. Pressing the insert key again toggles back to over-writing.

Sometimes a window asks you to enter a file name or other information longer than a single keystroke. While you are on such a line in a window, a completely independent insert action is available; it has no connection with the notice in the lower right corner of the screen.

Restore line

When you delete a whole line or part of a line, the text goes into a small buffer. The restore line command brings the text back at the cursor. Only the most recently deleted line is available.

Used with care, the combination of deleting a line, moving the cursor, and restoring a line is a convenient way to relocate a line of text.

Auto indent

The auto indent key combination moves the cursor to the column under-neath the first non-blank character on the preceding line. This is helpful when writing nested if-statements.

Tab and back tab

Unless you change the default, the tab key moves to the next fourth column position on the line. The back tab key combination moves to the left.

Go to line by number

This command tells you how many lines the file has at its current line width and lets you move to a specified line number. This command is helpful when the compiler reports an error on a certain line.

Reformat

Every screen line ends in one of two ways: it has a carriage return, or it is a word wrapped line. After awhile, word wrapped lines may present a ragged margin down the right side of your text. You can use the reformat command.

It rewraps lines to fit the current line width. This command is available in two forms. One operates from the beginning of the cursor line until a carriage return is encountered. A more sweeping method is to reformat the entire document; setting the line width on the Set menu accomplishes this action.

Reformat is most useful in text mode, in which you enter a carriage return only at the end of paragraphs. In program mode, every line normally ends with a return.

This command is a handy way to advance to the next paragraph, too.

Block Operations

A portion of text may be marked with two block marks. The block marker key inserts a mark at the cursor. Besides moving, deleting, and copying the block as listed on the Block menu, the Out menu will output the block to a disk file or the printer. In addition, when you have a split screen, the Split menu has an option for copying a block of text from the inactive screen to the cursor location in the active buffer.

One of the block options deletes all text except a marked block. By putting two block marks next to each other anywhere in the text and using this option, you can clear the entire buffer.

Entering Lines in a Window

When you specify a file name to be read or output, a new line width, or other information requested in a window, you are using the window line editor. It follows many of the same editing commands as the screen editor, like delete character, delete entire line, go to beginning of line, and go to end of line. While you are on the line, you can also toggle between inserting and overwriting; however, the insert status has no relation to the text editing status shown in the lower right corner.

Find and Replace

The find command asks you to enter a find and replace pattern. The pattern may have three parts separated by a backward tick mark. The first part is the fragment of text you want to find. Optional second and third parts specify a replacement pattern and the number of times you want to replace. To replace all occurrences, enter a huge number like 999.

A carriage return may be specified with the tab key.

After you enter the find pattern, you specify your find and replace commands. You may search forward (F) or backward (B), or search and replace (R), which is always forward. You may also specify whether to require that matching letters have the same case. Normally, "Any" does not match "any," but you can ignore case.

Some examples of find patterns:

`Hello`	F and B go to first instance after or before cursor
	R is invalid
`Hello'Hi`	F and B go to first instance
	R replaces first forward instance
`Hello'Hi'3`	F and B go to third instance (or as many as exist)
	R replaces three times (or as many as can find)
`Hello''`	F and B find; R *deletes* by replacing
`Hello''3`	F and B go to third instance (or as many as exist)
	R deletes three times (or as many as can find)
`'Hi'`	Invalid pattern does not specify what to find

The find pattern is remembered throughout the editing session. You can use the line delete command to erase it.

You may repeat your last find or replace operation without going through the menu by pressing the repeat find key. Only one operation is performed; this key ignores the count if any.

Getting Files

You may get a file from any drive and directory.

You may get an entire file into the buffer, or you may simply view it screenful by screenful.

If the editor reports that it is unable to open the file, it probably cannot find the file. You can edit the file name. A check of the directory may help you spot a misspelling or discover the file in another directory.

Note that when the screen is split, you get a file into the active buffer.

Outputting Text

The editor may fill in a default output file name based on a file you read earlier. However, you can edit the name to any file name you wish.

When you want to remember parts of a document, you can mark a block and output it to its own file.

If you are programming and crash the system, your text buffer is lost. It is a good idea to output the source text to a disk file frequently, especially before a test run of your program.

The Split Screen

By splitting the screen, you may work in two different files.

The editing cursor is active in only one screen. A single command switches the active cursor from top to bottom or vice versa.

First, decide where you want to divide the screen and place the cursor on that row. (The Workshop will automatically adjust the row if the dividing line is too near the top or bottom of the screen.) The bottom part of a divided screen is your view into a completely separate editing buffer. Its size is normally determined by a command in the Workshop parameter file. You can Get any disk file into the bottom portion. Normally, you bring in a file you need to consult for reference, although you can edit and output two files at once. The only communication between the screens is the command to move a block from the inactive screen to the active one at the cursor location.

Pay extra care to Get and Out file names when the screen is split. These commands, regardless of the default file names that may appear in their windows, always operate on the active half of the screen.

It is possible to read the same disk file into both halves of a split screen. When the screen is split, each portion has its own buffer. Editing changes affect only the buffer in which they are made. If you write a buffer to a disk file, it replaces that disk file. The situation can be confusing if you started with the same disk file in both halves of the screen. It is your responsibility to keep things straight!

You may remove the bottom screen two ways. One way is to hide it but continue to hold the text in its buffer. When you reopen it (perhaps divided at a different row), the text will still be there. The other way is to delete the bottom screen completely; it is your responsibility to Output the file first if you want to save it.

Startup Options for the C Workshop

When you start the C Workshop, you can select where it goes by using options after the command name *cw*.

```
cw -p35A
```
This option takes you to the tutor beginning at the specified screen, such as page 35A as shown here. Do not put a space between the *-p* and the page number.

```
cw -e
```
Go directly to the editor and compiler, bypassing the title screen and tutor. When you quit the editor, control returns to the operating system.

```
cw xmasltr.txt
```
Go to the editor and get the specified file. It is the only option that does not begin with a hyphen. If the file is not found, the effect is the same as though you went to the editor with the *-e* option.

Organizing Workshop Files on Disks

The C Workshop system contains many files, and as you write programs, you will create additional files. So long as you keep certain portions of the C Workshop system together, you may start the C Workshop from any drive and directory and store your files in different places.

CW.EXE starts the Workshop. The MS-DOS or PC-DOS operating system can find this file if it is in the current directory or an area specified in the operating system PATH= command.

Thereafter, CW.EXE finds all the files it needs in the current directory or in a directory called CWPATH. It searches the current directory for tutor and help .DOC files; if they are not there, it searches the CWPATH directory. The strictest rule is that these files must reside as a group in either the current directory or the CWPATH directory. Less strictly, files referenced by an #include directive may reside individually in the current or CWPATH directory.

The editor is not constrained: you can get and save files from virtually any part of your computer's storage.

You tell CW.EXE what to use for CWPATH in one of three ways. One way is to specify a CWPATH= command in the operating system environment, similar to a PATH= command. (Consult the MS-DOS rules for the SET environment command. Note that CWPATH is only one directory, not a list of alternatives.)

A second way is to have a parameter file CW.PAR in the current directory containing a line

```
CWPATH=path
```

Third, when asked for the Screens disk, you may specify the drive and directory at the last minute. You might reply

```
c:\cwdir
```

Note that a backslash is used to specify that cwdir is attached to the root directory.

CW.EXE needs to find the tutor and help .DOC files. Their default names are CTUTnn.DOC and CHELPnn.DOC. It also needs to find the file CWLIB.BIN. The program must find the files in the current directory or the specified CWPATH directory.

Suggested Hard Disk Use

If you have a hard disk and want to write your own programs, here is a suggestion for organizing the files.

Create a directory containing all the files supplied with the C Workshop. When you start your computer, or in an AUTOEXEC.BAT file, enter the command

```
SET CWPATH=this directory
```

Also include this directory in the PATH= command, so that the operating system can find CW.EXE.

For each programming project, create a new directory. Log onto it and enter

```
cw -e
```

Using this system, you may store your source and object files in their own directory, and the system will automatically find necessary files, such as the standard library, in the Workshop directory.

Systems with One Drive

If you have a system with one floppy drive and no hard drive, insert the working copy of the disk with CW.EXE into the drive and start the program. While you are using the tutorial, you will be asked to swap disks as needed.

When you edit and save programs, make sure you have the proper disk in the drive. Keep this point in mind when you swap a disk in to give the system a help file and later want to save your programs.

Never change diskettes while the operating system has a problem and asks you whether to Abort, Retry, or Ignore a disk error message. If you change diskettes then say retry or ignore, the operating system will probably leave the new diskette hopelessly scrambled.

The Parameter File

The optional parameter file CW.PAR is the key to customizing the C Workshop. Upon startup, CW.EXE looks for it in the current directory or in the CWPATH if you have set this path in the operating system environment with a SET command.

The parameter file consists of lines having the general form

```
option=value,value,value ;comment
```

Spaces are permitted, and upper and lower case are equivalent. The options discussed below allocate memory to different parts of the Workshop, select screen colors, choose certain compiler options, etc. CW.EXE reads each line and puts the values into effect. Comments following a semicolon are ignored.

For the most part, the program does not check values for errors. If the result is not according to your intention, inspect the parameter file and change it. Note that you can edit the file with the Workshop editor or virtually any other editor. However, you must restart the C Workshop to put new parameters into effect.

Parameter file options are discussed in the following sections. Specific figures for some options may be referenced in the READ.ME disk file.

Allocating Memory to the C Workshop

The C Workshop requires a minimum quantity of RAM memory. If more memory is available, you may let the C Workshop allocate it or decide yourself how to use it.

Each of the areas discussed below occupies at most 64K bytes of memory. Each requires a minimum amount. If there is not enough memory to meet the minimums, the Workshop will not run. The Workshop takes all the available memory it can use, unless you specify a maximum total for these four areas.

The four parts of the C Workshop that may be larger or smaller are the following:

• First and second editing buffers. These buffers hold the text you are editing in the top and bottom halves of the split screen. The first buffer must always exist and have at least 7K of RAM; the second buffer is optional.

• The object code area. This area holds your compiled and linked program. It requires 20K.

• The directory and miscellaneous area. This area holds the names when you use the Dir command and has other miscellaneous functions. It requires 10K.

You may alter the minimum demanded for each area with an appropriate line in the parameter file. The C Workshop will allocate available memory so that each area is at least your requested minimum. If you want to prevent the C Workshop from using additional memory, add up the minimum sizes (specified by you or the default minimum for each area) and put a line in the parameter file telling the C Workshop the total memory for all four areas.

The parameter file coding for these options is as follows.

    MEM=letter,size

where the letter specifies the memory area:

    E   first edit buffer
    S   second edit buffer
    O   object code area
    X   directory and miscellaneous area
    T   total to take for these four areas

and the size is given in kilobytes. For example,

```
MEM=E,64  ;allocate maximum 64Kb for edit buffer
MEM=T,178 ;areas E, S, O and X get no more than
178K
```

Video Specification

The editor may be told to write directly to video memory or to use the BIOS software interrupt for video display. The latter may be required for compatibility with other software operating simultaneously in the computer. The direct method speeds up editor display considerably. The default uses the BIOS, or it may be specified by

    VIDEO=0

Otherwise, the number is the ASCII hex value of the video memory segment.

```
VIDEO=B000    ;monochrome video buffer at B000
VIDEO=B800    ;color graphics buffer at B800
```

Note that hexadecimal values are specified without 0x or other notation.

You may specify the screen colors, too. These parameters use the attribute byte of the IBM PC display, in which bits 0-2 determine the foreground color and bits 4-6 the background color. One parameter, SCRN, is for the tutorial and editing screen. Another parameter, WDW, selects the attribute for the pop-up menu windows. The values are given in hexadecimal. For example,

```
   SCRN=07    ;white (or green or amber) on black
(default)
   WDW=13     ;cyan on blue in a color system
```

Compiler Options

Certain compiler options may be set in the parameter file. Normally, members in different structures may have the same name; a char is unsigned unless declared signed; comments do not nest; and the maximum length of a symbol name is 18 characters. Also, every time a function is invoked, the stack is checked for overflow into the heap area.

The following options change these defaults.

```
   ALLMEMB    ;member names are shared among all
structures
   SIGCHAR    ;a char is signed unless declared unsigned
   NEST       ;comments nest
   SYMLEN=8   ;maximum symbol length in characters,
not over 18
   NOSTCKCHK  ;do not compile a stack overflow check
into functions
```

Editing Parameters

Several features of the editor are governed by parameters. You may fix most of them on the Set menu, too.

Hard carriage returns may be displayed on the screen as the character of your choice or left invisible. Use CRWP for the symbol when in word processing mode and CRPROG for the symbol in programming mode. These options are also affected by a selection on the Set menu.

```
CRPROG=FA ;symbol with hex code FA for program
returns
```

The SOFT parameter determines the handling of soft carriage returns when a file is output to disk (screen display is always blank). The most common choices, specified in hexadecimal, are the following:

```
SOFT=8D    ;convert to return with high bit set
(WordStar)
SOFT=20    ;convert to a space upon output
```

The default is 8D.

Line width, for both buffers, may be specified.

```
LWIDTH=65 ;lines are 65 characters long
```

Note that the Set menu will change this value independently for the top or bottom edit buffer.

Tab width, normally four columns, may be altered.

```
TAB=8
```

When reading a file from another editor, the C Workshop normally converts tab characters to spaces. The tab may be preserved or assigned a different value.

```
TABTRAN=9    ;desired hex value
```

Customizing the Editor Keyboard

You may change the default keys for most editor commands by writing appropriate lines in the parameter file. Each command has an arbitrary number. The line in the parameter file associates one or more keys with a given command number. In other words, two keys may perform the same command.

The help screen for the editing commands will continue to list the default keys.

Lines in the parameter file are interpreted in order. No checking is done for keyboard conflicts.

The keys to which you may assign commands, and the way to name them in the parameter file, are the following:

• Control-letter combinations, for example, ^A.

• Control-function key combinations, specified CFn, where *n* is 0..9 (F10 is simply specified with a 0).

• Shift-function key combinations, specified SFn.

• Alt-function keys, specified AFn.

• Cursor pad keys, specified simply by letters:

H   Home
E   End
U   PgUp
DN PgDn
DE Del
I   Ins
MR right arrow ("move right")
ML left arrow
MD down arrow
MU up arrow

• Six of the cursor keys in combination with the control key are specified with a double carat: ^^H, ^^U, ^^DN, ^^E, ^^MR, and ^^ML.

The editing menu at the bottom of the screen is permanently assigned to the function keys. Of course, a program that remaps the keyboard and stays active while you use the C Workshop could change the meaning of these keys.

A parameter file line is of the form

ED=n,key,key

where *n* is the command number and the key or keys to activate the command are specified according to the above system.

The command numbers are referenced in the READ.ME file.

For example,

```
ED=38,CF0 ;command 38 activated by
control-Function 10
```

Print Margins

The dimensions used to print a page may be altered in the parameter file.

```
TOP=8      ;8 lines at top of page
BOTTOM=10  ;10 lines at bottom of page
PAGE=66    ;physical page has 66 lines
LEFT=7     ;7 columns left margin
```

The number of printed lines is the page length less the top and bottom margins. The right margin is determined by the line width and the left margin.

C Workshop Compiler Specifications

In general, the compiler conforms to the standard defined in *The C Programming Language,* by Brian W. Kernighan and Dennis M. Ritchie. This standard is commonly called "K&R" C.

Comments do not nest, except when the parameter file contains an option for this purpose.

Names have up to 18 characters, all significant, except when reduced by a parameter file option.

Data types occupy the following sizes:

```
char            8 bits
signed char     8
short           16
int             16
long            32
unsigned long   32
float           32
double          64
```

The `char` is unsigned, except the default may be made signed by a parameter file option.

Floats and doubles are represented in IEEE format.

Integer division and modulus divide the absolute values then attach a sign.

Declarations cannot initialize automatic variables.

Member names are unique to the structure template in which they are declared; that is, names may be re-used. This feature may be defeated by an option in the parameter file.

Bit fields are 16 bits wide only. They may be declared `int` (one bit is used to hold a sign) or `unsigned int`. Fields are allocated beginning from the least significant bit.

A .COM program may have up to ten command line switches, including the program name.

Runtime error messages

You may see these messages when your program executes.

Address 0 bad; check *ptr

The program altered location 0, which should never happen. The most common cause is using a pointer that has 0 instead of a valid address.

Stack overflow

The stack, which holds the return addresses for active functions and their local variables, has overflowed into the heap area. The program may be infinitely recursive, or there is not enough memory for all the local variables.

Long divide by 0

An attempt has been made to divide by 0 when performing division of `longs`.

Floating point underflow/overflow/divide by 0

The respective error has occurred during a floating point arithmetic operation.

Appendices

Chart of Operator Precedence and Associativity

()	[]	->	.							
++	--	*	&	-	!	sizeof	(cast type)	~		Unary, right to left
*	/	%								Multiplicative
+	-									Additive
<<	>>									Shift
<	<=	>	>=							Relational
==	!=									Equality test
&										Bitwise group
^										
|										
&&										Logical group
||										
?:										Conditional expr
=	+=	-=	*=	/=	%=	<<=	>>=	&=	etc.	Right to left
,										Statement join

Associativity is left to right except where noted opposite.

A Quick Primer on Hexadecimal and Binary Numbers

Decimal notation gives each position a weight: the digit to the left of the decimal point is in units, the next digit is in tens, etc. In the hexadecimal system the weight of each successive digit is 16 times its neighbor to the right.

The letters A through F are used for 10 through 15.

```
10A4 hexadecimal =
      4    x        1
   + 10    x       16
   +  0    x      256
   +  1    x     4096    = 4260 decimal
```

To convert a decimal number into hexadecimal, divide successively by 16. The first remainder is the units digit, the leftover after removing the multiples of 16. The next remainder is the sixteen's digit, and so on.

Hexadecimal numbers are preceded by 0x (C notation) or followed by H or h (assembly language notation).

A hexadecimal digit expands into four binary digits.

```
0   0000    4   0100    8   1000    C   1100
1   0001    5   0101    9   1001    D   1101
2   0010    6   0110    A   1010    E   1110
3   0011    7   0111    B   1011    F   1111
```

A byte holds eight bits. It takes two hexadecimal digits to represent the bit pattern of a byte. For example, A1 hexadecimal is 1010 0001 binary.

A word is usually 16 bits, requiring four hexadecimal digits.

Signed binary words use the most significant bit for the sign. A 0 is positive and a 1 means negative in two's complement. Two's complement simply means counting down: FFFFh is -1, FFFEh is -2, and so on. The formula is to subtract the absolute value from FFFF and add 1. For example, -3 is represented:

FFFF - 3 = FFFC and add 1 to get FFFD

If you write out this subtraction in binary, you see that it simply flips each bit of the subtrahend, an easy thing to make a silicon circuit do.

```
      1111 1111 1111 1111
  -   0000 0000 0000 0011
      ─────────────────────
      1111 1111 1111 1100    one's complement flips bits
  +                     1
      ─────────────────────
      1111 1111 1111 1101    two's complement
```

$$= 0\text{xFFFD or } -3$$

The range of signed binary words is from 0 to 32767 decimal on the positive side, while FFFF to 8000 represent -1 to -32768.

If only a byte is available, then the signed range is from -128 (80h) to +127 (7Fh). In a byte, -1 is FFh. To convert to a word, just propagate (duplicate) the sign bit through the high order positions: FFh becomes, in a word, FFFFh.

Math instructions of some computer processor chips take a byte and put it into a word without sign propagation; other computer chips and instructions do propagate the sign bit. There is a big difference between 00FFh and FFFFh.

In C, the corresponding matter to watch is the conversion from a character, represented in a byte, to an integer, often represented in a word. If a character byte is assigned to an integer word, will 0x8D become 0xFF8D or 0x008D? You must know! (By default, the C Workshop does not extend sign.)

The ASCII Code

The American Standard Code for Information Interchange (ASCII) is a widely used system of coding characters using the numbers 0 through 127 decimal. The 128 codes can be represented in seven bits of a byte, leaving the most significant bit (the "high bit") free for other interpretation.

The codes are grouped conceptually (indicated in hexadecimal):

Control codes (0..1F): Control characters, such as a carriage return (0D), line feed (0A), backspace (08) and other controls are used in different ways by different software. The last code, 7F, is considered a control code, too.

The control codes are assigned letters when speaking of them, not to be confused with the actual codes for letters. Code 1 is control-A, code 1A is control-Z. The rest are assigned certain punctuation symbols.

Printable characters: 20 (blank) .. 7E (~).
The digits '0'..'9':   30 hex .. 39.
Uppercase 'A'..'Z':   41 hex .. 5A.
Lowercase 'a'..'z':   61 hex .. 7A.

Note that each lowercase letter is a fixed amount greater than its upper-case letter.

The other codes represent various punctuation and special symbols.

Along with the space, the five codes for tab (09), line feed (0A), vertical tab (0B), form feed (0C), and carriage return (0D) are considered white space. A function that skips over white space, for example, could move across blanks, to the next line, and even to the next page if the input stream consisted of these various white space characters.

Index

If You Have A Problem Using the Software

If you cannot install or start the C Workshop, please review the first and last chapters. Check the disks for a file READ.ME, which has last-minute information. Be sure your computer has sufficient memory.

When you can start the C Workshop but have a problem with some part of it, attempt to reproduce the problem consistently. Test slight variations and note the results.

Registered licensees may write to Wordcraft. Tell us the version number of the software, displayed when the program starts; a description of the problem and how we can duplicate it; the serial number on the diskette label; and the computer, operating system version number, and amount of RAM memory installed. Wordcraft's address is in the READ.ME file.

Software Has Value

Many hours and considerable expense go into creating and sustaining the C Workshop. We do not steal your paycheck; please do not make unauthorized copies of our software.

Single User License

Customer is granted a non-exclusive license to use the licensed software on a single computer workstation at a time. You may make archival and backup copies only; no more than two copies may be in existence at any one time. The program is licensed to a single user. If a company or other institution has purchased the license, one person must be designated the sole assigned user.

Multiple Users

Libraries, departments and other groups that wish to have more than one assigned user need a multiple user license. Organizations desiring multiple licenses should contact Wordcraft.

Diskette Replacement

If a diskette in this package has a manufacturing defect, return it within ten days of purchase to Wordcraft. Enclose your registration if you have not already sent it.

The diskettes are 5 1/4", 360 kilobyte double density format. If you need 3 1/2", 720 KB format and do not have access to transfer facilities, send the original diskettes and $20 to Wordcraft (add 7% sales tax in California).

Limited Warranty

Publisher is not liable for any consequences of use or attempted use of program. The program is provided "as is." The warranty and liability are the minimum defined by applicable laws.

BEFORE YOU OPEN THE DISKETTE PACKAGE,
1) Read the license terms on the previous page,
2) Look through the book, and
3) Check the system requirements on the back cover.

WHEN YOU OPEN THE DISKETTE PACKAGE, YOU ACCEPT THE LICENSE TERMS.